READING & LEARNING STRATEGIES

FOR

MIDDLE & HIGH SCHOOL STUDENTS

SUSAN DAVIS LENSKI
Illinois State University

MARY ANN WHAM
University of Wisconsin-Whitewater

JERRY L. JOHNS
Northern Illinois University

KENDALL/HUNT PUBLISHING COMPANY
4050 Westmark Drive   Dubuque, Iowa 52002

Books by Jerry L. Johns

Basic Reading Inventory (seven editions)
Secondary & College Reading Inventory (two editions)
Literacy for Diverse Learners (edited)
Handbook for Remediation of Reading Difficulties
Informal Reading Inventories: An Annotated Reference Guide (compiled)
Literacy: Celebration and Challenge (edited)
Spanish Reading Inventory

Books by Jerry L. Johns and Susan Davis Lenski

Improving Reading: A Handbook of Strategies (2nd edition)
Reading & Learning Strategies for Middle & High School Students (with Mary Ann Wham)
Celebrate Literacy! The Joy of Reading and Writing (with June E. Barnhart, James H. Moss, and
   Thomas E. Wheat)
Language Arts for Gifted Middle School Students

Book by Jerry L. Johns and Laurie Elish-Piper

Balanced Reading Instruction: Teachers' Visions and Voices (edited)

Author Addresses for Correspondence and Workshops

Susan Davis Lenski
Illinois State University
239 DeGarmo Hall
Normal, IL 61790
E-mail: sjlensk@ilstu.edu
309-438-3028

Mary Ann Wham
Department of Curriculum and Instruction
University of Wisconsin-Whitewater
800 W. Main Street
Whitewater, WI 53190
E-mail: whamm@uwwvax.uww.edu
414-472-5377

Jerry L. Johns
Northern Illinois University
Reading Clinic—119 Graham
DeKalb, IL 60115
E-mail: jjohns@niu.edu
815-753-8484

To Order
Phone 800-228-0810   Fax 800-772-9165
www.kendallhunt.com

Interior photos by Susan Johns and Gary Meader
Cover images © 1998 PhotoDisc, Inc.

Copyright © 1999 by Kendall/Hunt Publishing Company

ISBN 0-7872-5607-2

Printed in the United States of America
10 9 8 7 6 5 4 3 2

Contents

Purpose of This Book

Reading & Learning Strategies for Middle & High School Students is a user-friendly, practical book grounded in solid knowledge about reading. It is intended for use in undergraduate and graduate secondary and content area reading courses as well as for workshops and inservice programs for teachers in middle and high schools. Reading teachers and specialists will embrace it as a valuable resource for their personal libraries.

Unique Characteristics

The characteristics of *Reading & Learning Strategies for Middle & High School Students* that make it a content book that is different from the ones already on your shelves are as follows.

- Straightforward organizational scheme
- Clear writing
- Useful strategies
- Helpful examples
- Content area examples
- Reproducible classroom resources

Content Area Strategies

There is at least one content area example for each strategy presented in this book; many strategies have examples gleaned from more than one subject. We tried to vary the content examples in each chapter so that you could see for yourself how to apply the strategies to your classroom instruction. However, there will be strategies with examples from middle and high school subjects other than your own. For those strategies that have examples from other subject areas, we urge you to adapt the strategies to fit your particular content and classroom. Virtually all of the strategies presented in this book can be applied to each of the subjects taught in schools.

Word to the Wise Teacher

Please use and adapt these strategies to make your instruction more responsive to the needs of your students. Through your thoughtful and conscientious use of this book, we know that your students will become more effective readers and learners—the base for knowledge learned throughout their lives.

How to Use This Book

Take a few minutes to get acquainted with *Reading & Learning Strategies for Middle & High School Students*.

A **Quick Reference Guide** is placed on the inside front cover and continues to the inside back cover. Beneath each chapter title are three to five goals for students.

Go Ahead—choose a specific goal and find it on the page number listed.

You will see that each chapter is arranged in the same format:

- Overview
- Numbered section heading
- Boxed student learning goal
- Background information
- Numbered teaching strategies

There is a **numbered section** heading (e.g., 2.1 Creating Interest).

Chapter 2

Promoting Reading Engagement

Overview

A common concern among content area teachers is finding ways to encourage students to read their textbooks. Although capable of obtaining content knowledge through classroom discussions, lectures, and projects, many students will do almost anything to avoid reading a chapter of text (Vacca & Vacca, 1996). In order to elude their text assignments, students may resort to memorizing class notes, reading summaries, or hoping for an exam that requires little reading or understanding of the text material. Of course, as educators, we want our students to be able to read their textbooks. We also want students to choose to read the text in order to extend their learning and enhance their knowledge. It is important for students to become active, strategic readers who choose to participate in reading activities. Readers who are active participants in the learning process can be described as engaged readers.

9

2.1 Creating Interest

> **Goal**
>
> To help students develop an interest in a topic.

Background

When you capitalize on your students' interests, they are likely to be motivated to learn more about a topic, have improved attitudes toward the topic, and show increased reading engagement. Most of your students probably are capable readers, but many may choose not to read their content texts. There is a very strong tie between interest and motivation, and, by focusing on students' interests, you will increase the extent of student involvement. Research by Hidi and Baird (1988) indicates that interest in text increases long-term recall of information and improves comprehension of the reading material. One way to improve attitudes and create interest simultaneously is by personalizing subject matter. Such personalization will give students the message that learning is related to their world. The challenge is to tap into your students' existing knowledge about a topic while arousing their interest in the topic. In other words, students with interest in a particular subject are likely to be more highly motivated to seek additional information about that subject. The following strategies are designed to develop students' interest in a topic.

TEACHING STRATEGY 1

Anticipation Guide

The purpose of an Anticipation Guide (Herber, 1978) is to activate students' thoughts and opinions about a topic and to link their prior knowledge to the new material. Because Anticipation Guides are flexible strategies, they can be used effectively with any content area text as well as with nonprint media such as videos. Anticipation Guides provide an excellent springboard for class discussion and lead students into their reading or viewing with a sense of curiosity about the topic. Although an Anticipation Guide can be completed individually, assigning it to a small group promotes the collaborative aspect of learning.

Directions and Examples

1. Identify the major concepts that you want your students to learn from text materials and think about what your students may already know or believe to be true about the topic. For example, when beginning a chapter on pollution in your text *Earth Science* (1993), think about your students' existing knowledge related to pollution and about the concepts you want them to learn from the text. You might consider the following aspects of the chapter to be important:

    The implication of human activities on the environment.
    The major types of pollution and their impact on human health.
    The effects of acid rain on people, plants, water, and materials.

The **goal** for the section is identified in the box.

Background information is given to aid in reaching the goal.

Teaching strategies form the heart of this book. These strategies are carefully described and use examples from various content areas. For each goal, you will find one or more strategies.

Resources are listed with some sections as a reference tool.

Technology Tips provide web site addresses perinent to some sections. Please note that web sites are accurate at the time of publication. We cannot guarantee how long these sites will remain online.

Appendix Material

Appendix A lists various professional organizations organized by discipline to help you find a network of content area specialists in your field.

Appendix B provides a list of resources (books, web sites, and journals) for content area teachers to supplement the use of textbooks in the classroom.

Appendix C provides you with information on ways to determine readability of texts using readability formulas both manually and with computer software.

Appendix D shows you how to develop cloze tests manually or with computer software to determine whether the readability of classroom materials fits the reading ability of your students.

Appendix E lists the professional books referenced in *Reading & Learning Strategies* as well as the middle and high school content area texts we've used as examples.

Susan Davis Lenski is an Associate Professor at Illinois State University (ISU) where she teaches undergraduate and graduate courses in reading and language arts. She is also the Director of the ISU-Wheeling Professional Development School.

Dr. Lenski brings 20 years of public school teaching experience to her work as a professor and writer. During her years as a middle school teacher, Dr. Lenski developed a program that integrated reading instruction with content area subjects. In recognition of Dr. Lenski's program, the International Reading Association presented her with the Nila Banton Smith Award, a national award given each year to one secondary teacher who has been instrumental in infusing reading into the content areas.

As a professor, Dr. Lenski has been actively engaged in research and writing. She was awarded the Outstanding Researcher Award for the Illinois State University College of Education for her work on reading and writing from multiple sources. She has co-authored four books, one of which is *Improving Reading: A Handbook of Strategies* (with Jerry L. Johns).

Mary Ann Wham is an Associate Professor at the University of Wisconsin-Whitewater. She teaches undergraduate and graduate courses related to reading and the language arts. Prior to her position in Whitewater, Dr. Wham was director of the Rockford College Reading Clinic in Rockford, IL where she worked with middle and high school students involved in reading improvement.

Dr. Wham is a member of the editorial board of *The Reading Teacher* and serves on the Board of Directors of the Mid-Western Educational Research Association. She conducts inservices and workshops for practicing teachers and makes frequent presentations at regional and national reading conferences. Dr. Wham has contributed a number of articles to reading journals regarding effective classroom literacy instruction. This is her first book.

Jerry L. Johns is a Distinguished Teaching Professor at Northern Illinois University. He directs the Reading Clinic and teaches undergraduate, graduate, and doctoral students. As a public school teacher, Dr. Johns taught students at a wide variety of grade levels and served as a reading teacher for students in grades four through eight.

Dr. Johns has served on numerous committees of the International Reading Association and was a member of the Board of Directors. He was also president of the College Reading Association and the Illinois Reading Council.

Dr. Johns has been invited to consult, conduct workshops, and make presentations for teachers throughout the United States and Canada. He has also prepared nearly three hundred publications. His *Basic Reading Inventory* and *Improving Reading* (with Susan Davis Lenski) are widely used in undergraduate and graduate classes as well as by practicing teachers.

Note from the authors

You may find this book different from other content area books. We don't expect you to start reading at the beginning of the book and read sequentially through the chapters. Instead, we encourage you to use the QUICK REFERENCE GUIDE to identify a teaching goal that you think will be appropriate for a specific lesson you want to teach. Use the goal, background, and strategies to guide your thinking as you plan and implement teaching lessons. As you have need for additional teaching strategies, thumb through the book and stop when you identify a strategy that looks interesting. You will find that this book provides a wide variety of ideas and teaching strategies.

As we were writing this manuscript, we were continually astonished to learn how many wonderful strategies for teaching in content areas exist, yet how few are used in middle and high schools. We believe that many strategies are not being used because they have not been written in a form accessible to content area teachers.

Reading & Learning Strategies is our attempt to adapt reading strategies for different content areas and to present them in such a way that teachers can easily use them in their instruction. We hope that you find this book easy to use, that it helps you teach students in your content area, and, most importantly, that middle and high school students are encouraged to read texts to learn.

We have included our addresses on the copyright page, and we invite and encourage you to share your successes and concerns with us so that future editions of this book can be continually updated to provide a useful teaching tool.

Sue Lenski
Mary Ann Wham
Jerry Johns

Acknowledgments

We are grateful to colleagues, teachers, and other professionals who have assisted us with the preparation of this book. Our special thanks are extended to Laurie Elish-Piper, a talented colleague at Northern Illinois University, who graciously agreed to write one of the chapters. Kate McCabe, the former Reading Clinic secretary, typed several parts of the book. Rachel Becknell, the new Reading Clinic secretary, worked with the existing files to bring several parts of the book to completion. Dorie Cannon, a Reading Clinic Assistant, joyfully assisted with numerous aspects of the project. Kristiina Montero, Northern Illinois University, read numerous drafts of manuscripts and prepared the finishing touches to several parts of the book. Jeffrey L. Welcker, the principal at Sycamore High School, graciously arranged classroom visits. Teachers at the school were generous in sharing their books and materials.

A number of teachers and graduate students were willing to share their resources, provide content examples, react to drafts of our writing, and assist in various ways that strengthened the book. We are pleased to acknowledge the excellent assistance of these wonderful individuals:

Carolyn Bailey, Rockford Illinois
Jennifer Bolander, Illinois State University
Linda Bookout, Streator District #44
Heather Carlson, Northern Illinois University
Dawn Cavanaugh, Sycamore High School
Dave Claypool, Northern Illinois University
Mary Coleman, Northern Illinois University
Mary Engleken, Wheeling District #21
Annette Johns, Kishwaukee College
Becky Karls, Glen Westlake Middle School
LaVonne Knapstein, Wheeling District #21
Ken Kubycheck, Elgin District #46
Christine Kutz, University of Wisconsin-Whitewater
John Liedtke, Jefferson Middle School
Phil Makurat, University of Wisconsin-Whitewater
Peggy Nink, Streator District #44
Marsha Riss, Metcalf Laboratory School
Marilyn Roark, Palatine, Illinois
Anne Marie Rubendall, Sycamore District #427
J. Suzanne Oliver Sheets, Westview Elementary School
Ellen Spycher, Illinois State University
Karol Squier, Fontana, Wisconsin
Carolyn Strzok, Huntley Middle School
Christine Wolff, Wheeling District #21
Roslyn Wylie, Illinois State University

Sue, Mary Ann, and Jerry

Content Area Examples

This grid shows the range of content area examples given in *Reading & Learning Strategies*.

Middle School	= Grades 4-8
High School	= Grades 9-12
First Number	= Chapter Number
Second Number	= Specific Teaching Strategy

Level	**Literature/English** (American, British, World, Contemporary, Grammar)
Middle School	4-9, 5-2, 6-8, 6-14, 7-9, 7-12
High School	2-4, 2-6, 2-8, 2-9, 4-7, 5-13, 6-1, 6-2, 6-6, 6-7, 6-13, 7-4, 7-10, 9-5

Level	**Science** (General, Biology, Earth, Chemistry)
Middle School	2-1, 4-3, 4-6, 5-6, 5-13, 5-14, 6-9, 8-4, 8-5, 9-2, 9-7
High School	2-7, 2-12, 3-3, 3-8, 3-10, 4-1, 4-9, 4-10, 4-13, 4-17, 5-11, 7-9, 7-12, 8-2, 8-4, 8-6, 8-7, 8-9, 9-8

Level	**Mathematics** (General, Algebra, Geometry)
Middle School	2-1, 3-7, 5-1, 5-14
High School	2-5, 4-12, 4-15, 5-4, 6-7, 8-7

Level	**Social Studies** (American History, World History, Government, Geography, Economics)
Middle School	2-2, 2-3, 2-4, 2-8, 4-5, 5-5, 5-13, 6-1, 6-5, 6-9, 8-3, 9-11
High School	2-6, 2-10, 2-11, 3-1, 3-2, 3-6, 3-9, 3-11, 3-12, 3-13, 4-2, 4-4, 4-8, 4-11, 4-14, 4-16, 5-7, 5-9, 5-12, 5-15, 6-1, 6-4, 6-12, 6-13, 7-13, 8-4, 8-9, 9-6, 9-10, 9-12

Level	Fine and Applied Arts (Music, Art, Foreign Languages, Business, Technology)
Middle School	6-1
High School	3-4, 3-5, 3-7, 3-8, 6-3, 7-1, 7-8, 7-11, 9-3

Level	Physical and Personal Growth (Physical Education, Parenting, Driver's Education, Health, Personal Growth, Career Development)
Middle School	6-8, 6-15, 7-7, 9-13
High School	2-11, 5-8, 5-10, 5-15, 5-16, 6-9, 7-6, 9-1, 9-4, 9-9

Chapter 1

Reading to Learn

Overview

Reading to learn is an important skill in our society. Indeed, reading is essential. We encounter print in all aspects of our lives, and we use print to access information. For example, many of us read newspapers and magazines to keep current in the world. We rely on printed signs as we drive to work or use public transportation. When we go to the grocery store, we read labels on food packages and magazines at check-out stands. Even television commercials use printed words to convey their advertising messages. The ability to read to learn is one of the fundamental skills for the times in which we live.

People in all walks of life rely on reading. As a matter of fact, the literacy demands of many jobs in our society are increasing. In the past, many jobs did not require workers who had high literacy skills.

Now, however, even jobs that traditionally have been held by people who did not have high literacy skills require increasing degrees of reading and writing abilities (Mikulecky & Drew, 1991). Because our society is so reliant on print, these increasing literacy demands make sense. For example, when someone takes a car in for repairs, a car mechanic needs to be able to access information from technical manuals in order to repair certain car problems. The mechanic could ask a co-worker for suggestions as a means to find out how to fix the car, and workers often do obtain information from each other. But workers who can only learn new information by asking other people are at a distinct disadvantage. Reading texts is an important avenue for learning in all walks of life.

The reason we rely so much on the printed word is that we learn through language. In our society, we use spoken and written language to learn. Each of the content areas (e.g., science, social studies) consists of specialized vocabulary. Even mathematics, which is generally written in symbolic language, is translated into words when it is processed in the brain. Word problems are an example of the symbolic language of mathematics translated into real situations and words. In the following example, the mathematical formula for the question is $(x)(y) = 48$, but to determine the answer and to discuss the solution, we use words.

> David plans to build a rectangular patio with 48 square tiles. Each tile has an area of 1 square foot. He does not want to cut the tiles so the length and width of the patio must be whole numbers. What are all the possible measurements for the length and width of the patio?

▶ From *Math trailblazers: A mathematical journey using science and language arts.* (1998). Dubuque, IA: Kendall/Hunt, p. 144.

We encode this mathematical message in words because we use language to think. As a result, every content area is reliant on language and print in varying degrees. Students use reading print sources as a tool for learning in every content area.

Reading to Learn in Content Areas

Although students will use many methods to learn your subject, reading to learn is an important skill in each of your content areas. When you want your students to learn about polymers, for example, you might tell them the information; you could use strategies to access students' background knowledge and have students discuss what they know; you could assign students to interview scientists; you could have students conduct an internet search; or you could have students read a textbook selection. Reading content texts is not the only way for students to learn about content material, but reading texts is one of the tools that students use to learn.

Reading print sources is an essential skill to learn new information in all subjects. Even though there are other ways to learn, reading cannot be replaced.

The beauty of reading is that it's so versatile. When you want to learn about something, you can read brochures, manuals, web sites, books, and so on. When you read, you don't have to read every word or even every page. You are in control of what information to access, how to access it, and what speed you use to read. When you think about personal control of information, think about the difference between watching a sports event in person and watching a television broadcast or a videotape of the event. When watching the event in person, you are able to see the action in real time. You cannot speed up or stop the action. Viewing events on videotape is popular because you can listen to a commentator, watch instant replays, rewind or stop the action, and fast forward parts you don't want to watch. Reading is similar in that readers have control over what they read and how they read it. Reading to learn is about as useful a tool for all areas of life as any that exists. Reading, therefore, should be one of the primary tools students use to learn about your content area subject.

Content Area Literacy

Because one of the most important purposes of reading in middle and high schools is for students to read to learn your content information (Brozo & Simpson, 1995), students must have the ability to read content texts, or to be content literate. Content literacy is the combination of having general literacy skills, background knowledge in the content, and reading skills that apply specifically to a particular content field (McKenna & Robinson, 1990). The following diagram illustrates content literacy as the relationship between general literacy skills, content knowledge, and content-specific literacy skills.

General Reading Ability

The general ability to read is an important component of content area literacy. Sometimes middle and high school teachers think that the students they are teaching should be able to read well enough so that no more reading instruction is necessary. In one sense, this is true. Most students in middle and high schools are able to read at a basic level (Mullis, Campbell, & Farstrup, 1993). Some teachers believe that when students encounter more difficult print in middle and high school textbooks, they should be able

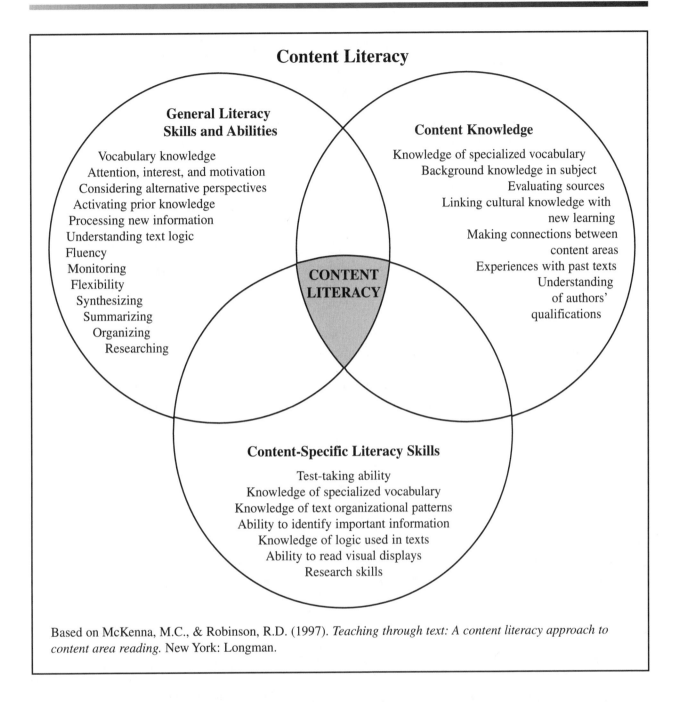

Content Literacy

General Literacy Skills and Abilities

Vocabulary knowledge
Attention, interest, and motivation
Considering alternative perspectives
Activating prior knowledge
Processing new information
Understanding text logic
Fluency
Monitoring
Flexibility
Synthesizing
Summarizing
Organizing
Researching

Content Knowledge

Knowledge of specialized vocabulary
Background knowledge in subject
Evaluating sources
Linking cultural knowledge with new learning
Making connections between content areas
Experiences with past texts
Understanding of authors' qualifications

CONTENT LITERACY

Content-Specific Literacy Skills

Test-taking ability
Knowledge of specialized vocabulary
Knowledge of text organizational patterns
Ability to identify important information
Knowledge of logic used in texts
Ability to read visual displays
Research skills

Based on McKenna, M.C., & Robinson, R.D. (1997). *Teaching through text: A content literacy approach to content area reading.* New York: Longman.

to read the text without difficulty (Feathers, 1993). This seems logical. However, it doesn't usually happen that way. Here's an analogy that may help illustrate how complex skills need to be taught. Let's say you (or a son, daughter, or friend) learned how to do a front dive off a one-meter diving board. You might be able to do that dive on a higher board without much trouble. But being able to do a front dive does not automatically mean you can do a more compli-

cated dive, say a back somersault. To learn this new skill, you would have to learn a whole set of more complicated physical moves.

The same principle holds true with content area reading. As students progress through the grades, they encounter more difficult texts and need more than basic reading skills and abilities. For example, read the following passages from an elementary science textbook and a high school biology textbook.

Elementary Science Example

Growing Green Plants

You've probably eaten many different kinds of seeds. Beans, peas, and corn are seeds. So are nuts such as acorns. You know apples and oranges have seeds. But you probably don't know that some pine cones have seeds. Perhaps you've puffed on a dandelion and blown some of the seeds away. What may have happened to the seeds?

From *Science and technology: Changes we make.* (1985). San Diego, CA: Coronado, p. 202.

High School Biology Example

Flowering Plants May Appear Very Different

Flowering plants are divided into two large classes—the monocots and the dicots. In monocots, the embryo contains a single cotyledon. The monocots include grasses and grain-producing plants such as wheat, rice, and corn—the chief food plants of the world. The pasture grasses that feed cattle, another source of human food, are also monocots. Without monocots, the human population never could have reached its present state.

From *BSCS Biology: An ecological approach.* (1998). Dubuque, IA: Kendall/Hunt, p. 330.

In the elementary passage, notice that the vocabulary is simple, the sentences are short, the text is personalized, and the ideas are basic. Now look at the example from the high school science text. Notice the complexity of the language and thoughts. Students need to have better reading skills to read this text, skills that do not necessarily come without instructional intervention.

Reading instruction needs to continue as students enter middle and high schools because reading is not a skill that is learned once and for all. As students encounter more complex texts, they need to learn more advanced reading skills to be able to construct meaning from those texts. An example of a complex reading skill that middle and high school students need to be able to learn is the ability to understand difficult sentence structure and technical vocabulary. When middle and high school students encounter content texts, however, they need to be able to keep reading even when the information is difficult to understand.

There are many general reading skills that help students construct meaning as they read content area texts. Among the reading skills that aid com-prehension of content area texts is the skill of summarizing text (Alvermann & Qian, 1994). When students summarize, they sift through information, differentiate important from unimportant ideas, and synthesize that information into their own words, thus personalizing and processing the text (Dole, Duffy, Roehler, & Pearson, 1991). The ability to summarize, therefore, is a general reading ability that helps students learn from texts.

As middle and high school students read more difficult texts, they must continue to develop general reading ability. Middle and high school teachers should teach general reading skills that support their content area learning. That doesn't mean that middle and high school teachers are reading teachers. It means that when students could benefit from learning a more sophisticated skill to enhance their ability to learn from content area texts, the teachers should teach that skill in the context of their own content area.

Content Knowledge

Some texts are easier to read than others. We find that true in our own lives. Most of the reading we do is easy for us. For example, when we read books or articles in our content areas, we have little or no difficulty understanding what we are reading. However, when we try to read material outside of our content areas, we are likely to experience difficulty. Think of the last time you read a computer manual or a legal contract. The reading may have been difficult if you didn't have enough knowledge about the content. Content knowledge, or background knowledge, therefore, is another factor in content literacy.

Content knowledge is important because what a person already knows about a subject is probably the most influential factor in new learning (Anderson & Pearson, 1984). As people learn new information, they organize that data into meaningful patterns. Then they use those patterns to interpret new data and construct meaning from text. The following sentence illustrates how background knowledge is used to influence meaning (Bransford & McCarrell, 1974).

The notes were sour because the seam split.

When reading that sentence for the first time, many of us will probably have difficulty constructing meaning. However, those of us able to activate our knowledge of bagpipe music will understand the meaning of the sentence. Our background knowledge makes it possible for us to read and understand the text.

Each content area is based on a different perspective on life and has a specialized language and different priorities. Consider for a moment taking a vacation to the Himalayas. If you are a history teacher, you might be most interested in the history of the countries found in that region. If you are a sociologist, you might be interested in the cultures of the mountain people. An English teacher might be interested in the writings of the people or in writing a poem. An artist might be interested in painting a picture, a musician in the music of the people or in composing a song, and a physical education teacher in the stamina necessary for mountain climbing. Each content area has a distinctly different perspective on the same experience. This perspective provides people in the same content area with shared knowledge and a vocabulary made up of terminology that describes the experience, but this shared knowledge and terminology may be unfamiliar to others outside of their content area.

There are many ways you can increase your students' content knowledge so that they can learn more easily from texts. One of the most important ways for students to increase background knowledge is through wide reading. When students read texts from your content area, they increase their ability to understand future texts. They also begin to learn some of the specialized vocabulary in your subject. Having students read easy texts builds their background knowledge and ability to understand more complex texts.

Another example of increasing content knowledge is through the teaching of content-specific vocabulary. Content area texts are loaded with new terminology. Each content area has its own terminology that is necessary for reading and learning new information. For example, consider the following passage.

People lived in Italy as early as the Old Stone Age, and a Neolithic culture had developed there before 3000 B.C. After 2000 B.C. waves of invaders swept through the mountain passes and overran the peninsula. As in Greece these invaders came from north of the Black and Caspian Seas.

▶ From *World history: People and nations.* (1990). Orlando, FL: Harcourt Brace Jovanovich, p. 144.

In this passage, comprehension hinges on the knowledge of many concepts that are integral to history and not necessarily important to other content areas. Some of the specialized vocabulary that students would need to understand are the words *Neolithic, invaders, B.C.,* and *peninsula.* Although some students could construct meaning from the passage without knowing the meaning of these terms, comprehension and learning are enhanced when students know content-specific vocabulary. Therefore, another important component of content area literacy is the knowledge students have in the specific content area.

Content-Specific Reading Skills

Because content area subjects have unique terminology and different types of texts, each content area requires students to have content-specific reading skills. Consider the different types of reading found in various content areas. Some content area subjects have many visual displays such as maps, charts, and graphs. Other content area subjects, especially mathematics, rely on symbolic language. Different content subjects find expression in different organizational structures. Whatever the structure, most content area reading in schools can be found in content area textbooks rather than in other types of expository reading materials (Alvermann & Moore, 1991).

Textbooks are the staple of content area reading in schools. A survey of high school students reported that students use textbooks from three to five days per week (Lester & Cheek, 1997/1998). Textbooks, however, may not be written for easy reading. Most textbooks are written by experts in their subjects. However, an expert in biology may have difficulty explaining difficult science concepts in language students can understand. Many textbook publishers include teachers on textbook writing teams, but textbooks still tend to be difficult to read. Textbooks often are poorly organized, have abrupt shifts in topics, have subheadings unrelated to material contained in the sections, and may try to cover too much information (Feathers, 1993). Because textbooks are difficult for students to read, some middle and secondary teachers may not require students to read very much. However, students need to be able to learn content material by reading content information. Content area teachers need to be in control of informational learning and should not let themselves be controlled by difficult textbooks.

Students can learn how to read textbooks, especially material that is specifically related to the subject they are studying. For example, you can teach students how to read your content textbooks by teaching them text organization. When students are able to use organizational patterns in content writing, they increase their comprehension of text (Alvermann & Qian, 1994). When students understand the organizational structure of text, they can more easily understand the relationship between the ideas that are presented. For example, if a history chapter is divided into a cause-effect structure when describing the Spanish-American War, students who understand the structure can more easily follow what is presented as a cause and what is presented as an effect. Understanding text organization is a content-specific skill that promotes learning.

The final component of content literacy is content-specific reading skills. The best person to teach these skills is the content teacher. By learning content-specific reading skills, students learn content information more effectively. Therefore, if you spend time teaching students to use the skills necessary to read

your content area textbooks, you will help students learn.

Creating A Learning Environment

As content area teachers, you create a learning environment for your students by modeling the importance and joy of reading to learn. The atmosphere you create within your classroom as well as your own behavior speaks to students about the value you place on learning. If you openly display the pleasure that reading gives you and demonstrate to students that reading provides a pathway to a world of information, you are providing them with a positive example about the value of learning. A learning environment is one in which the joy of literacy is fostered and nurtured (Goodman, 1986).

Students need to see themselves as readers, writers, and learners in order to be motivated to pursue literacy activities. In your classroom, the atmosphere you create can either enhance the pursuit of literacy or discourage it. By providing students with activities that allow them to experience personal, individual, and social interests, you will help them develop the sense that they are part of a supportive, learning community (Oldfather & Wigfield, 1996). This community spirit is enhanced when your students work collaboratively with classmates to solve problems and seek information.

Students will be motivated to read content materials when they are in an environment that allows them to have some choices about their learning. Being participants in determining their learning goals in a content area classroom empowers as well as motivates students. Research provides discouraging evidence that students' motivation to learn declines as they enter middle school and frequently continues to decline throughout high school (Oldfather, 1992). A key element in this decline is the decrease in student classroom interaction as they advance into middle school and the increase in teacher-centered instruction (Oldfather, 1992). When students lose their voice and their opportunities for self-expression, they begin to feel a loss of control over their learning and consequently a loss of interest in their learning.

The environment that students experience in your classroom is a major component in determining whether students will pursue literacy activities and progress toward becoming lifelong learners. A print-rich and idea-rich atmosphere that provides opportunities for stimulating conversations with other students and teachers may make the difference between students who can learn from text and those who can read but choose not to despite their cognitive abilities (Guthrie, McGough, Bennett, & Rice, 1996).

As future community members, students who desire to read will have an impact on workplace productivity and community involvement (Guthrie, McGough, Bennett, & Rice, 1996). Your classroom provides students with the opportunity to experience a small version of the large community they will encounter as young adults. By creating an atmosphere within your classroom that encourages active participation in reading, you are preparing your students for the real world and providing them with the tools that may make the difference between success and failure in their lifetimes. Within the context of a supportive classroom, students will become motivated and inspired to develop their reading and learning skills as they engage in content learning.

Encouraging Lifelong Learning

When students experience a learning environment in classrooms with teachers who model the importance and joy of reading, they are inspired to become lifelong learners. As educators, our goal is to support the development of learners who will choose to engage in literacy activities both inside and outside of our classrooms. By providing students with opportunities for self-discovery, by encouraging them to develop a sense of responsibility for their own learning, and by urging them to take risks knowing that they will usually succeed but sometimes fail, we are developing the qualities in them that are necessary for becoming lifelong learners.

As educators, our goals are to provide students with the tools to construct meaning from text, to make social, political, and moral connections outside their texts, to think for themselves, and to act democratically and compassionately (Sturk, 1992). Reading is not a skill that is learned once and for all time but one that evolves and grows as we do, allowing us to be informed citizens and lifelong learners.

One of the finest compliments that can be paid to an individual is to say that he or she is curious. This comment indicates a desire for knowledge which we can nurture within our classrooms.

We have the ability to provide students with opportunities for a wealth of experiences that support diversity, increase problem-solving abilities, encourage investigation, and allow them to use their literacy talents to become responsible citizens. We want to teach our students "to make intelligent choices, to think and analyze critically and to choose to go on learning—in all areas of their lives—even when they are not in the classroom or taking formal course work" (Routman, 1994, p. 17). You have the chance within your content area classroom to provide opportunities for students to become active learners, critical readers, writers, speakers, listeners, and thinkers. You can be the catalyst that sparks the desire to make learning a lifelong pursuit among your students.

Conclusion

What could be more exciting than the information and concepts you have to teach in your subject area? Your goal is for students to become knowledgeable in your subject and to become interested in the world around them from the perspective of your content area. However, you may be faced with unmotivated, disinterested learners who have difficulty learning from you or from texts. In an enlightening article titled "Seventeen Reasons Why Football is Better than High School," Childress (1998) makes the point that many middle and high school students were emotionally absent from their classes but came alive after school. Childress suggests that students can become more interested in learning content area subjects by approaching school learning as coaches approach learning how to play football. Football coaches approach teaching their players through both team spirit and individual instruction. This interesting analogy holds true with content area literacy. Students may be disengaged from learning from texts for a number of reasons. However, success breeds success. Therefore, if you emphasize the content literacy skills such as increasing general ability to read in the content area, building content knowledge, and teaching content-specific literacy skills, students will have the tools for learning from text. This book was written for you, the content area teacher, to provide you with reading and learning strategies that can facilitate your students' content literacy. We believe this book will help you teach your students how to learn all content area subjects through reading texts.

TECHNOLOGY TIP

Web Sites with Links to Content Literacy Sources

Content Area Literacy
http://miavx1.muohio.edu/~andrewcs/conlit.htmlx

Content Literacy Information Consortium
http://www.ced.appstate.edu/clic

Kathy Schrock's Guide for Educators
http://www.capecod.net/Wixon/wixon.htm

You can create a learning environment that encourages your students to actively participate in reading.

Chapter 2

Promoting Reading Engagement

Overview

A common concern among content area teachers is finding ways to encourage students to read their textbooks. Although capable of obtaining content knowledge through classroom discussions, lectures, and projects, many students will do almost anything to avoid reading a chapter of text (Vacca & Vacca, 1996). In order to elude their text assignments, students may resort to memorizing class notes, reading summaries, or hoping for an exam that requires little reading or understanding of the text material. Of course, as educators, we want our students to be able to read their textbooks. We also want students to choose to read the text in order to extend their learning and enhance their knowledge. It is important for students to become active, strategic readers who choose to participate in reading activities. Readers who are active participants in the learning process can be described as engaged readers.

Reading engagement doesn't just happen. It is facilitated by a combination of factors that include affective components such as motivation, self-esteem, self-confidence, interest, and attitude. Furthermore, your students' previous experiences in other classrooms will have an effect on their level of reading engagement in your classroom (Afflerbach, 1996).

Motivation is the most important element in creating an environment for students that promotes reading engagement. Few students, however, are motivated when a teacher says, "Read Chapter 10 and answer the questions on page 257." Current research related to motivational theory (Gambrell & Morrow, 1996) suggests that three factors enhance the chances that students will be motivated to engage in reading and learning: having challenging reading assignments, having the opportunity to choose what is read, and collaborating with other students on work related to reading and writing activities.

Selecting challenging reading assignments is the first step toward creating an environment where students are motivated to read. Reading assignments for students should be challenging but not overwhelming. In other words, the assignments should be at a level that is not too difficult for comprehension to occur but not so easy as to be boring. (See Appendices C and D for determining textbook appropriateness.) It is important that students believe they are capable of completing their reading assignments without undue stress. When students believe that they can accomplish a task, they are more apt to approach it with enthusiasm, confidence, and anticipation. Being able to successfully interact with text increases the likelihood that students will participate in the assigned activity and become engaged readers.

Choice is the second component in motivation. Students who have the opportunity to make choices feel empowered and experience a sense of control over their learning. Providing a variety of material on the same subject written at different levels or in different styles encourages readers who struggle.

Opportunities to find out about a subject by doing research on the internet give students alternative modes of investigation and may increase the odds that they will become engaged in their learning.

Collaboration or social interaction, the third element in motivating students, is a fundamental aspect of Vygotsky's (1978) contextual view of learning. Frequently this element can be provided by allowing students to collaborate with each other as they work. According to Vygotsky (1978), learning is a social process and is enhanced by peer interaction, because peers can provide essential feedback and encouragement as well as a sense of team spirit.

Another essential aspect of reading engagement involves students' self-concepts and self-esteem. Promoting self-esteem among your students involves instilling in them the desire to complete an activity successfully. A desire for success is related to intrinsic and extrinsic motivation. Intrinsic motivation pertains to being motivated to engage in an activity for its own sake, while extrinsic motivation refers to being motivated by external factors such as a reward or simply the intent to comply with instructions. Of course, your goal is probably to increase your students' intrinsic motivation. A study by Oldfather and Wigfield (1996) indicated that intrinsic motivation is most often enhanced by activities involving self-expression. Written, oral, and artistic self-expression are all modes that can enhance students' self-esteem and self-confidence. Activities of this type allow students to express their individuality as they demonstrate in a variety of ways that they have learned the material.

Finally, to promote reading engagement, the attitudes and interests of students deserve attention. If you can tap into your students' interests, a positive attitude toward the assignment will probably emerge. By focusing on your students' interests, you will increase the extent of their involvement. Through careful planning and implementation of meaningful activities and strategy instruction, you can effectively contribute to your students' engagement in reading.

2.1 Creating Interest

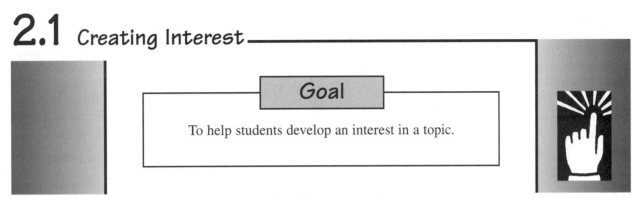

Goal

To help students develop an interest in a topic.

Background

When you capitalize on your students' interests, they are likely to be motivated to learn more about a topic, have improved attitudes toward the topic, and show increased reading engagement. Most of your students probably are capable readers, but many may choose not to read their content texts. There is a very strong tie between interest and motivation, and, by focusing on students' interests, you will increase the extent of student involvement. Research by Hidi and Baird (1988) indicates that interest in text increases long-term recall of information and improves comprehension of the reading material. One way to improve attitudes and create interest simultaneously is by personalizing subject matter. Such personalization will give students the message that learning is related to their world. The challenge is to tap into your students' existing knowledge about a topic while arousing their interest in the topic. In other words, students with interest in a particular subject are likely to be more highly motivated to seek additional information about that subject. The following strategies are designed to develop students' interest in a topic.

TEACHING STRATEGY **1**

Anticipation Guide

The purpose of an Anticipation Guide (Herber, 1978) is to activate students' thoughts and opinions about a topic and to link their prior knowledge to the new material. Because Anticipation Guides are flexible strategies, they can be used effectively with any content area text as well as with nonprint media such as videos. Anticipation Guides provide an excellent springboard for class discussion and lead students into their reading or viewing with a sense of curiosity about the topic. Although an Anticipation Guide can be completed individually, assigning it to a small group promotes the collaborative aspect of learning.

Directions and Examples

1. Identify the major concepts that you want your students to learn from text materials and think about what your students may already know or believe to be true about the topic. For example, when beginning a chapter on pollution in your text *Earth Science* (1993), think about your students' existing knowledge related to pollution and about the concepts you want them to learn from the text. You might consider the following aspects of the chapter to be important:

    The implication of human activities on the environment.
    The major types of pollution and their impact on human health.
    The effects of acid rain on people, plants, water, and materials.

2. Create four to six statements relating to the major concepts of the text. The most effective statements are those about which students have some knowledge but do not have complete understanding. Write the statements on the chalkboard or an overhead transparency, or use a computer with an LCD panel and present the Anticipation Guide to your students, as in the following example.

   _____ 1. Because of water pollution, some fish do not have enough oxygen to survive.

   _____ 2. Most pollution is caused by legal, everyday activities such as brushing your teeth.

   _____ 3. The coal producing plants in the Midwest are responsible for much of the acid rain.

   _____ 4. Every year more than 40,000 people in the United States die from diseases related to air pollution.

3. Explain to students that they are about to read a new section of text. Say the following:

> Before you read the text, I want you to respond to a series of statements based on the text material. As you read the statements, put a check mark next to those that you believe to be true or with which you agree.

4. After students have completed the Anticipation Guide, proceed with class discussion. Urge students to share their opinions about the validity of the statements based on their prior knowledge. Then have students read their texts.

5. A middle school math Anticipation Guide follows.

Middle School Math Example

Anticipation Guide

Directions: Below are some statements about bank loans from your text *Consumer Math* (1983). Read each statement carefully and place a check mark in front of those statements with which you agree or believe to be true. Be prepared to defend your thinking when we discuss the statements.

   _____ 1. To get a loan from a bank, you may have to pay interest at the time the loan is made.

   _____ 2. Sometimes banks discount loans.

   _____ 3. Some banks lend money on a discount basis rather than on an interest basis because they make more money that way.

   _____ 4. Some loan repayment schedules require increasing payments each month.

TEACHING STRATEGY 2

People Search

People Search (Hemmrich, Lim, & Neel, 1994) is a strategy designed to promote collaboration among the students in your classroom. It uses an interview technique for implementation and creates interest in a topic as it increases students' motivation to learn more about a topic. Additionally, it supports social interaction and helps foster positive attitudes toward learning. This interaction among students is a source of enjoyment and is an excellent way to introduce a new unit of study. It has also been used effectively as a way of reviewing concepts developed during a topic of study.

TECHNOLOGY TIP

Pitsco's Ask An Expert

Ask An Expert is a comprehensive list with links and information about contacting professionals who will answer students' questions.

http://www.askanexpert.com/askanexpert

Directions and Example

1. Decide on the topic or theme of your People Search. This strategy can be implemented as a way of introducing a new course, as the beginning of a unit, as an introduction to a new chapter of study, or as a review technique.

2. Prepare 10 to 20 relevant statements or questions about the topic. If you are introducing a new subject to your students, your statements might be more general. For example, if you are beginning a study of the United States government, you might use the following statement.

    Find someone who . . .
    can name the vice president of the United States.

    If, however, you are continuing a unit of study about the United States government, your statements might be more specific. An example of this type of statement follows.

    Find someone who . . .
    can name the main job of the vice president.

3. Duplicate copies of the People Search and distribute a copy to each student.

4. Tell students they are to walk around the room and interview their classmates to find someone who can answer the questions or perform the required tasks. Tell them that once someone has answered a ques-

tion or responded to a statement in the appropriate space, they are to ask the person to sign his or her name next to the answer. Remind them that they must have as many different signatures as possible.

5. Set a time limit of 10 or 15 minutes for completion of the People Search.

6. Have students share the success of their People Search at the end of the allotted time. This can be done as a whole class activity or in small groups.

7. The following example is based on *World Regions* (1991).

Middle School Geography Example

People Search

Find someone who . . .

1. knows the name of an economic system in which businesses and factories are owned by individuals. _____

2. knows to which nation most of Canada's exports go. _____

3. can name the three major river systems of Latin America. _____

4. knows the country of the *mestizos*. _____

5. can identify Pablo Neruda's "claim to fame." _____

TEACHING STRATEGY 3

Problematic Situation

Mathison (1989) suggests that asking students to solve a paradox or a problem is one of the primary elements in sparking students' interest about a topic. A Problematic Situation (Vacca & Vacca, 1996) promotes lively classroom discussions as it compels students to delve into their prior experiences and share their knowledge with their classmates, thus increasing their interest in a topic. As teachers, you can design problematic situations specifically related to a particular text. By creating a problem to be solved, you can develop an exciting and imaginative introduction into text material. This particular strategy provides an avenue for arousing students' natural curiosity and prepares them for text in which a problem/solution scenario exists or can be developed by the teacher.

Directions and Example

1. Identify a topic from your text about which you can develop a problematic situation for students to analyze. Prepare a short paragraph describing the problem using an example from your content area or use the example that follows. The following example has been developed for a middle school geography class.

Problematic Situation

The year is 1946 and you are a citizen of Argentina. Your country is ruled by a dictator whose name is Juan Peron. He has maintained power by creating labor unions, schools, and new industries. His wife, Eva Peron, has helped him by encouraging workers to give money to the government's programs. However, with his power as a dictator, Peron has taken control of the press, businesses, labor unions, and the army. Sometimes people are arrested and killed without cause. If people are seen as enemies of the government, they frequently "disappear." Some opposition to the Perons is developing. People you know have reason to believe that the Perons are stealing money that the workers have given to the government. But life is better than it used to be. Although you are poor, you're not as poor as you once were because you have a job.

Adapted from *World regions.* (1991). Chicago: MacMillan/McGraw-Hill, p.171.

2. Place students into mixed ability groups and read the problematic situation to them. Then present a written copy of the problem to each group of students. This may be done by distributing a handout, by writing the problem on the chalkboard or an overhead transparency, or by using a computer with an LCD panel. An example of a problem follows.

   A revolution or a coup against the Perons is developing. You have been asked to join the effort to overthrow the Perons, whom you have come to believe are corrupt. What will you do? Will you continue to live as you are, knowing that some of your money is being misused? Or will you become part of the revolt that is brewing? Upon what will you base your decision? How will it impact your family? What will happen if you decide not to join the revolt and the revolution is successful?

3. Instruct students, within their groups, to generate possible solutions to the problem. Tell them to imagine that they are the person facing the dilemma in the problematic situation. Be sure to provide them with enough information so that they will focus their attention on the key concepts within the text as they discuss and develop their solutions. For example:

   I think I'll take my family and leave the country. I can't stand living where dishonest people rule. I want my family to be safe and my children to grow up in an environment that gives them good values.

4. Have each group record all of their responses as they discuss them. As students make their lists, encourage them to discuss the merits and difficulties of each presented solution, as in the following example.

   Leaving the country is not going to be easy. Where will we go? How will we get extra money for travel?

5. Encourage whole class sharing of the solutions after the small groups have completed their assigned task. After completing a Problematic Situation, students are ready to read their texts and supplement their existing information with additional material.

6. Ask students to read the text passage, looking for information that supports their solution during reading. Encourage students to modify their proposed solutions if they discover new information that influences their original decisions.

7. Have the class discuss the merits of each group's revised solutions.

TECHNOLOGY TIP

Sharing Problem-Solving Ideas

Students can contact other students and share ideas for solving problems by logging on to KEYPALS.

http://www.ozemail.com.au/~reed/global/keypal.html

TEACHING STRATEGY 4

Story Impressions

Story Impressions (Denner & McGinley, 1986) is a prereading strategy primarily designed to create interest in upcoming narrative text. It can, however, be used with expository text. Story Impressions involve your students in using key concepts from the story or passage in order to develop their impressions of how these elements will fit together. In addition to creating interest, this strategy helps students develop anticipatory outlooks about the text that will be confirmed or modified as they read. When students write their Story Impressions, they become interested in how the author will use the words in the actual text.

Directions and Examples

1. Explain to students that the purpose of this activity is to look at a series of words taken from the text and to determine whether they can predict how the author will use the words in the selection.

2. Identify and write a list of words on the chalkboard or an overhead transparency, or use a computer with an LCD panel. The following example has been taken from the poem "To Be of Use" (*Literature & Language,* 1994).

people	fire	task	clean	food
forward	satisfies	fields	worth	real
haul	used	work	patience	

3. Ask students to brainstorm the ways that the words might be used in a poem. For example, one student might say:

<u>People</u> might <u>work</u> in their <u>fields</u> for <u>food</u>.

4. Direct students to write their own selection incorporating the list of Story Impression words. They may choose to write a poem or a short narrative paragraph using the words. Ask them to underline all of the words their Story Impressions include. After completing their stories, students might enjoy sharing their writing in small groups as in the following example.

> <u>People</u> <u>work</u> with <u>patience</u> if they have a <u>task</u> that compels them to move <u>forward</u>. They'll even <u>haul</u> <u>food</u> for a living or fight <u>fires</u> in the <u>fields</u>. Hard work is <u>worth</u> the <u>effort</u>, particularly if it's <u>clean</u> work and satisfies your soul. It's satisfying to be involved in <u>real</u> work and, even if it's difficult, you get <u>used</u> to it.

5. Have students read the author's version and compare their Story Impressions with the actual piece.

6. Story Impressions can also be used with expository text. The following key words are taken from *World Regions* (1998). The section describes Great Britain and the monarchy. The directions for implementation are the same as for narrative text. Students may find a Story Impression using expository text to be more difficult because they need to rely primarily on their prior knowledge. However, you will find, through a whole class discussion of the words, that many of your students have a surprising depth of knowledge.

Middle School Geography Example

Story Impression

Key Words

constitutional monarchy	prime minister
king or queen	House of Commons
British Parliament	$40 million
House of Lords	public functions
aristocrats	loyalty

Written Example

<u>British Parliament</u> has two parts: the <u>House of Lords</u> and the <u>House of Commons</u>. The members of the House of Lords are called <u>aristocrats</u>. The Parliament is led by the <u>prime minister</u>. Great Britain is called a <u>constitutional monarchy</u> because it has a <u>king or queen</u>. I think they mainly appear at <u>public functions</u> and, even though it costs Great Britain about <u>$40 million</u> a year to support them, there is a strong sense of <u>loyalty</u> to them among most of the English people.

2.2 Promoting Positive Attitudes

Goal
To help students develop positive attitudes toward content area topics.

Background

Attitudes have been defined as "those feelings that cause a reader to approach or avoid a reading situation" (Readence, Bean, & Baldwin, 1992, p. 54). Attitudes toward reading are commensurate with feelings about reading. It stands to reason that students' feelings about reading will probably correlate positively with the amount of reading they are willing to do. By providing activities for students that are enjoyable as well as challenging and manageable, you can encourage students to have positive attitudes toward reading and your content area. For learning to occur within your classroom, students need to have positive attitudes about themselves as learners and must believe that they are capable of succeeding academically (Graves, Juel, & Graves, 1998).

The old adage "nothing succeeds like success" can be applied to your classroom. Try to offer activities to your students that virtually ensure successful experiences in the course. Students must experience success in the vast majority of activities in which they participate if they are to progress academically (Brophy, 1986).

Activities that allow students to participate in aspects of self-expression can help develop positive attitudes toward a content area. Written, oral, and artistic self-expression activities are all avenues that promote students' sense of being valued within their classroom. Marzano (1992) has presented four ways that teachers can promote positive attitudes among students. They include instilling in students feelings of acceptance, providing a classroom that is comfortable and orderly, involving students in activities that they value, and explaining with clarity what you expect them to do.

Positive attitudes often go hand in hand with self-awareness and self-expression. By providing students with experiences that acknowledge that their feelings and opinions are important, you are empowering them as learners. The following strategies are designed to build positive attitudes toward content material while communicating to students that you value their thoughts and opinions.

TEACHING STRATEGY 5

Writing An Autobiography

This strategy, Writing An Autobiography (Countryman, 1992), can easily and effectively be applied to any content area. All students bring some sort of history to every subject. For example, in social studies, all students have experienced interactions with other people; in history, all students have a family with a unique personal background; and in math, everyone has a math autobiography because all of us use math in our everyday lives.

Writing an autobiography enhances engagement among students because it enables them to assume more responsibility for what goes on in their classroom. Even students for whom mathematics may have been a negative experience feel empowered as they write about themselves in relationship to the subject matter.

Suddenly, the impersonal world of mathematics becomes one that engenders feelings. Students often are surprised to find that their classmates share many similar experiences and attitudes toward a subject (Countryman, 1992).

Another benefit of this strategy is that teachers learn about their students in a personal, individual way. For example, autobiographies reveal information about confidence levels, self-esteem, and attitudes. Most important, autobiographies bring laughter into the classroom as students share their experiences. When learning becomes engaging, teachers are on their way to producing learners who are enthusiastic and willing to be active participants in the academic journey.

TECHNOLOGY TIP

Biographies

Over 20,000 short biographies from the Cambridge Dictionary of Biography can be searched. There are also more lengthy biographies with pictures and videoclips based on the programming from the nightly Arts & Entertainment series.

http://www.edge.kennedy-center.org

Directions and Example

1. Introduce and discuss the idea of writing autobiographies. Tell students that an autobiography is an author's account of his or her own life. Use the following example or adapt it to fit your content area.

    > Today we are going to focus on one aspect of your life—your experience with mathematics. I want you to tell me about your successes with math. How have they been important in your life? Consider what you like about learning math. What do you not like? If you could teach this class for one day, what would you teach your classmates? What would you personally like to learn this year in the area of mathematics?

2. Model writing your own content area autobiography and read it to the class. In addition to being presented with a model, your students will enjoy knowing that you, too, have feelings about your experiences with your content area.

3. Give your students ample time to complete their autobiographies. Perhaps one class period can be devoted to writing rough drafts and another period used for revisions.

4. Place students in small groups after the autobiographies have been completed. Ask them to share their autobiographies with their group members. Some of your students may be comfortable sharing their writing with the entire class.

5. Collect the autobiographies and read them if you wish to gain insights about your students and their attitudes toward the subjects you are teaching. An example of a mathematics autobiography is presented on the following page.

High School Mathematics Example

Autobiography

Until the time I was in junior high school, I sort of liked math. I liked it because everything made sense and seemed to fit together very neatly. Then I met Mrs. Brynwood in eighth-grade algebra. Nothing has been the same for me since then as far as math is concerned. I still don't get the abstract principles that she tried to teach us. And besides, who needs to know the value of x in real life? Last semester, however, I took geometry from Mr. Phillips. He is cool and so is his class. He really makes learning fun, and if I didn't get it, he figured out a different way to help me understand it.

If I could teach this class for one day, I would teach the students in here how to figure out the cost of going to college. Like how do you know how much you should pay for tuition? And if you only go part-time do you just pay a percentage of the tuition? These are things I'd like to learn about this semester.

TEACHING STRATEGY 6

Opinionnaire/Questionnaire

Opinionnaire/Questionnaire (Reasoner, 1976) is designed to examine students' attitudes and experiences related to selected issues. In addition to encouraging students to examine their own attitudes towards a subject or event, this strategy enables students to interact with their classmates as they interview them. Opinionnaire/Questionnaire is another strategy that promotes social interaction among your students, thereby helping to promote positive attitudes toward learning while developing interest and increased motivation.

Directions and Example

1. Look over your text and identify ideas or events on which you wish to focus your instruction. Write a series of questions designed to tap students' opinions, attitudes, and prior knowledge related to the subject.

2. Use an example from your content area or the following example. It is designed to generate information about students' attitudes towards the Holocaust in a high school literature class reading *Anne Frank: Diary of a Young Girl* (1995) and studying the Holocaust in *World History* (1994).

Opinionnaire/Questionnaire

1. What words would you use to describe concentration camps?

    _____ death factories   _____ relocation facilities

    _____ hard labor camps   _____ historical fiction

    _____ jails   _____ punishment

    _____ other

2. Why do you think that the Nazis hated Jewish people?

    _____ They were afraid of them.

    _____ The Nazis felt superior to the Jews.

    _____ Nazis were just naturally mean.

    _____ The Nazis didn't hate the Jews. They were just following orders.

3. Which of the following statements do you believe to be true?

    _____ Auschwitz was the largest Nazi-operated camp.

    _____ One hundred individuals were reduced to ashes each day.

    _____ Prisoners who worked hard were allowed to go free.

    _____ There was usually enough food to go around in the concentration camps.

    _____ Blue-eyed blonds were spared.

3. Tell students that they are going to survey their classmates to find out their opinions and knowledge about the topic.

4. Provide all students with a copy of the Opinionnaire/Questionnaire and ask them to interview their classmates.

5. Divide the class into small groups and ask them to share and compare their responses.

6. Ask each group to write a summary for each part of the Opinionnaire/Questionnaire, incorporating elements of summary writing. (For ideas on how to teach summary writing, see Section 7.4.)

7. Collect the summaries and develop a class summary or book that can be reviewed at the end of the unit. Students will enjoy seeing how their attitudes and knowledge have changed during their course of study.

TECHNOLOGY TIP

This Day in History

Choose the month and day to learn about events that happened throughout history.

http://www.historychannel.com/thisday

2.3 Arousing Curiosity for Topics

Goal

To help students become curious about content area topics.

Background

After you have determined the important concepts in the text that you are asking your students to read, ask yourself *why* they would want to read it. You want to spark your students' curiosity about the subject matter. When your students' curiosity about a topic is aroused, they will naturally become interested in the topic and begin to consider adding new information to what they already know. Building a bridge between new and known material is a necessary element for comprehension.

The text that you are asking your students to read must be manageable, not too difficult and not too easy (see Appendices C and D for determining textbook appropriateness). Arousing your students' curiosity will help them develop questions about the topic and seek answers to their questions as they read. When students actively seek information, they naturally use cognitive strategies, one of the hallmarks of an engaged reader. The following strategies are designed to arouse your students' curiosity about a topic as they become interested in the topic.

TEACHING STRATEGY 7

Possible Sentences

Possible Sentences (Moore & Moore, 1986) is a strategy that uses some of the vocabulary words that will be encountered in the text in order to arouse students' curiosity. Students will become curious about the text when they make predictions about the text's contents. In addition to motivating students to read the upcoming text and to determine the accuracy of their predictions, Possible Sentences encourages students to think about the relationships among a variety of words from the assigned selection.

Directions and Examples

1. List the important vocabulary for the text selection on the chalkboard or an overhead transparency, or use a computer with an LCD panel. Pronounce each word. These words should be core words from the selection and should be able to be defined by their use in the selection. The following example is based on *Biology* (1981).

heart	circulates	arteries	oxygen
pump	blood vessel	cells	veins

2. Ask students to select pairs of words from the lists and, for each pair, to write a sentence that they think might appear in the text.

3. Pick several students to write their sentences on the chalkboard or an overhead transparency, or use a computer with an LCD panel. Ask them to underline the words that they have included from the list. An example follows.

    1. The <u>heart</u> is a muscle that pumps <u>blood</u>.
    2. <u>Blood</u> circulates through our <u>blood vessels</u>.
    3. <u>Arteries</u> carry blood toward the heart, and <u>veins</u> carry blood away from the heart.
    4. <u>Cells</u> in the body store <u>oxygen</u>.

4. Ask students if anyone disagrees with any of the sentences. Encourage discussion about these sentences.

5. Have students read their textbook selection to verify the accuracy of their sentences. Then have students evaluate each sentence through class discussion and, if there are any incorrect sentences, invite a student to offer a corrected sentence. In this example, students will find that sentence 3 needs to be modified. The new sentence might read as follows: <u>Arteries</u> carry blood away from the heart, and <u>veins</u> carry blood toward the heart.

6. Ask for additional sentences based on the information that has been presented in the text.

7. Students may wish to record the sentences in their notebooks for further study.

TEACHING STRATEGY 8

Probable Passages

Probable Passages (Wood, 1984) is a writing strategy that is very similar to Possible Sentences in that it involves students in making predictions about their upcoming reading assignment. However, Probable Passages focuses on larger sections of text. One of the attributes of this strategy is that it lends itself well to both narrative and expository writing. It also can be used effectively for a collaborative effort among small groups of students.

Directions and Examples

1. Determine the main concepts in the text selection that you have chosen for your students to read. Then decide if the text has an identifiable organizational pattern such as problem-solution or cause-effect.

2. Identify key words within the selection and categorize them under the text structure labels. The following example is based on an expository text selection from *Africa* (1998). The organizational pattern found in the selection is cause-effect.

Middle School Social Studies Example

Probable Passage

Cause	Effect
Olaudah Equiano	best
captives	capable
died	healthiest
Africans	disaster
journey	strong
freedom	youngest

3. Write the words on the chalkboard or an overhead transparency, or use a computer with an LCD panel and explain to your students that you have placed the words in categories according to the text structure. (See Section 4.2 for information on teaching text structures.)

4. Then provide students with the cause portion of the text selection leaving blanks for the words under the cause label above. Have students fill in the blanks of the first part of the Probable Passage by selecting words from the cause list, as in the following example.

> Captured _____ were branded with hot irons and transported as _____ on filthy shelves stacked from floor to ceiling. They were given little food or water on the _____ across the Atlantic. As many as 20 percent of the slaves _____ during the crossing. _____ _____ described this horrible experience in a book he wrote about his life. He proved luckier than most African slaves. In time, he was able to buy his _____.

5. Provide students with the effect portion of the Probable Passage. Write an opening sentence that suggests the contents of the second part of the text passage or the effect. For example:

> The country of Africa suffered as a result of the practice of slavery.

6. Ask students to select words from the effect list and write a paragraph about the effects of slavery on Africa. For example:

> The country of Africa suffered as a result of the practice of slavery. Although some Africans grew wealthy, the slave trade was a disaster for the country. The people who were sold as slaves were the youngest and healthiest workers from the region. When a country loses its most capable and best young people, it is difficult for it to remain a strong nation.

7. Direct students to read the actual selection.

8. Ask students to edit their work in order to correct any contradictory statements or add any missing information.

9. An example of a Probable Passage using a high school literature text follows. In this example the text structure categories have been grouped according to the elements of the story (setting, characters, problem, and resolution).

High School Literature Example

Probable Passage

Directions: Place the key words below into the appropriate categories. Then read the incomplete Probable Passage and see if you can place the appropriate word or words in each blank.

Key Words

Bellevue Hospital complicated convalescence bumbled
operating room operating jitters surgery
Dr. George Walters guilt appendectomy
Mr. Polansky responsibility

Categories

Setting   Characters   Problem

Bellevue Hospital Dr. George Walters operating jitters
operating room   Mr. Polansky   surgery
              appendectomy
              bumbled

Resolution

complicated convalescence
guilt and responsibility

Incomplete Probable Passage

This story takes place in the _____ at _____. Two doctors,

_____, and the narrator are about to perform an _____ on _____.

Suddenly the narrator, who is the chief surgeon, develops a bad case of _____.

Although the _____ is _____, the operation is completed. As a result,

however, the patient endures a _____ and the surgeon is left with feelings of

_____.

Based on Nolen, W. (1994). The first appendectomy. In *Literature & Language* (pp. 478–482). Evanston, IL: McDougal, Littell.

TEACHING STRATEGY **9**

Character Quotes

Character Quotes (Buehl, 1995) is a strategy that motivates students to analyze the personality traits of characters in a literature selection and sparks their curiosity about the selection. Students enjoy becoming "amateur psychiatrists" as they attempt to describe the type of person who could voice the selected comments.

Directions and Example

1. Preview a story or novel to identify several quotations by a character that illustrate different elements of his or her personality. Select quotations that will encourage students to develop varying descriptions of what kind of person this character might be. Write each quotation on a separate slip of paper or note card as in the following example.

   > I guess all of you want to make just as much of yourselves as you can.

   > Now eat as much as you want, Boyd. I want to see you get filled up.

   > Boyd, Johnny has some suits that are a little too small for him, and a winter coat. It's not new, of course, but there's lots of wear in it still. And I have a few dresses that your mother or sister could probably use. Your mother can make them over into lots of things for all of you.

   > There are many little boys like you, Boyd, who would be very grateful for the clothes someone was kind enough to give them.

   > Don't think I'm angry, Boyd. I'm just disappointed in you, that's all. Now let's not say anything more about it.

   > I'll bet he's strong though. Does he . . . work?

   ▶ From Jackson, S. (1992). After you my dear Alphonse. In *Language & Literature* (pp. 456–458). Evanston, IL: McDougal, Littell.

2. Organize students into cooperative groups with three or four students in each group. Give each group a different quotation to consider. Each group then has the responsibility to generate as many words as possible that might describe this character. For example, students might use some of the following words to describe the character: condescending, prejudiced, generous, curious, and self-serving.

3. Ask a member from each group to read a quotation to the entire class and share the list of qualities and traits that he or she associated with the character. Write these qualities on the chalkboard or an overhead transparency as they are presented. Then tell students that all of the quotations were uttered by the same individual.

4. Assist the students in making some generalizations about this character or individual. Have the students work again in their cooperative groups to write a preliminary "personality profile" of this character by using the qualities and traits listed by the entire class. The summary should contain four or five statements that integrate important qualities from the list. An example of a personality profile for a character from "After You My Dear Alphonse" is presented on the next page.

Personality Profile

The character whose words we analyzed seems to mean well, but she sounds very self-serving and smug. She speaks to Boyd in a condescending manner and seems to assume that he needs her help. We get the impression that she doesn't really know him but is making judgments about him perhaps because of the way he is dressed or the color of his skin. We think she probably believes that she is doing the "right thing" when, in fact, her comments are very insulting.

5. Direct students to begin reading the story, novel, or other text assignment. After completing their reading, they can return to their "personality profiles" to discuss what new qualities or traits they might add. Students can also discuss how they would change the profiles to make them better match the true nature of the character.

Does this student appear confident about revising a personality profile? How can the teacher help?

2.4 Encouraging Motivation

Goal

To help students become motivated to learn.

Background

Motivation is a key component of reading engagement. It is enhanced by challenge, choice, and collaboration. Educators and researchers agree that, if we can motivate students to learn, we increase the chances that they will view academic achievement as a worthy pursuit. The "Ten Commandments of Motivation" (Irwin & Baker, 1989) are presented below to help you as you plan lessons in your content area.

1. Never give a reading assignment without thinking about how to motivate your students.
2. Never use reading as a form of punishment.
3. Increase the rewards and decrease the effort needed to complete an assignment.
4. Give students some choices about what they read.
5. Follow reading assignments with activities that allow students to work together and to use what they've learned.
6. Give students a purpose for reading.
7. When possible, use reading material related to students' interests.
8. Show students how the material relates to real life.
9. Be enthusiastic about the reading material.
10. Provide for success!

The strategies in this section are designed to motivate students to participate actively in their learning.

TEACHING STRATEGY 10

K-W-L

K-W-L (Ogle, 1986) is designed to engage students in becoming active learners as it motivates them to purposefully seek information from their texts and other sources. It can be used effectively as a prereading strategy because it activates students' prior knowledge about a subject and also helps them organize their thoughts and questions before they begin to read. K-W-L involves three basic steps: determining what students already **K**now about a topic; determining what they **W**ant to learn about a topic; and, after reading, assessing what they have **L**earned about the topic. This strategy lends itself well to follow-up activities such as the construction of graphic organizers and summary writing.

Directions and Example

1. Introduce the K-W-L strategy prior to assigning a reading selection with a new unit of study. Explain to students that, when they begin to study new material, it is important to determine prior knowledge or

what they already know about the material. Use an example from your content area or use the following example. In this example, the new topic is the country of Cuba from the text *Latin America* (1998).

2. Ask students to brainstorm what they know about the topic as you record the information under **K.** The following list is an example of sentences describing what students know about Cuba.

Cuba

K	W	L
Cuba is 90 miles from Miami. Castro is the dictator. The government is communist. They grow sugar.		

3. Ask students what they would like to know about the topic. Some of their questions will arise from curiosity and others from a real desire to know more about the country. Record their questions under the **W** portion of the graph. The following list is an example of questions students asked about Cuba.

Cuba

K	W	L
Cuba is 90 miles from Miami. Castro is the dictator. The government is communist. They grow sugar.	What language do Cubans speak? What is Cuba's major industry? What is the capital of Cuba? Why are so many Cubans leaving Cuba?	

4. Direct students to read the selection. When they have completed their reading, they are ready to return to the chart and record the answers to their questions in the column labeled **L** as in the following example. For unanswered questions, students should place question marks on the chart.

Cuba

K	W	L
Cuba is 90 miles from Miami. Castro is the dictator. The government is communist. They grow sugar.	What language do Cubans speak? What is Cuba's major industry? What is the capital of Cuba? Why are so many Cubans leaving Cuba?	Spanish sugar cane Havana ?

5. Involve students in follow-up activities designed to extend their learning. Questions that were not answered in the **W**ant to know column provide opportunities for further reading and research.

TEACHING STRATEGY 11

Decisions!

Activities that students find particularly motivating are those that relate to their lives and the lives of people they know. Students must make decisions throughout their lifetimes. This particular activity ties decision-making to their course work and encourages them to link their personal experiences and knowledge to the text. Being able to make personal connections to information greatly increases comprehension and long-term memory of the material.

Directions and Example

1. Examine your text and determine what information can be incorporated into situations that students might actually experience.

2. Write several short vignettes that incorporate elements of the text material. For example, in a government class studying the United States Constitution, you might think about the fifth amendment and write the following vignette.

> Rose Slender was accused of murdering her husband. She was tried and acquitted (found, in the jury's opinion, not to have murdered her husband). Three years later, her former mother-in-law found more evidence of Rose's guilt. She demanded that Rose be tried again. Rose's lawyer said that a retrial was unconstitutional.

3. Duplicate and distribute handouts for each of your students. One handout will contain the vignettes, and the other will be a response sheet for recording information regarding students' opinions and decisions. An abbreviated example of a response sheet follows.

Middle School Social Studies Example

Response Sheet

City of Red River Courts

Case	Who is the case against?	What part of the United States Constitution is involved?	How does the amendment apply to the case?	What is your decision?
1	Rose Slender	fifth amendment	can't be tried again for the same crime	Rose Slender doesn't have another trial.
2				

4. Have students read each vignette and respond to the questions on the response sheet. Students may wish to work in pairs for this activity.

5. Ask them to record their decisions on the appropriate response sheet. After students have completed their work, divide the class into groups of three or four students and ask them to discuss their decisions with their group members.

6. An example of Decisions! from a career development course follows.

Decisions!

Directions: The following scenarios from *Career Directions* (1991) focus on work behaviors that may affect career development. Read each scenario and decide if the individual's behavior is positive or negative. Then decide what effect the behavior will have on future success in the workplace. Record your answers on the sheet labeled Apex Toy Company. The first one is done for you.

1. Lucretia never comes to work early and never stays a minute beyond quitting time at 5:00 p.m. She will not take any work home with her. Also, Lucretia makes sure to use every minute of her allotted lunch time and never misses a coffee break regardless of her workload.

2. Although Charlie works on a word processor with a spell checker, he always carefully reads over his work for possible errors before submitting it to his boss.

3. Marcia could not solve a customer's problem. Rather than asking a fellow employee for assistance, Marcia told the customer that she was sorry and suggested that the customer seek assistance in another department.

4. Although Maria is a member of a team working on a project, she prefers to do most of the work herself rather than consulting her team members. She is sure that this will provide quality control and will enable her team to present an excellent final product.

Response Sheet

Apex Toy Company

	Name of Employee	Behavior Exhibited	Positive/Negative Trait	Effect on Future
1.	Lucretia	clock watcher	negative	may indicate lack of commitment
2.				
3.				
4.				

Based on *Career directions.* (1991). St. Paul, MN: EMC.

TEACHING STRATEGY 12

Structured Question Guide and Process Sheet

The Structured Question Guide and Process Sheet (Crawley & Mountain, 1995) serves as a motivational tool as students draw on their prior knowledge, form generalizations, and discuss those generalizations with their classmates. When engaging in the activities of this strategy, students use cognitive skills such as predicting, observing, inferring, analyzing, and making deductions (Crawley & Mountain, 1995).

Directions and Example

1. Decide on a unit of study and determine the aspects of the unit that are important and will be of interest to your students.

2. Think of a question that relates to the topic and use it as you develop your Structured Question Guide. Use an example from your content area or the following example from *Biology* (1981). In this example, students are about to begin a unit in biology on the effects abusive substances and activities have on the body. This example is based on the following question:

   What effects do you think the listed substances and activities have on your body?

3. Select key words from a chapter with a cause-effect text pattern. List the key words under column A.

4. Tell students to list the effect of each key word in column B. Ask them to note the seriousness of the effect in column C.

High School Biology Example

Structured Question Guide

Directions: In your text *Biology* (1981), we are reading about substance and activity abuses. What effects do you think these substances and activities have on your body? Use your prior knowledge to rate (1 through 6) the seriousness of their effects, with 1 representing the most harmful effects and 6 representing the least harmful effects. You may wish to add additional abusive substances and activities to the list.

A	B	C
Substance/Experience	**Effects**	**Ratings**
alcohol	impaired judgment	2
tobacco	increased heart rate	4
sleep deprivation	hallucinations	3
narcotics	depression	1
sedentary lifestyle	weight gain	5
other _____		

5. After students have completed the Structured Question Guide, divide the class into groups of three or four students so that they can compare their answers. They should use the Process Sheet to guide their discussions. The following is an example of a Process Sheet.

High School Biology Example

Process Sheet

- How do your answers compare with your group members' answers?

- Did any of your group members list additional harmful substances or abusive behaviors?

- Did all of your group members list the same harmful effects? Were there any effects that were different?

- Compare the ratings listed in Column C. Were the ratings different among your group members? Why do you think your ratings were different?

6. After discussion, students should prepare a written summary of the results obtained by their group members.

TECHNOLOGY TIP

Why Files

Every two weeks an article is posted that focuses on current science topics in the news. You can use these articles with students to generate discussions in the classroom.

http://whyfiles.new.wisc.edu

As students enter middle school, they may need help in understanding more complex stories and novels.

Chapter 3

Building Vocabulary

Overview

Most content area teachers recognize the strong relationship between vocabulary knowledge and comprehension of text. They know that if their students have a well-developed content vocabulary, they will understand written materials within their content area more easily. Consequently, many teachers spend a portion of time with vocabulary instruction. Vocabulary knowledge has become a strong focus of research among educators during the past two decades. No longer do we believe that memory is built sequentially from an accumulation of facts. Rather, meaning relies on building relationships between words and ideas (Beck & McKeown, 1991).

Knowing words actually involves four different vocabularies: speaking, writing, reading, and listen-ing. Speaking and writing are expressive vocabularies, while reading and listening are receptive vocabularies (Baumann & Kameenui, 1991). In order for a word to be used in expressive vocabulary, it must be adequately learned so that it is retained in memory and easily retrieved in speaking and writing (Crowder, 1976). By contrast, our receptive vocabulary involves associating a meaning with a given label when we read text or listen to conversation (Kameenui, Dixon, & Carnine, 1987). Effective vocabulary instruction will develop students' vocabularies in all four areas.

As a content specialist, you must determine which vocabulary words your students need to learn in order to comprehend their textbooks. Once you have decided on the words that are important to teach, it is necessary to select methods for instruction. Regardless of the particular strategy selected, class discussion of the new words should always be conducted in order to help students process the meanings of the words more deeply. As you teach students new words, it is important that you teach not only the denotative, or general meaning of the words, but also the connotative definitions. Connotative definitions are the range of meanings a word may have, determined by the specific context in which it occurs (Readence, Bean, & Baldwin, 1992). Providing opportunities for class discussion often facilitates students' understanding of the connotative definitions of words.

In order to be effective, vocabulary instruction must be meaningful. A basic premise of effective instruction in any area is that students need to relate new information to what they already know. This principle is equally applicable to vocabulary instruction. Not only is it important for students to understand the meaning of a word, but they must also develop ownership of the word by interacting with it in some individual and personal way (Stahl, 1986). Strategies that activate prior knowledge focus on semantic relatedness and involve presenting new words in relation to words of similar meaning. Relating new words or concepts to those already within the learner's schema or background knowledge allows the learner to develop a personal connection. Strategies such as Semantic Feature Analysis (Johnson & Pearson, 1984) and the Knowledge Rating Scale (Blachowicz, 1986) focus on activities that require students to think deeply about words and relate to them on a personal level.

Because different methods of teaching words are appropriate in different circumstances, there is no one best method for teaching new words (Graves & Prenn, 1986). For example, if you are a science

teacher and wish to teach your students the meanings of a few key words, you might choose to use a definitional approach. This approach would involve presenting selected words prior to asking your students to read the text and directing them to categorize the words as they compare their properties and characteristics. List-Group-Label (Taba, 1967) and Concept of Definition Maps (Schwartz & Raphael, 1985) are two strategies that facilitate this process.

A goal of effective instruction is to help students experience enjoyment and satisfaction as they build their vocabulary knowledge. This goal can be achieved by developing activities that allow students to play with words through word games linked to content topics. Challenging students to complete a Magic Square provides an opportunity for collaboration and enjoyment among students as it fortifies links to their background knowledge.

A final major component of effective vocabulary instruction is to help students increase their vocabulary knowledge independently. Effective instruction in this area will include many activities that are student directed as well as some that are teacher directed (Carr & Wixson, 1986). When you involve students in class discussions that incorporate new vocabulary and provide opportunities for students to apply the newly acquired vocabulary to a different situation, you are helping students become independent learners. All vocabulary instruction should help students develop the ability to acquire new vocabulary independently.

Different methods of teaching words are appropriate in different circumstances, and different word learning activities result in different levels of word knowledge (Graves & Prenn, 1986). This chapter is designed to present strategies that help students link new words to what they already know, understand relationships among words, and develop their existing vocabularies.

3.1 Linking Vocabulary to Background Knowledge

> ## Goal
>
> To help students link vocabulary to their background knowledge.

Background

Effective vocabulary instruction involves assisting students in relating new vocabulary to what they already know. Helping students make ties to new vocabulary words that are personally meaningful aids in long-term retention of the words. Additionally, relating new vocabulary to previous experiences frequently leads to increased reading comprehension (Carr & Wixson, 1986). There are a variety of simple strategies that can be used in your classroom to help students make these personal ties. One such strategy, developed by Gipe (1979), guides students as they read a short passage that uses an unknown word in a defined context. After reading the passage, students are asked to respond in writing to a question or statement with information from their personal experience that further develops the meaning of the unknown word. For example, if the new word were *barbarian,* you might ask students to write down something a barbarian might do if he or she came to their home for dinner. Making this personal tie enhances students' ability to remember the meaning of a new vocabulary word.

Students should be active participants in creating semantic connections between their prior knowledge and new vocabulary. Asking themselves "What do I already know about these words?" should be their first strategic step when new vocabulary is introduced. As they preview an upcoming reading selection, they can also ask themselves "What do I see in this selection that gives me a clue to what these words might mean?" Encourage your students to make preliminary predictions about the relationship between the new words and the topic of their content reading selection. These predictions demonstrate for students that words are not isolated elements but "parts of rich semantic networks" (Blachowicz, 1986, p. 645) and that vocabulary learning is a crucial element in understanding textbook material.

TEACHING STRATEGY 1

Knowledge Rating Scale

The Knowledge Rating Scale (Blachowicz, 1986) is a prereading activity designed to introduce a list of potentially unknown content words to your students. The Knowledge Rating Scale uses a survey format to have students determine their knowledge of a word or concept. As students complete the survey and participate in class discussions, they become aware of how much they already know about the subject to which the words are related. Additionally, using a Knowledge Rating Scale activates students' existing background knowledge and helps them begin to forge links with the new vocabulary concepts. As their teacher, you will be able to gauge the depth of your students' existing knowledge and note what areas need special attention during your instruction.

Directions and Example

1. Select a list of important vocabulary words from a new unit or a chapter of text. Prepare a handout for each of your students that lists the vocabulary words followed by three columns labeled *Know It Well, Have Heard/Seen It,* and *No Clue.*

2. Divide the class into mixed ability groups of three or four students to provide students with opportunities to share their diverse background knowledge.

3. Have students consider each word on the Knowledge Rating Scale and place an X in the appropriate column next to the word. Ask students to look carefully at each word. Tell them that, if they think that they can define the word, they should place an X in the first column under *Know It Well.* If they have heard of the word or have seen it, but are unsure of its meaning, they should place an X in the second column under *Have Heard/Seen It.* If it is totally unfamiliar, they should place an X in the third column labeled *No Clue.* The following vocabulary words were taken from *American Government* (1999).

High School Government Example

Knowledge Rating Scale

	Know It Well	Have Heard/Seen It	No Clue
interdependence		X	
refugee	X		
nuclear proliferation		X	
international laws		X	
ethnic intolerance	X		
religious intolerance	X		
chemical weapons			X
biological weapons			X
United Nations	X		
human rights		X	

4. After students have completed the Knowledge Rating Scale, ask them to write down definitions for the words they have marked in the *Know It Well* column.

5. Lead the class in a discussion about the words for which students have definitions. As students read the chapter in the following days, direct them to add definitions for unknown words and confirm or, if appropriate, change the definitions they have written.

TEACHING STRATEGY **2**

Exclusion Brainstorming

Exclusion Brainstorming (Blachowicz, 1986) is a strategy designed to guide students as they think about what they already know about concept words related to a particular topic. It is a user-friendly technique, easy to implement, and easy for students to understand. Additionally, it accommodates reluctant readers and those students who may be unfamiliar with the topic.

Directions and Example

1. Place the title of a selection or a topic on the chalkboard or an overhead transparency, or use a computer with an LCD panel. Use an example from your content area or use the following example from *World History* (1994).

2. Underneath the topic or title, list a mixture of words or phrases—five that are related to the topic, five that are not related to the topic, and five that are ambiguous. List the words in random order. An example follows.

Topic: Chernobyl
Mixture of Words and Phrases

Kiev	rain forests	radiation
illness	energy	exposure
greenhouse effect	death	accident
meltdown	global warming	world climate
nuclear power	thyroid cancer	conservation

3. Ask students to eliminate those words and phrases that they think are not related to the topic or would not be included in a selection about the topic. Ask students to explain their decisions. In this example, students should eliminate the following words and phrases.

Words Unrelated to the Topic

greenhouse effect	conservation
global warming	rain forests
world climate	

4. Next, ask students to choose the words and phrases that they think are most likely to appear in the selection and that are related to the topic. Once again, be sure to ask students to explain their decisions. An essential component of any brainstorming activity is for students to explain why they think the way they do (Blachowicz, 1986). In this example, the words and phrases related to the topic are listed below.

Words Related to the Topic

Kiev	accident
nuclear power	radiation
meltdown	

5. Have students choose those words and phrases that are somewhat ambiguous. The words and phrases that are ambiguous are listed below.

Ambiguous Words

thyroid cancer   death
illness   energy
exposure

6. Assign the related reading selection and ask students to look for the vocabulary words as they read. Direct students to make particular note of the ambiguous words and phrases to see if they can determine how they are used in the selection.

7. After students have completed the reading assignment, discuss the meanings of the ambiguous vocabulary words and how they relate to the selection. Encourage students to share their knowledge about the meanings of the words. For any words that are still unknown, ask students to determine their meanings by using their dictionaries and the context in which the words are presented.

TECHNOLOGY TIP

SAT Vocabulary Words

Visit the interactive site for learning advanced English vocabulary words for the SAT.

Net Sage Wordwave Page
http://www.dezines.com/words/

TEACHING STRATEGY 3

List-Group-Label

List-Group-Label (Taba, 1967) was originally developed as an aid to students encountering technical vocabulary in science and social studies classes. This strategy, which emphasizes word relationships, is based on the idea of organizing words and concepts into categories as a way of linking them to previously learned terminology. Additionally, it activates students' prior knowledge when they brainstorm words related to the topic. List-Group-Label is a three-part strategy that consists of listing, grouping and labeling, and follow-up discussion.

Directions and Example

1. Select a concept that you wish to clarify from a chapter in your content textbook.

2. Ask students to brainstorm all of the words they can think of that are related to the topic. Record students' responses on the chalkboard or on an overhead transparency, or use a computer with an LCD panel. Select an example from your content area or use the following example from *Earth Science* (1993). Below is a list of words brainstormed by students studying earthquakes.

faults	tremors	tidal wave	rocks
epicenter	seismologists	magnitude	plates
California	death	warning systems	South Carolina
seismic waves	destruction	cracks	Richter scale

3. Ask students to decide if any of the words can be grouped together. Invite students to share their reasoning as they present a possible grouping. One student might say that the following words should be grouped together because they all deal with things or people that warn about an earthquake.

> warning systems
> seismologists
> magnitude
> Richter scale

4. Divide the class into groups of three or four students and ask them to place all of the words into categories. Remind them that the words they place together must have something in common. This is the grouping portion of the activity.

5. Ask students to title or label each group in order to indicate the shared relationship of the words within the group, as in the following example.

Locations	Indicators	Elements	Aftermath
California	warning systems	rocks	death
South Carolina	seismologists	plates	destruction
	Richter scale	faults	tidal waves
	magnitude	cracks	
		tremors	
		seismic waves	

6. After students have completed their categorization, have the class discuss their categories and share reasons for placing words together. This is the discussion portion of the activity.

7. Students are now ready to read the chapter on earthquakes in their text. This activity will provide you with information about your students' background knowledge and can guide the depth of your instruction.

8. Encourage students to add words to their categories or move words from one category to another as they read.

3.2 Defining Words

Goal

To help students learn the definitions of words.

Background

When teachers give their students a list of seemingly unknown words and ask them to find the words in dictionaries, write down definitions for them, and use the words in sentences, they are not involving their students in a meaningful instructional activity. Too often, students will comply with the instructions, complete the exercise, and immediately forget the definitions for which they have arduously searched. In other words, no personal connection to the new words is being forged through participation in this activity. Teachers need to help students define and categorize these new words and assist students in making personal connections. Every content area has vocabulary that is unique to its subject matter. These special and technical vocabulary terms provide the framework for learning the information specific to a particular subject.

It is impossible for teachers to predict all of the words that their students will need to know in order to gain meaning from a text selection. Stahl (1986) has developed three guidelines for determining which words may need special instruction.

First, decide how important each word is to understanding the text. If the word is one that will probably not be encountered again, that word can be ignored. For example, in *Exploring Art* (1992, p.180), the following sentence appears: "This work was done with quick drying *duco* paint." Although the word *duco* may not be in the students' vocabulary, it is not a word that is necessary to teach because it does not affect the meaning of the passage. If, however, comprehension of the material hinges on understanding a particular word, it is important to select this word for special instruction. In the sentence "When applied thickly, oil paint is *opaque*," it might be necessary to teach the word *opaque* because it is important for understanding the meaning of the sentence.

Second, try to decide if students can figure out the meaning of the word through the context in which it is presented. If the word is well defined in context it is not imperative that you teach it. The following example taken from *Biology* (1981, p. 42) defines *theory:* "If an hypothesis continues to generate successful predictions, it may be promoted to the status of a *theory*. A theory is any hypothesis that is supported by many observations." If, however, the text does not clearly define the word, you may wish to select the word for teaching.

Third, decide how much time you need to spend teaching a particular word. If the word represents a concept that is not within students' understanding but is closely related to a known word, it can be taught relatively easily by providing examples that establish the connection. For example, the word *parsimonious* may be an unfamiliar word to many of your students. However, the word *stingy* is one that most of them will recognize. Making the connection between the two words for your students will assist them in learning and remembering the meaning of *parsimonious*. Discussion may motivate them to pursue further vocabulary exploration as they become more conscious of new words (Stahl, 1986).

Magic Squares

The purpose of Magic Squares is for students to match a content term with its definition. Magic Squares provide a challenging yet enjoyable way for students to think about word definitions as they solve a simple math puzzle based on a particular number combination. Magic Squares can be used as an opportunity for students to predict the meanings of new words by seeing the words in context or as a review for important definitions from a chapter of text.

Directions and Example

1. Construct an activity sheet that has two sections, one for content area terms and one for definitions.

2. Direct students to match each term with its definition. As they do this, students consider the numbers denoting the terms as well as the letters denoting the definitions.

3. Instruct students to put the number of a word in the proper space of the Magic Square that is marked by the letter of its definition. For example, the definition of Dali (word 2) is B, a Spanish Surrealist painter, so the number 2 goes in the box labeled B. If students' answers are correct, they will complete a Magic Square. The numerical total will be the same for each row across and each column down in the square. In the following example from *Art Scholastic* (1993), the magic number is 18.

Magic Square

Definitions

A. turning something familiar into something strange
B. Spanish Surrealist painter
C. joining images in impossible combinations
D. Belgian Surrealist
E. art movement based on radical ideas and dream-like images
F. the range from light to dark
G. use of space
H. things are not where they naturally belong
I. surface quality

A	B	C
D	E	F
G	H	I

Content Terms (Answers)

1. Scale
2. Dali
3. Texture
4. Magritte
5. Composition
6. Surrealism
7. Juxtaposing
8. Value
9. Transformation
10. Dislocation

Answers

A	B	C
(9)	(2)	(7)
D	E	F
(4)	(6)	(8)
G	H	I
(5)	(10)	(3)

4. Vacca and Vacca (1996) offer the following patterns for Magic Square compositions (p.166).

7	3	5
2	4	9
6	8	1

0*   15**

9	7	5
1	8	12
11	6	4

3*   21**

7	11	8
10	12	4
9	3	14

5*   26**

* extra terms needed in answer columns   ** magic number

TECHNOLOGY TIP

Vandelay Games: Word Gamer's Paradise!

Here's an opportunity to play a variety of word games.

http://www.inxpress.net/~lnp/

TEACHING STRATEGY **5**

Concept of Definition Map

A Concept of Definition Map (Schwartz & Raphael, 1985) is a strategy designed for teaching the definitions of key vocabulary concepts. Its purpose is to help students develop a rich, in-depth understanding of a concept through the use of a graphic structure. This strategy is particularly effective when introducing a text selection with an important concept that you are especially interested in your students remembering. The Concept of Definition Map focuses on the key components of a concept: its class or category, its properties or characteristics, several illustrations or examples, and an example of a comparison (Schwartz, 1988).

Directions and Example

1. Identify a term or concept from your text that is necessary to teach in order for students to better comprehend the selection. In this example, the students are learning about the concept of savings bonds from *Economics Today & Tomorrow* (1995).

2. Write the term on the chalkboard or an overhead transparency, or use a computer with an LCD panel and place the term or concept that you wish to teach in the center of the Concept of Definition Map.

3. Guide students in completing the Concept of Definition Map as you ask them the following questions.

   What is a savings bond? (category of the concept)
   What are some things you know about a savings bond? (properties of the concept)
   What is an example of a savings bond? (an example of the concept)
   What is it like? (an example of a comparison)

4. Direct students to use their textbooks and background knowledge for adding information to the Concept of Definition Map.

High School Economics Example

Concept of Definition Map

Category

savings accounts

Comparison	**Concept**	**Properties**
cash	U.S. Savings Bond	pays interest
checking account		bought at a bank
money market account		taxes deferred

Examples

U.S. Savings Bond worth $50.00

5. After students have completed the map, ask them to write a definition of the concept, using their map as a guideline. An example of a definition for the term savings bond follows.

> Definition: A savings bond is like having a savings account. It can be bought at a bank and the interest is exempt from taxes until the bond is turned in for cash.

6. A blank Concept of Definition Map follows.

Concept of Definition Map

Category

_____

Comparison

_____

_____

_____

Concept

_____

Properties

_____

_____

_____

_____

Examples

_____

_____

_____

Four Square

Four Square is easy to implement and is effective in helping students learn the definitions of new words. In Four Square students make a personal connection to a new word, thus increasing the likelihood that the word will be retained in their long-term memory.

Directions and Example

1. Draw a square with four quadrants on the chalkboard or an overhead transparency, or use a computer with an LCD panel.

2. In the top left quadrant, write a vocabulary word that you want students to learn.

3. Ask students to suggest words or phrases that they personally associate with the vocabulary word. Write one of the personal associations suggested by students in the upper right-hand quadrant.

4. Write a brief definition of the vocabulary word in the lower left quadrant.

5. Next, ask students to suggest a word or phrase that does *not* define the vocabulary word. Write this word or phrase in the lower right-hand quadrant. The following example is from *American Government* (1999).

High School Government Example

Four Square

Vocabulary Word détente	Personal Association French for relaxation
Definition decrease in tension between countries	**Opposite** strained relations

6. Invite students to develop several Four Square vocabulary examples using words from their text that are important for understanding content material.

3.3 Understanding Relationships Among Words

Goal
To help students understand the relationships among words.

Background

The complexity of learning new words is compounded by the variety of word level knowledge that students bring with them to the classroom. Four different relationships representing four different levels of knowledge exist between words or concepts and students' schemata or background knowledge (Herber, 1978). These four relationships are known word/known concept, new word/known concept, known word/new concept, and new word/new concept.

In the first relationship, words represent a concept that students know and can explain. For example, when beginning a unit on "Native Americans in Crisis" in *The Americans* (1999), many high school students are probably familiar with *Native Americans* and *crisis*. During instruction you will expand their knowledge base and refine these concepts for them.

In the second relationship, new word/known concept, the task is to apply new words to familiar concepts. For example, you might introduce words such as *mobility* and *assimilation*. These words may not be familiar in the context of Native Americans and crisis.

The third relationship requires students to learn a new concept but use a familiar word to describe or talk about it. For instance, the concept *counting coup* will probably be unfamiliar to students even though they may have some background information about tribal warfare.

The final kind of word-learning task is the most complex as it involves both new words and new concepts. You might focus on the Pacific Railroad Act of 1873 and the exodusters—African Americans who moved from the post-Reconstruction South to Kansas in large numbers. Students are unlikely to be familiar with either the word or the concept in this example.

There is a common thread running through all content subjects. All students need a variety of experiences in order to develop and enhance their vocabularies beyond specific content areas. The strategies in this section are designed to provide opportunities for students to use new words in meaningful contexts as they develop a deeper understanding of the relationships among words.

TEACHING STRATEGY 7

Semantic Feature Analysis

A Semantic Feature Analysis (Johnson & Pearson, 1984) is an effective strategy for helping students visualize the relationships among concepts. This activity helps students as they build bridges between new concepts and known concepts that are already part of their background knowledge. As students complete a Semantic Feature Analysis, they establish conceptual frameworks that help them understand the meanings of the words in new contexts. When students participate in this activity, they analyze words and concepts by identifying and comparing their various properties. Through the use of a matrix or a grid, students will be involved in developing their categorization skills as they determine the similarities and differences between related words. A Semantic Feature Analysis is designed to provide a systematic procedure for establishing categories and developing significant relationships among new words and concepts.

Directions and Example

1. Select a topic or category from your text that you want your students to analyze in some depth. Write the name of the topic on a chart, the chalkboard, or an overhead transparency, or use a computer with an LCD panel. To demonstrate the Semantic Feature Analysis, use an example from your content area or use the following example. This particular example focuses on the topic of the art media used by a variety of artists.

2. List terms related to the topic down the left side of the grid. In this example, the names of the artists are listed.

3. List features or properties related to the topic across the top of the grid. In this example, types of art media are listed. The following example is from *Exploring Art* (1992).

High School Art Example

Semantic Feature Analysis

Art Media

Artists	print making	watercolor	acrylic	oil	sculpture	charcoal
Mary Cassatt						
Henri de Toulouse-Lautrec						
Wassily Kandinsky						
Henri-Charles Manguin						
Georgia O'Keeffe						

4. Discuss each topic word as you read it aloud. Remind students of the definitions of the feature words written across the top of the grid, briefly discussing each one.

5. Guide your students through the matrix. Ask them to decide how each topic word relates to each feature on the top of the matrix. In this particular example, students are to decide if a listed artist used a particular medium. Ask students to place a plus (+) on the grid if the feature relates to a topic word, a minus (−) if it does not, and a question mark (?) if they are unsure.

6. After you have completed this initial phase of the Semantic Feature Analysis, direct students to read the appropriate chapter in their textbooks. In this example, students can also be encouraged to look for the names of additional artists and art media. As they do this, they will expand their vocabulary related to the subject and build their background knowledge.

7. Discuss the selection with the class and add their suggestions to the appropriate areas of the grid. Below is an example of a Semantic Feature Analysis based on words from *Transition Mathematics* (1992).

Semantic Feature Analysis

Geometric Figures	Features			
	Convex	Exactly 4-Sided	Contains Right Angle	Contains Straight Line Segments
parallelogram	−	+	?	+
circle	+	−	−	−
obtuse triangle	+	−	−	+
polygon	?	?	?	+
quadrilaterals	?	+	?	+
nonagon	?	−	?	+
acute triangle	+	−	−	+
right triangle	+	−	+	+

8. A blank Semantic Feature Analysis Chart follows.

Semantic Feature Analysis Chart

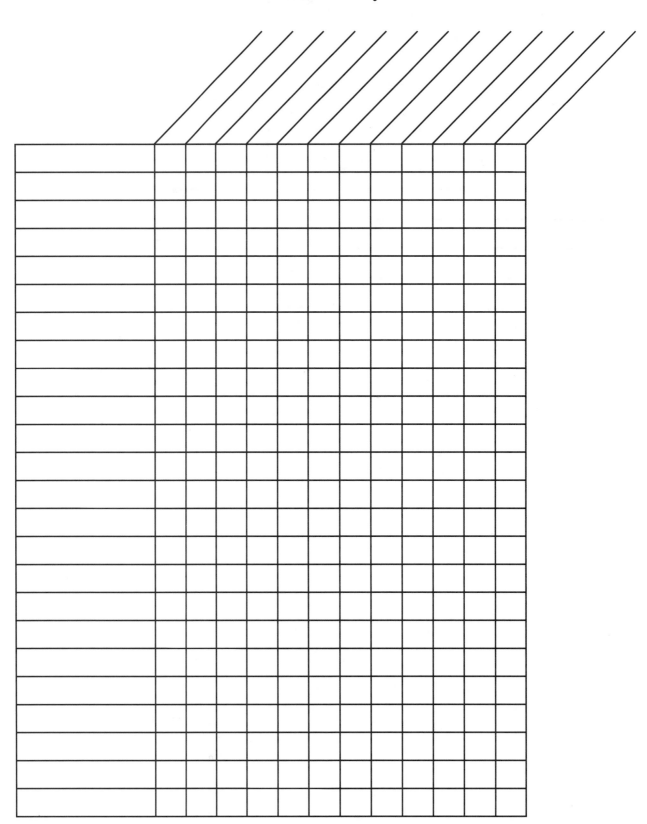

Word Sort

A Word Sort (Gillet & Kita, 1979) requires students to organize and classify words based on their prior knowledge about the words. It is a simple activity that lends itself well to small group collaboration. The object of a Word Sort is to group words into categories according to some shared feature. Word Sorts can be conducted in two ways: closed and open. In a Closed Word Sort, the teacher predetermines the categories for the students and thus establishes the criterion that the words must have in common in order to form a group or category. In an Open Word Sort, there are no predetermined categories and thus no shared characteristics have been decided in advance. Students are asked to decide for themselves what the words have in common and to group them accordingly. Word Sorts can be used before reading as a predictive exercise or after reading as a way of extending understanding of the concepts (Vacca & Vacca, 1996).

Directions and Examples

1. Select 12 to 15 interesting words from a chapter in your content textbook. The words should be ones that you have determined are related to some of the important concepts in the chapter. Write the words on sets of note cards, on the chalkboard, or on an overhead transparency, or use a computer with a LCD panel.

2. Divide the class into groups of three or four students. Tell the students that they are going to participate in a Closed Word Sort and are to sort the words according to the categories you have established. If using cards, distribute a set to each group. Use an example from your content area or use the following example from *Biology* (1981).

High School Biology Example

Closed Word Sort

Categories

Animalia   Plantae   Protista

Words to Sort

anemone	whisk fern	diatom
bobcat	paramecium	hornwort
horsetail	millipede	dinosaur
lady beetle	trypanosoma	planarian

---

3. Allow about 10 minutes for students to sort the words. Ask a student from each group to share one of their group's categories. Continue until all categories have been discussed. Invite students to explain why they sorted the words as they did.

4. To conduct an Open Word Sort, tell students to group the selected words into categories by looking for shared traits among them. The above example would be an Open Word Sort if the categories were omitted. In this case, students would need to establish their own categories for the words.

5. Following is an example of words for an Open Word Sort using terms selected from *Accounting* (1992).

Words to Sort

accountant	charter	manufacturing business
accounting clerk	corporation	merchandising business
accounting system	fiscal period	partnership
business entity	general bookkeeper	profit
capital	going concern	service business
certified public accountant	loss	sole proprietorship

6. After students have completed the Word Sort, invite a student to share one of the categories. An example follows.

Types of Businesses Operated for Profit

manufacturing business	partnership
merchandising business	sole proprietorship
service business	corporation

TEACHING STRATEGY 9

Magnet Words

Magnet Words, adapted from Magnet Summaries (Buehl, 1995), has students identify key vocabulary terms from a text selection. As students select their words, they are focusing on the main concepts presented in the chapter. Thus, students are provided with opportunities for enhancing two important skill areas: their understanding of key vocabulary terms and the relationship of the words to each other. Students work in small groups to identify the Magnet Words, which provides them with the chance to work collaboratively.

Directions and Example

1. Use the idea of magnets as you introduce the concept of Magnet Words to your students. For example, make the following comments.

> Magnets attract metal objects and magnet words attract information or details to them. Look over your text assignment and see if you can identify some magnet words that the details in the passage "stick to." Most of the information in each section of your text will be connected to the magnet words in that section.

2. After students have completed reading a short selection of text, ask them to suggest possible Magnet Words from the text selection. Initially, students may need you to model selecting the Magnet Words from a selection.

3. Write the Magnet Words offered by your students on the chalkboard or an overhead transparency, or use a computer with an LCD panel. The following words were taken from *World History* (1994):

Nile River   pharaohs   society   religion

4. Distribute four note cards to each student and ask students to write one Magnet Word on each card.

5. Ask students to recall some important details from the passage related to each magnet word. Write these details beneath the appropriate magnet word. As you write them, ask students to follow the same procedure on the appropriate note card.

Nile River	**Pharaohs**	**Society**	**Religion**
shaped Egyptian life	Egyptian kings	nobles	maat
linked diverse lands	immortal	peasants	Osiris
fertile farming	pyramids	slaves	Akhenaton
	first illness		
	middle kingdom		
	second illness		

6. Divide the class into groups of three or four students of mixed ability. Ask students to record additional details from the passage related to each of the Magnet Words.

7. Model writing a short paragraph that incorporates a Magnet Word. Although additional details can be added from the text, students should be sure that the Magnet Word forms the structure of the paragraph. An example follows.

> The Nile River shaped Egyptian life. It linked diverse lands from the highlands of eastern Africa to the Mediterranean Sea. The river brought water to Egypt from the distant mountains, plateaus, and lakes of central Africa. When the river receded each year in October, it left behind a rich, wet deposit of fertile black mud perfect for farming.

8. Ask each group of students to share a paragraph using a Magnet Word. Encourage class members to offer suggestions for effectively incorporating other words relating to the Magnet Word into the paragraph.

TECHNOLOGY TIP

Unusual Words

Interested in learning some unusual words? Learn about the history, quirks, curiosities, and evolution of the English language.

World Wide Words Home Page
http//www.clever.net/quinion/words/

TEACHING STRATEGY **10**

Word Analogies

Analogies provide students with the opportunity to establish relationships between familiar concepts and new ideas. For example, in social studies, students studying the culture of Mexico can compare it with the culture of the United States. Analogies promote creative and divergent thinking. Additionally, using analogies in your vocabulary instruction provides students with a powerful visual framework for comparing two relationships. There are many types of analogies you can use to help students understand the relationships among words. The following types of analogies are recommended for content area instruction (Vacca & Vacca, 1996).

Types of Analogies

Part to whole	battery : flashlight :: hard drive : computer
Cause and effect	fatigue : yawning :: itching : scratching
Person to situation	mother : home :: teacher : school
Synonym	obese : fat :: slender : thin
Antonym	poverty : wealth :: sickness : health
Geography	Chicago : Illinois :: Denver : Colorado
Measurement	pound : kilogram :: quart : liter
Time	March : Spring :: December : Winter

Directions and Example

1. Explain to students that analogies are a comparison of two similar concepts.

2. Model the reasoning process involved in completing an analogy, as some of your students may find this type of thinking difficult. For example, tell students that analogies are like mathematical equations; the sides are balanced. Provide the following sentence and explain to students that it contains an analogy.

   March is to Spring as December is to Winter.

3. Tell students that March is the beginning of springtime and December is the month when winter begins. Therefore, the relationship between March and Spring is similar to the relationship between December and Winter. Then, using colons, write the analogy on the chalkboard or an overhead transparency. Be sure that students understand that the single colon (:) stands for *is to,* and the double colon (::) stands for *as.*

4. Provide students with several other partially completed examples from the list above or use examples from your content area.

5. Encourage students to talk about the relationship in each pair and to discuss the type of analogy it is. Model this procedure for them. For example, say the following: Pound is to kilogram as quart is to liter. Pounds and kilograms measure weight and quarts and liters measure capacity.

6. After students are comfortable with the concept of analogies, prepare an analogy exercise using material about which you wish to enhance the depth of their vocabulary and concept knowledge. The following example is from *Biology: The Study of Life* (1993).

High School Biology Example

Word Analogies

Directions: See if you can complete the comparisons between a factory complex and a cell.

1. Computer center : product production :: _____ : protein production.
    (nucleus)

2. Electrical outlets and generators : factory energy :: _____ : cell energy.
    (mitochondria)

3. Machines : factory products :: protein synthesis : _____.
    (ribosomes)

4. Boxes : products :: cell packaging : _____.
    (golgi apparatus)

5. Garbage cans : factory garbage :: _____ : cell waste products.
    (lysosomes)

Based on *Biology: The study of life*. (1993). Englewood Cliffs, NJ: Prentice-Hall.

---

7. Invite students to construct their own analogies using additional material from the chapter.

3.4 Developing Independence in Vocabulary Acquisition

Goal

To help students develop independence in extending their knowledge of words.

Background

There are nearly 400,000 graphically distinct word types in books used in schools. This does not include proper names, of which there are an estimated 100,000 (Nagy & Anderson, 1984). It is estimated that students learn approximately 3,000 new words per year during their school years, and a high school senior's vocabulary contains approximately 40,000 words (Nagy & Herman, 1987). Clearly, the vocabulary learning challenge for students is extensive.

A goal in teaching any subject is for students to become independent learners and eventually assume responsibility for their own learning. However, this will not happen automatically. We must scaffold instruction so that students develop the ability to learn from texts and other sources independently. Scaffolding instruction involves supporting learners as they develop the ability to learn without us. We must provide the necessary support or scaffolds while students develop the confidence to learn independently. It is essential that students develop the use of strategies that will provide them with the tools they need.

One way in which students learn new words is through using the context in which the word appears. Artley (1943) wrote that it is context, not the dictionary meaning, that gives each word its unique flavor. By teaching students to consider the context as they determine word meanings, you help them further develop their independent vocabulary strategies.

In order for students to develop independence as they increase their vocabularies, they should sometimes be allowed to select the words they wish to learn, define the words in their own terms, and engage in word play so that they gain an appreciation for a versatile vocabulary (Moore, Moore, Cunningham, & Cunningham, 1994). This section will present several strategies designed to assist students in developing independence in extending their word knowledge.

TEACHING STRATEGY 11

Vocabulary Self-Collection

Vocabulary Self-Collection (Haggard, 1986) is designed to promote growth in both the students' general vocabulary and content area vocabulary. This strategy facilitates long-term retention of words that are used in a variety of academic disciplines. Students work in teams to choose the vocabulary words they believe are important to the meaning of a text selection, thus expanding their vocabulary as they assume responsibility for their own learning.

Directions and Example

1. After students have completed reading and discussing an assigned text selection, divide the class into groups of three or four students. Ask students to go through the text selection and identify one word that they think should be studied further by the class. Encourage students to pick words they believe are important to understanding the content. Model the procedure by selecting a word and presenting it to the class.

2. Explain that each group is to choose an individual to present the selected word and its definition.

3. Write the word you selected and those selected by the students on the chalkboard or an overhead transparency, or use a computer with an LCD panel. As you record each word, invite students to present its definition from its original context. Use the following example from *The Americans* (1999) or an example from your textbook.

    conquistadors: Spanish explorers who claimed new colonies for Spain during the 16th century.

4. Discuss each word's meaning adding whatever information is necessary in order to clarify the definitions. Urge students to draw upon their prior knowledge as well as their textbooks as they verify their definitions. Use the following example as a guide.

    conquistadors: Spanish explorers who crossed the Atlantic to claim new colonies for Spain during the 16th century. They traveled first into the Caribbean islands and along the coasts of Central America and South America. Then they swept through Mexico and south to the tip of South America.

5. Complete the discussion and instruct students to review the list and eliminate words that are duplicates, words they already know, and words that they do not think are important to the comprehension of the text selection.

6. Ask students to define the remaining words and record them in their vocabulary journals or notebooks.

TEACHING STRATEGY 12

Morphemic Analysis

Word parts (roots and affixes) provide another form of assistance for students as they unlock unfamiliar words. Using these parts to determine meaning is sometimes called morphemic analysis. A morpheme is defined as the smallest unit of meaning in a language and can occur in two forms. The word *book* is known as a free morpheme; it can stand alone and is often known as a root word. The suffix *-s* is called a bound morpheme; it has no inherent meaning, but when it is added to a word, as in *books,* it means more than one. In the word *precede,* both *pre-* and *cede* are bound morphemes because they have no meaning when used in isolation. Many morphemes are consistent in the way that they modify a root word. For example, *re-* in *rewrite* generally means *again,* so using the prefix *re-* at the beginning of a word usually means doing something again.

A large number of morphemes combine to form many familiar words from the science, math, and social studies content areas: monocots, pentagon, polyhedrons, biosphere, androgyny (Alvermann & Phelps, 1998).

If you help students increase their knowledge of morphemes, they may be able to use them in determining the meanings of unknown words, thus increasing their independence in extending their vocabulary knowledge.

Directions and Example

1. Model the process of determining the meaning of an unknown word by examining the morphemes within the word. Use a word from your content area or the following example.

2. Write the following word on the chalkboard or on an overhead transparency, or use a computer with an LCD panel.

monotheist

3. Divide the word into its morphological components and identify the meaning of each component.

mono theist

mono = one
theist = god worshiper

4. Write the word in the context of the sentence in which it was found in *World History* (1994, p. 40). Discuss the meaning of the word *monotheist* in the sentence and compare it to the word *polytheist*.

   While other groups in the Fertile Crescent were polytheists, the Jewish people became monotheists.

5. Model your thinking by saying the following: I know that *mono* means one, and I know that *theist* means god worshiper, so the Jewish people must have worshiped one god. The other people in the Fertile Crescent worshiped more than one god because I know that *poly* means more than one.

6. Invite students to determine the meanings of the italicized words in the following sentences by using the procedure you have modeled in step 3.

   On November 9, 1918, Kaiser William II *abdicated* his throne and Germany became a republic.

   The Nile River provided a *transporting* link between Upper and Lower Egypt.

   Sojourner Truth was *previously* called Isabella Baumfree.

   Europe's *revival* would have been impossible without improved farming methods.

7. Encourage students to use their knowledge of morphemic analysis to increase their independence in extending their vocabulary knowledge.

Developing your vocabulary

Learn about the Latin and Greek elements used in English.

http://www.wordfocus.com/

TEACHING STRATEGY **13**

Contextual Redefinition

Contextual Redefinition (Readence, Bean, & Baldwin, 1992) is a strategy designed to assist students as they use context to determine the meanings of unknown words. Contextual Redefinition stresses the necessity for using syntax or word order in predicting word meanings and making informed decisions about an author's intent. When using this strategy, students have another method for developing independence in their reading.

Directions and Example

1. Identify several words in conjunction with a reading assignment. Select words that students must understand in order to adequately comprehend the text selection. Use an example from your content area or the following example. The following words have been selected from *World History* (1994).

utopia	Huguenot
Reformation	theocracy
predestination	geocentric theory

2. Using the chalkboard, an overhead transparency, or a computer with an LCD panel, present the words in isolation, pronounce them, and ask students to provide a definition for each word.

3. As students present their definitions, they should try to provide a rationale for their thinking. Although trying to determine meaning without context seems to be counterproductive in teaching the strategy, this particular activity demonstrates the difficulty in determining the meanings of words presented in isolation. Record the definitions given by students. For example, one student might use the following definition.

   A utopia is like the perfect place to be. I read about a place that was supposed to be like that in *The Giver* (Lowry, 1993).

4. After all of the definitions have been recorded, present the words in the sentences taken from the textbook or in the sentences you have constructed. If the textbook presents the word in a manner that provides information for determining its meaning, use it. Otherwise, create your own sentences. An example follows.

    Utopia was an imaginary perfect society.

    The *Reformation,* a religious crisis in the Roman Catholic Church, was started by Martin Luther.

    John Calvin's *predestination* doctrine stated that God has known since the beginning of time who will be saved.

    Calvin hoped for a *theocracy*, a government controlled by church leaders.

    Geocentric theory, or earth-centered theory, was defended by Aristotle.

5. Once again, ask students to provide definitions for the selected words. As students determine the words' meanings, they should use the context in which the words are presented. Students should provide a rationale for their definitions. For example, one student might say:

    Predestination means that your path in life is set at the time you're born. That would fit Calvin's beliefs about everything being set since the beginning of time.

6. Have students use their dictionaries in order to confirm the definitions constructed using context clues. Students should share the dictionary meanings with the entire class and compare them with their own definitions. Point out to students that the quality of their definitions increased from their initial encounter with the words in isolation to their use of context in determining meaning.

Chapter 4

Comprehending Texts

Laurie Elish-Piper

Overview

The purpose of reading is to construct meaning and understand what is read. If your students are not able to understand what they are reading in your class and content area, they are not gaining the knowledge and experiences they need to be successful learners in your classroom. While you may effectively use hands-on learning, discussion, and technology in your teaching, your students still need to be able to read and understand various types of content-related texts, such as textbooks, trade-

books, novels, online texts, newspapers, magazines, and other written materials.

Reading begins before the reader looks at the first word in a text. Readers bring their unique experiences and background knowledge to reading tasks in a network of prior knowledge, called schema. By connecting their background knowledge and previous experiences to what they are reading, students are better able to understand content area texts (McNamara, Miller, & Bransford, 1991). This type of connection between the reader's own life and the text is very important in helping students understand and think about the texts in their content classes. In short, what students already know about a topic will affect their comprehension and learning of new material.

Effective readers are strategic readers. They apply various strategies while reading, and they read many types of text for different purposes (Paris, Wasik, & Turner, 1991). Effective readers have metacognitive awareness and control over their own reading processes (Baker & Brown, 1984). This means that they understand their own thinking and reading, and they effectively make choices and select appropriate strategies as they read. Strategic readers have a variety of strategies from which to choose, and they select those that most appropriately fit the text they are reading. Strategic readers monitor their reading to make sure they are comprehending what they read. They ask themselves questions while they are reading, and they consider whether what they are reading makes sense. They view reading as an active process that requires them to think, monitor their understanding, and apply strategies to "fix-up" their comprehension when they encounter comprehension problems.

Successful readers also know how texts are organized, and they use this information to enhance their comprehension. For example, novels and fictional stories are organized according to story grammars that include components such as setting, characters, goal, problem, and resolution. Informational texts, on the other hand, are organized according to patterns such as cause-effect, description, problem-solution, and sequence (Armbruster, Anderson, & Ostertag, 1989). If your students become aware of these patterns, they will have a framework for approaching and comprehending texts more effectively.

In addition, successful readers understand signal words and phrases that provide important clues about how texts are organized. Consequently, if your students understand that their social studies reading assignment is organized around a problem-solution pattern, they will be better prepared to identify the problem and solution as well as focus on the important components of the problem-solution relationship. Some texts, however, have no discernible pattern, and students need to be aware of this fact so they can select other strategies and techniques to assist them with understanding what they read.

Reading does not end when your students have finished reading a text. Understanding key ideas, reacting to what they have read, and extending what they have read are important aspects of the reading process. By providing opportunities for students to discuss, write, and engage in projects after reading, you enable students to react to their reading by connecting it to their personal responses. In addition, students can deepen their understanding of what they read by putting ideas into their own words, applying what they have learned, and making judgments about ideas and concepts from the reading.

The strategies in this chapter promote comprehension and can be applied to a variety of content areas. The chapter provides multiple opportunities for your students to apply these strategies in meaningful contexts so that students will begin to internalize and use them while reading independently. Promoting comprehension is a key goal of all content area teachers. While accomplishing this goal is not easy, you will begin to notice improved comprehension as a result of teaching your students strategies for preparing to read, using text structure, monitoring understanding, and extending meaning.

4.1 Accessing Prior Knowledge

Goal

To help students use prior knowledge to comprehend texts.

Background

By accessing their background knowledge, or schema, students can create a frame of reference for what they are about to read (Anderson & Pearson, 1984). They can also make connections between what they know and what they will be reading. Your students will find learning new information much easier if they can develop clear connections between new information and their background knowledge.

The schema theory of comprehension explains how prior knowledge helps students assimilate new information into what they already know about the topic (McNamara, Miller, & Bransford, 1991). Schema can be described as the abstract mental frameworks that organize knowledge into memory. As your students learn new information, they connect new ideas with their prior knowledge. In addition, they may reorganize their schema to incorporate new information into the framework. If students have prior knowledge about a specific topic, that information will allow them to approach the topic with confidence, make inferences as they read, and focus on the big ideas in the text rather than getting lost in the details (Brozo & Simpson, 1995). Students' background knowledge is an essential component in comprehension.

The strategies in this section are designed to help students access their prior knowledge and prepare for reading. By engaging students in these strategies, you will help lay the groundwork for their comprehension of texts.

TEACHING STRATEGY 1

Prereading Plan (PreP)

The Prereading Plan, called PreP for short, was developed by Langer (1981) to generate students' interest in content area reading and to access and determine the level of background knowledge that students bring to a reading assignment. PreP guides students to make associations with a topic, reflect on their associations, and reformulate their knowledge. You will probably find that students have differing levels of background knowledge about the topic to be studied. Based on this information about students' background knowledge, you can develop appropriate instruction to meet the needs of students, thus increasing the likelihood that students will comprehend the text they are asked to read.

Directions and Example

1. Select a section of text students will be reading. Examine the text for key words and concepts students will need to understand from the reading. Determine a central concept that will be the main focus of the strategy.

2. Once the central concept is identified, introduce PreP to students. Explain to students that the strategy will help them activate their background knowledge and better understand their reading. Model PreP by using an example from your content area or the following example from "Continuity Through Heredity" in *BSCS Biology: An Ecological Approach* (1998).

3. Identify the main topic of the reading selection. Tell students that they will be reading a new chapter from their textbook. Explain that before reading students should access their prior knowledge so that they will understand the text better. Tell students that they can access their prior knowledge before they read by thinking of words and phrases that they associate with the topic.

4. Divide the class into groups of three or four students. Have students list ideas and concepts about the central theme, focusing on any ideas that come to mind when they hear the key concept. Give students five minutes to list ideas; then have students share their initial lists with other members of the class.

5. As students share their ideas, write them on the chalkboard or an overhead transparency, or use a computer with an LCD panel. Try to organize or group the ideas as students share them. Group ideas by making lists or by constructing a semantic map to show how ideas are connected. Consult the following example to see the types of responses students may generate at this stage of the strategy.

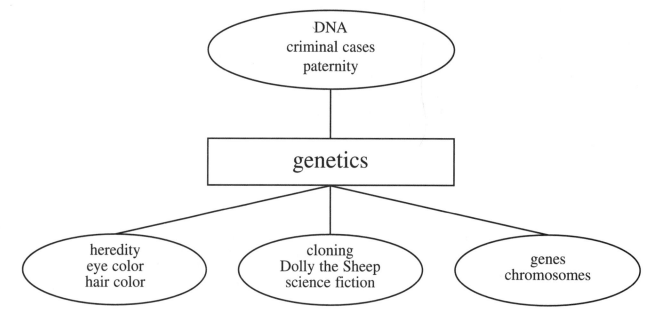

6. Assist students as they reflect on their initial associations with the topic. Ask students to explain their reasons for the associations they suggested for the semantic map. Explain to students that, by listening to ideas that other students share, they will develop an awareness of the networks of associations possible for the term. As students discuss the main concept, add new ideas to the semantic map. Encourage students to explain their thinking by asking them the following questions:

What made you think of _____?

How is _____ related to _____?

What do you know about _____ and _____?

7. Next, guide students to reformulate their knowledge about the topic. The following questions can be used at this stage of the strategy:

    Based on our discussion about _____, what new ideas do you now have about _____?

    Is there anything we need to delete or change from our earlier list of ideas about _____?

8. Add these ideas to what is already written. Because students have had a chance to access their background knowledge and to consider ideas shared by their classmates, responses during this stage of the PreP strategy often are more refined and detailed than earlier responses. During this stage, clarify any misinformation or gaps in ideas shared by students. If students have not shared ideas related to one or more of the key words and concepts, guide students by using questions such as those listed below.

    What do you think of when you hear the term _____?

    What do you know about _____?

9. Explain to students that when they use the PreP strategy they access their prior knowledge. Tell them to use the PreP activity to help them construct meaning as they read.

TECHNOLOGY TIP

Organizing Ideas

Storyspace is a hypertext program that facilitates outlining, mapping, and linking texts.

Eastgate Systems 800-562-1638

TEACHING STRATEGY 2

Text Preview

Students who preview a text before reading are in a strategic position to take control of their learning and comprehension. Using the text preview strategy before reading helps students consider what they already know about a topic they will be studying. By helping students activate their prior knowledge about the topic, the Text Preview prepares students to understand what they will be reading.

Directions and Examples

1. Identify a section of text that may be challenging for students. This strategy works best for texts that contain organizational aids such as headings, subheadings, chapter introductions, summaries, chapter

questions, pictures, diagrams, and other graphics. Begin modeling this strategy using a think-aloud procedure with the following example or create one from your content area.

> Notice that Section 1, "Earth's Growing Population," in Chapter 6 of our textbook *World Geography: People and Places* (1989) contains many useful organizational aids. These organizational aids are helpful for preparing to read and while reading the textbook.
>
> By using a prereading strategy called the Text Preview, you can figure out the kinds of information the text will contain and how it will be presented. In addition, the text preview will help you determine what is important to understand as you read.

2. Guide students through the organization of the chapter, focusing their attention on the important organizational aids in the chapter or section. For example, the textbook will probably contain a title, an introduction, headings, words in bold type, graphics, and chapter questions. Demonstrate this process by saying the following to students:

> This section has a title, introduction, headings, words in bold type, graphics, and chapter questions. These organizational aids will be very helpful as you get ready to read the textbook. They indicate important information and let you know how key concepts are connected.

3. Direct students to look at the title and make predictions about the subject of the chapter. Provide time for students to share their predictions.

4. Tell students that this textbook also contains an introduction that will provide an overview of what the section will be about. Provide time for students to silently read the introduction. Ask them to list the major ideas that they think will be covered in the section. Provide time for students to share their ideas. Pose questions such as those listed below to help guide students through this step.

> What seems to be the major focus of the chapter according to the introduction?
> What are the key ideas mentioned in the introduction?
> Based on the information in the introduction, what do you think you will learn in this section? Why do you think so?

5. Have students skim the section and look at the headings printed in large, bold type. Ask students to think about the kinds of information that will be contained under each of the headings and why. Guide them through the first section heading to model the process they should use when doing this activity. Use the example below or create one for your own content area.

> First, I will skim the section and look at the headings printed in large, bold type. I will think about what types of information will be contained in each of these sections.
>
> For example, if I turn to page 111 and look at the heading "Population Growth," I can ask myself questions such as the following ones:
>
> What will this section be about and why?
> What ideas do I already have about population growth?
>
> I think the section will be about how and why populations grow. I think it might also describe problems of overpopulation in an area. I know that population growth can be a problem for animals, like when too many deer survive the winter and there is not enough food for them in the

spring. I also know that population growth can be a problem for humans when they need to expand the roads, increase food supply, and provide water for lots of people.

I will also look through the paragraphs under this heading to see if there are any words in bold type. Under this heading, there are several words and phrases in bold type. They are *birthrate, death rate, standard of living, life expectancy,* and *population explosion.* I can ask myself the following questions:

> Do I already know any of these words?
> Do these words give me any clues about the subject of this part of the section?

6. Instruct students to continue this pattern of looking at headings and words in bold type until they have worked through the remaining headings in the section. Provide time for students to share their findings and ideas.

7. Direct students' attention to graphics in the section and provide time for them to discuss the types of information the graphics provide and why they might be included in the section. Model this process for them using the following example or create an example from your content area.

> On page 112, I see a photograph with a caption. What can I tell about the population of the area in the picture? I wonder why the textbook's authors included this picture in this section of the chapter.

> Figure 6-1 on page 113 looks important. What types of information does this figure provide? Why might the authors include a figure about actual and projected world population growth in this section of the text? Does this figure give me any additional ideas about what this section might be about? Why?

Ask students to look at any remaining graphics in the section. Encourage students to ask themselves questions such as those listed below.

> What types of information does the graphic provide?
> Why did the authors include it in the section?
> What does the graphic tell me about the types of information that will be in the section?

8. Inform students that the questions at the end of a section are very helpful when preparing to read. Tell students that these questions will help them understand what is important in the section and what they should understand when they finish reading the section. Model this stage of the strategy by using the following example or create an example from your content area.

> At the end of the section, I see the "Content Check" questions. I know these questions are important because we often discuss them in class. Sometimes similar questions are on a test. The first question asks me about some vocabulary words from the section. What important terms should I know and understand after reading this section? I should probably make a list of these words so I can pay attention to them when I read the section.

9. Ask students to look at the remaining questions and have them consider what they will be expected to know after reading the section. Remind students that the Text Preview strategy is an important prereading technique. Encourage them to think about the ideas from the Text Preview strategy as they read.

TEACHING STRATEGY 3

Anticipation/Reaction Guide

An Anticipation/Reaction Guide (Herber, 1978) enhances students' comprehension by activating their background knowledge, focusing their attention on key concepts to be addressed in the text reading, and inviting them to react to ideas in the text. An Anticipation/Reaction Guide is composed of a series of statements that supports students' opinions or challenges their beliefs about the topic of the text. The statements invite multiple responses based on students' experiences and opinions. Students mark whether they agree or disagree with a specific statement prior to reading about the topic. The real impact of this activity lies in the discussion that occurs after students have marked their responses. During this discussion, the teacher activates and agitates students' thoughts by asking open-ended questions such as "Why do you feel that way?" or "What ideas help to support your view?" Students then read the text to see if their responses change after reading or if their responses agree or disagree with the author's ideas. Another discussion occurs after reading to encourage students to discuss how and why their ideas and opinions changed after reading the text.

Directions and Example

1. Analyze the text to be read. Determine the major ideas students will need to consider.

2. Write those ideas in short, declarative sentences. Try to focus the statements on experiences that relate to students' lives. Limit the number of statements from four to six so ample time can be devoted to thinking about and discussing each statement fully.

3. Arrange the statements in an order and format that will elicit predictions and invite student participation.

4. Present the Anticipation Guide to students by providing a handout or by writing it on the chalkboard or an overhead transparency, or by using a computer with an LCD panel. Use the following example or create one from your content area.

Middle School Science Example

Anticipation/Reaction Guide

Directions: Before reading the section, read the following statements. Put a check mark in the "Before Reading" column next to each statement with which you agree. Be prepared to discuss your responses. After you read the section, put a check mark in the "After Reading" column next to each statement with which you agree. Be prepared to discuss your responses.

Before Reading   After Reading

_____ 1. Water belongs to everyone.   _____

_____ 2. There is plenty of water for people to use around the world. _____

_____ 3. Animals can migrate if there is not enough water.   _____

_____ 4. Droughts mainly affect people and animals in desert climates. _____

_____ 5. The availability of water impacts the lifestyles of humans. _____

_____ 6. Pollution is the greatest threat to the availability of water. _____

Based on *Ecology: A systems approach—water.* (1998). Dubuque, IA: Kendall/Hunt.

5. Give students a few minutes to respond to each of the statements and to consider how they will explain and support their responses.

6. Discuss each statement. Ask students to support their responses.

7. Explain to students that as they read the text they should consider their ideas from the Anticipation/ Reaction Guide and whether their views have stayed the same or have changed after reading the text.

8. After students complete the reading, engage them in a follow-up discussion to determine whether their responses have changed and why.

TEACHING STRATEGY 4

Think Sheet

The Think Sheet strategy helps students compare and contrast their prereading ideas with ideas from the text (Clewell & Haidemenous, 1982). By examining their own background knowledge and questions about a topic to be studied, students will be better prepared to read. After reading, students compare and contrast their ideas and questions with information from the text to help them make connections between their prior knowledge and ideas in the text.

Directions and Example

1. Select a text passage that students will be reading. Formulate a central issue about the topic to be studied.

2. Present the Think Sheet to students. Explain that students should record their questions about the central issue in the first column. Model this process by using the following example from *The American Nation* (1991) or create an example from your content area.

Think Sheet

Central Issue:

My Questions	My Ideas	Text Ideas

3. Explain that content area reading often has a central issue. In this passage, the central issue is that many things influenced the involvement of the United States in World War I. Have students generate questions about the central issue and write them on the Think Sheet. Examples of questions follow.

> When and where did World War I take place?
> Were things better for the United States after World War I?
> How many casualties were there, and how did this affect the United States?

4. Tell students that the second column focuses on what students know about the central issue before reading the textbook. Ask students to list their own ideas about the central issue on their Think Sheets. Model this stage of the strategy by using the following example or create one from your content area.

> The second column asks me to list ideas that I already know about the central issue. Let's see. I know that World War I started without the United States. I know that the United States only got involved later. I know that a ship sinking had something to do with the United States getting into the war.

5. Explain to students that they should read to find answers to their questions and also to determine whether their ideas are supported or negated by the text. Ask students to record important ideas from the text in the third column of the Think Sheet as they read.

6. After students have completed the text reading, ask them to share what they learned from the text. Guide students to make connections among their questions, their ideas, and the ideas in the text by posing questions such as the following ones.

> What did the text say about your question?
> What questions were not answered by the text?
> What ideas from your Think Sheet did the text support?
> What ideas from your Think Sheet did the text negate?
> Were there some ideas that were only partially supported or negated? Explain.

Literature Discussion Online

American Literature Survey Site provides students with an opportunity to discuss great works online.

http://www.en.utexas.edu/~daniel/amlit/amlit.html

This adult is helping the student to make predictions about what will happen in the story. After reading a section, they will discuss the accuracy of the prediction and make new predictions.

4.2 Using Text Structure

Goal
To help students use text structure to comprehend texts.

Background

Various types of texts are structured differently. Effective readers are aware of the structures of texts, and they can use this information to help them anticipate, monitor, and comprehend what they are reading (Taylor & Beach, 1984). Authors use a structure, or organization of ideas, to present their writing in a way that communicates with the reader (Pearson & Camperell, 1994). By helping your students develop an awareness of the common text organizational patterns, you will provide them with an important tool for comprehension. If your students understand and can identify text structures, they will be more likely to understand, remember, and apply the ideas they encounter in their reading (Weaver & Kintsch, 1991).

Fiction and nonfiction texts are structured differently. Fiction texts are organized around the concept of a story grammar that includes setting, characters, goal, problem, and resolution. Many of your students may already be familiar with the organization of fiction because, during the elementary school years, they received a great deal of instruction on reading fiction. They will need assistance, however, with developing a clear understanding of the more complex fictional stories and novels they will be reading during their middle and high school years. In addition, more complex aspects of plot development, such as initiating events, internal responses, character motivation, and theme, may be new to middle and high school students.

Nonfiction texts are often more difficult for students to comprehend because they may not understand how these texts are organized. Nonfiction texts are generally organized around five common text patterns: description, sequence, compare-contrast, cause-effect, and problem-solution. Authors often use signal or flag words to help readers identify the text structure being used. For example, an author may use words such as *because, since, therefore, consequently,* and *as a result* to signal that the cause-effect text structure is being used (Vacca & Vacca, 1996). Most informational writing is complex, including content area textbooks, and several text structures may be used in a section of text. If you are aware of the text structures used in a specific text, you will be more able to help your students become aware of signal words and text structures. Helping your students to identify and understand common text structures will enhance their comprehension.

Graphic Organizers

Graphic Organizers are pictorial representations of how ideas in a text are connected and organized. They help students understand main ideas in what they read, how ideas are related, and how important details support main ideas. Graphic Organizers serve purposes similar to outlining, but they provide more flexibility and capitalize on students' interests and facility with visual representations (Vacca & Vacca, 1996).

TECHNOLOGY TIP

Building Relationships Among Ideas

Learning Tool is a hypertext program that allows writers to build relationships among ideas.

Intellimation 800-346-8355

Directions and Example

1. Tell students that when they understand the ways texts are organized, they will be able to organize the information and understand it better. Explain to students that by using Graphic Organizers they can organize information more readily.

2. Select a passage that you want students to read. Explain to students that you will be modeling the use of Graphic Organizers to help them understand how the information is organized, thus promoting better comprehension.

3. Explain that there are five main patterns for organizing content texts: description, sequence, compare-contrast, cause-effect, and problem-solution. Write these words on the chalkboard or an overhead transparency.

4. Model how to use a Graphic Organizer using examples from your content area or use the following example.

> We will be using a Graphic Organizer for a section of our textbook *A More Perfect Union* (1991). The section is titled "The Sectional Conflict," and it describes how the North and South felt about slavery. We will be using the Compare-Contrast Graphic Organizer for this activity.

5. Present the Compare-Contrast Graphic Organizer by displaying it on the chalkboard or an overhead transparency. Explain that one item being compared goes in each circle, and the overlapping area contains information that the concepts have in common as in the following example.

Compare-Contrast Graphic Organizer

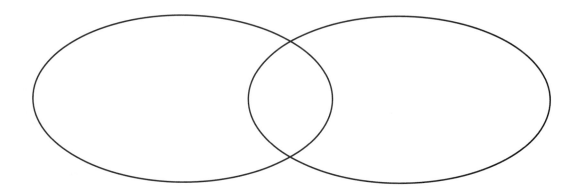

6. Model for students how to read the text and identify important information to include in the Compare-Contrast Graphic Organizer. Continue to use examples from your content area or use the following example.

Compare-contrast pattern means that the text will present two different concepts and how they are alike and how they are different. Skim the section. Note that the text presents information about the North and the South. The introduction also states that the text will be comparing how the people in the North and the South felt about slavery during the Civil War. This information will be helpful as you start to fill in the Compare-Contrast Graphic Organizer. Fill in a title and label each of the circles to show what you are comparing and contrasting.

**Compare-Contrast Graphic Organizer for
North and South Positions on Slavery Issue**

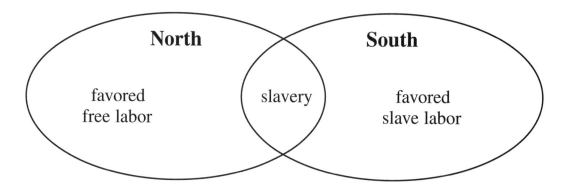

7. Read the first section aloud and demonstrate for students the thought processes you use to identify important information from the text. Continue to use examples from your content area or the following example.

After reading the first part of the section, I learned that the North and South had different opinions about the labor system. The North favored a free labor system, and the South favored a slave labor system. This is the main idea in this part of the section. I will add it to the compare-contrast chart.

While that is an important difference, I also learned that when I compared the North and South, they had something in common. They both needed a lot of labor to build their new and growing economies. I can add this to the compare section of the Graphic Organizer. I can continue to use the same strategy as I read the other parts of the text.

8. Ask students to read the remaining parts of the section and fill in important comparisons and contrasts between the North and South on their Graphic Organizers. Then have students in small groups discuss their compare-contrast charts to clarify and expand on their comparisons. Students may also include some comparisons that are not important. Such comparisons should be deleted.

9. In future lessons, introduce other Graphic Organizers to help students learn how to use them for other text organizational patterns. (Several Graphic Organizers are provided on the following pages.) Provide modeling and practice so students can learn how to use Graphic Organizers to understand text organizational patterns and improve their comprehension of texts.

Graphic Organizer for Description

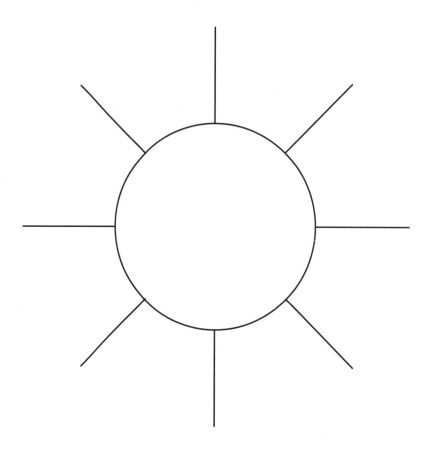

Graphic Organizer for Sequence

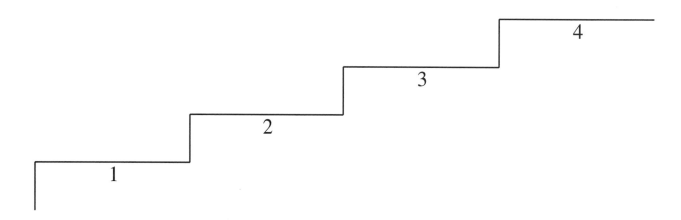

Graphic Organizer for Cause and Effect

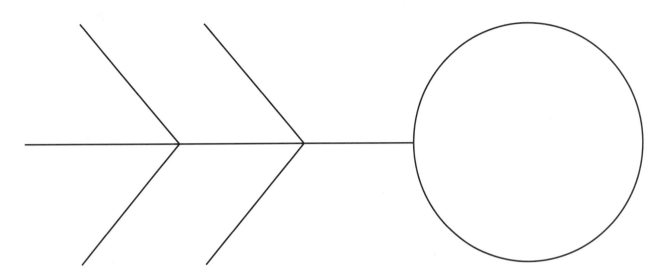

Graphic Organizer for Problem and Solution

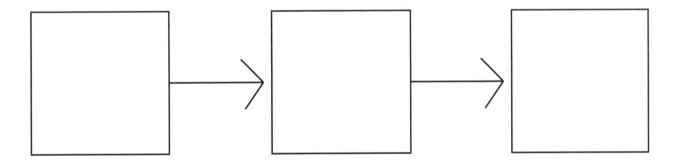

TEACHING STRATEGY 6

Idea-Maps

An Idea-Map is a strategy that helps readers see how information in an expository text is organized (Armbruster, 1986). The visual nature of the Idea-Map strategy helps students see and understand the organizational pattern of a text and how the various components fit together. Depending on the text to be studied, different forms of Idea-Maps can be used. For example, Idea-Maps can be designed for use with description, compare-contrast, sequence, cause-effect, and problem-solution patterns (Johns & Lenski, 1997).

Directions and Examples

1. Select a passage that you want students to read and learn. Determine the organizational pattern of the text. Select the appropriate Idea-Map for the text. Several types of Idea-Maps are included at the end of these directions.

2. Tell students that you will be demonstrating how to use a strategy called Idea-Maps to help them understand how their content textbooks are organized.

3. Explain that there are five main patterns for organizing content texts: description, sequence, compare-contrast, cause-effect, and problem-solution. Write these words on the chalkboard or an overhead transparency.

4. Model the Idea-Map strategy using examples from your content area or use the following example from *Science Interactions* (1995). Tell students that the first step in using an Idea-Map is to identify the text's organizational pattern. Model how to determine the text's pattern as in the following example.

   We will be reading section 11-2 from our science textbook. This section focuses on how the digestive system works. Skim through the section. You'll notice that there are a series of steps that occur in the digestive system. This is a good clue that the text is using the organizational pattern of sequence.

5. Present the Idea-Map for sequential text patterns by displaying it on the chalkboard or an overhead transparency.

Sequence Idea-Map

TOPIC:
↓
↓
↓
↓

6. Model for students how to read the text and identify the important information to include in the Idea-Map. Begin with the topic for the section. Continue to use examples from your content area or the following example.

> Sequencing ideas means that they need to be in order, just like the steps in a science experiment. As you read this section on digestion, look for the important steps. As you identify steps in the sequence, write them on the Idea-Map in the order they were presented.
>
> First, read the introduction of the section to clarify the topic of the section. The title of the section is "Digestion: A Disassembly Line." As you read the introduction, notice that the word *digestion* is in bold type and a definition is provided. The definition says "Digestion is the process that breaks down carbohydrates, fats, and proteins into smaller and simpler molecules used by the cells in your body" (p. 351).
>
> It seems like the topic of the section is digestion—a process that breaks down fats, carbohydrates, and proteins for use in the body. Fill that in on the topic section of the Idea-Map.

7. Continue to model the process for comprehending the passage by identifying details in order. Use examples from your content area or use the example provided below.

> Look at the next part of the section; it has a heading called "The Mouth." As you read this part, notice that digestion begins in the mouth. The passage also states how the teeth, saliva, and enzymes begin to break down the food. This seems like an important first step in the digestion process, so add it to the Idea-Map.
>
> The next section of the passage has a heading "From Mouth to Stomach." As you read this part, notice that the passage states that food travels from the mouth down the esophagus to the stomach. This is the next important step in digestion, so add it to the Idea-Map.
>
> Your Idea-Map should look something like the one that follows.

Sequence Idea-Map

TOPIC: Digestion is a process that breaks down carbohydrates, fats, and proteins for use in the body.
Digestion begins in the mouth with the teeth, saliva, and enzymes breaking down the food. ↓
Next, the food moves from the mouth down the esophagus to the stomach. This process is called peristalsis. ↓
↓
↓

8. Tell students that they can use the same techniques that you modeled to fill out the rest of the Idea-Map. Provide time for students to read the rest of the section and fill out the remainder of the Idea-Map.

9. Ask students to share and refine their Idea-Maps. Remind students that the Idea-Map is a helpful tool that uses text structure to improve their comprehension.

10. In future lessons, introduce other Idea-Maps that are appropriate for your texts. (Additional Idea-Maps can be found on the following pages.) Provide sufficient modeling and practice opportunities so students can learn how to use the Idea-Maps to improve their understanding of text structures and content texts.

Practicing idea mapping is an appropriate way to improve understanding of text structures and content texts.

Description Idea-Map

TOPIC:

Compare-Contrast Idea-Map

TOPIC:		TOPIC:
	=	
	=	
	=	
	≠	
	≠	
	≠	

Problem-Solution Idea-Map

PROBLEM:	→	SOLUTION:

Cause-Effect Idea-Map

CAUSE:	→	EFFECT:

TEACHING STRATEGY 7

Story Maps

Story Maps are graphic organizers for fictional texts. Fictional texts have a different text structure than informational texts. Fictional texts are organized around the elements of fiction: setting, characters, theme, and events in the plot. Many middle and high school students are familiar with the elements of fiction because they have had many experiences reading stories and identifying the stories' elements. However, as middle and high school students read more sophisticated stories with subtle plots, they should be reminded to identify the structures of the stories to enhance their comprehension.

TECHNOLOGY TIP

Learning Elements of Literature

Elements of Literature web site provides definitions of literary terms.

http://fur.rscc.cc.tn.us/OWL/ElementsLit.html

Directions and Example

1. Remind students that as they read they should identify the elements of fiction to help them understand the story.

2. Write the elements of fiction on the chalkboard or an overhead transparency. Include blank spaces after each term as listed below.

    Setting (time and place) _____

    Main characters _____

    Minor characters _____

    Problem _____

    Events _____

    Solution _____

    Theme (main point of story) _____

3. Review the elements of fiction using a story or book that students have read. Tell students that the setting is the time and place the story took place. If students are reading "The Ransom of Red Chief" by O. Henry in *Prentice-Hall Literature: Bronze* (1991), for example, tell them that the setting is in west-

ern Illinois during the westward expansion. Have students complete the blank next to the term setting. Then have students identify the major and minor characters in the story and write the names of the characters on the blanks. After that, have students identify the problem in the story, the events in sequence, and the solution. Finally, have students identify the theme of the story.

4.   Tell students that they should use what they know about the way fiction is organized to help them understand the story. Invite students to explain how the Story Map can help them understand the story. Encourage students to use Story Maps to identify and record a story's elements during reading.

5.   A blank copy of a Story Map follows.

Many students are familiar with the structure of fiction books because they read them for pleasure.

Story Map

Title

Setting

Characters

Problem

Events

▼

▼

▼

Solution

Flag Words

Flag Words help students identify text patterns and understand what they are reading. Teaching students common Flag Words and the signals they provide helps students become more skilled readers of content area texts. Tomlinson (1995) suggests teaching Flag Words through modeling and application activities. Teaching specific Flag Words that signal common text patterns helps students understand how text is organized and enhances their comprehension.

Directions and Example

1. Select a section of content text and identify the main organizational pattern used. Develop a list of common Flag Words for this organizational pattern.

2. Make photocopies of the text section so students can write on the text.

3. Explain to students that authors use Flag Words to give readers clues about how the text is organized and what information is important. Use examples from your content area or use the following example to model this strategy for students.

> Flag Words can help you understand the text *World Geography: People and Places* (1989). We will be reading a section called "Population Issues." This part of the text is mainly organized using a problem-solution pattern. We have a list of Flag Words that we will use to help you better understand how the text is organized and what ideas are important. The following are Flag Words:

> because
> since
> therefore
> consequently
> as a result of
> this led to
> so that
> nevertheless
> accordingly
> if . . . then
> thus
> subsequently

4. Model the process of identifying Flag Words and then annotating the text to focus on important ideas. Continue to use examples from your content area or use the example provided below.

> As I begin to read the section, I am looking for Flag Words from the list. I see the word *therefore* in a sentence. It says, "One of the most basic needs threatened by overpopulation is food; therefore, many countries have programs for population control" (p. 119).

> I will highlight the word *therefore,* and in the margin I will write a brief note called an annotation to remind myself of this important idea. I will write "overpopulation and limited food = problem;

population control = solution." I can continue to use this same technique as I work through the text section.

5. Distribute the photocopies of the text section to students. Provide them with highlighter markers or colored pens to identify Flag Words and to write brief annotations in the margins.

6. Provide time for students to read the section and highlight and annotate the text.

7. Ask students to share the Flag Words they identified and the annotations they wrote. Discuss how this strategy is helpful when they are reading and studying.

8. In future lessons, introduce and model Flag Words for other text patterns. (See box below for Flag Words.)

9. After multiple experiences with various text patterns and their common Flag Words, students will begin to identify text patterns and Flag Words on their own. A list of sample Flag Words is provided in the box.

Flag Words for Text Patterns

Description	Sequence	Compare-Contrast	Cause-Effect Problem-Solution
for instance to begin with also in fact for example in addition characteristics of	on (date) not long after now as before after when first second next then last finally	however but as well as on the other hand not only . . . but also either . . . or same as in contrast while although more than less than unless similarly yet likewise on the contrary	because since therefore consequently as a result of this led to so that nevertheless accordingly if . . . then thus subsequently

4.3 Monitoring Understanding

Goal

To help students monitor their understanding while reading.

Background

Effective readers monitor their comprehension as they read. They consider whether what they are reading makes sense, the questions they have about the text, and what they expect to happen next. Effective readers are actively engaged in thinking while they are reading. They ask themselves questions such as "Do I understand what I'm reading?" and "What is the main idea of what I am reading?"

Metacognition is an important aspect of monitoring comprehension while reading. Metacognition refers to the awareness of one's own thinking processes, and it contains two major components: knowledge and regulation (Flavell, 1981). Knowledge includes self-knowledge, or how one thinks, and task knowledge, or the students' knowledge about skills, strategies, and resources needed to complete a task. The second component of metacognition is self-regulation, which involves the ability to monitor and regulate comprehension (Baker & Brown, 1984).

Baker (1991) has identified six areas that will help students develop comprehension monitoring. Students should be on the lookout for the following items:

- Words they don't understand.
- Information that doesn't connect with what they already know.
- Ideas that don't fit together because they don't know who or what is being described.
- Ideas that don't fit together because they don't know how the ideas are related.
- Ideas that don't fit together because the ideas seem contradictory.
- Information that is missing or not clearly explained.

You can help your students become actively involved in their own reading by teaching them specific strategies to monitor and regulate their comprehension. In addition, you can encourage the use of comprehension-monitoring strategies by creating a classroom climate where you focus on helping students learn how to learn. By providing opportunities for students to reflect on and discuss their learning, you will help your students become more aware of how they read, comprehend, and learn.

TECHNOLOGY TIP

Teaching Comprehension

Big Sky Language Arts Lesson Plans include comprehension-monitoring lessons.

gopher://bvsd.k12.co.us:70/11/Educational_Resources/
Lesson_Plans/Big%20Sky/language_arts

Directed Reading-Thinking Activity (DR-TA)

The Directed Reading-Thinking Activity (DR-TA) actively involves students in a prediction-reading-verification-prediction process (Stauffer, 1969). This strategy can be applied to fiction or content texts. The goal of the DR-TA is for students to integrate the prediction-reading-verification-prediction process into their independent reading. The teacher uses the following questions:

- What do you think is going to happen?
- Why do you think so?
- Can you prove it?

Directions and Examples

1. Select a fictional text that students will be reading. Identify the key elements of the text such as setting, plot events, goal, problem, and solution. This information will help you determine appropriate stopping points for the DR-TA.

2. Use the following time line to assist you with determining appropriate stopping points in the DR-TA. It is important to limit the number of stopping points so you do not interrupt students' comprehension or interest in the story. At the stopping points, ask students to make predictions about the story and then to support or explain their predictions. As you progress to the next stopping point, ask students to reconsider their earlier predictions in light of new information they have learned from reading the story. Also, invite students to make and support new predictions.

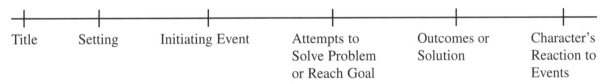

| Title | Setting | Initiating Event | Attempts to Solve Problem or Reach Goal | Outcomes or Solution | Character's Reaction to Events |

3. Model the DR-TA strategy for students using examples from your content area or use the following example from the story "Flowers for Algernon" in *Literature & Language* (1994). Ask students to read the title and predict what the story will be about. Have students share their predictions with a classmate.

4. After students have predicted the contents of the story from the title, have them provide evidence for their predictions. Have them ask the following questions: Why do I think so? and What clues did I use to make my prediction? Model the questioning by providing an example similar to the following one.

> I predict that the story "Flowers for Algernon" will be about someone who receives flowers for a special reason. I know that you give someone flowers for special occasions or when someone is sick. I think Algernon must be the main character because his name is in the title. I think Algernon will get flowers for a certain reason, but I need more information to figure out this reason. When I read the first part of the story, I will pay careful attention to see if my predictions are right.

5. Next, ask students to read a portion of the text to a predetermined stopping point. Tell them that you will be discussing their initial predictions and asking them to make new predictions. Continue to use examples from your content area or the following example.

I will read from page 268 to the bottom of page 271. After I finish reading, I need to ask myself "Do my predictions about the title still make sense?" and "What do I think will happen next in the story?" Finally, I need to ask myself "What part of the story gave me a clue?"

6. Invite students to make and support their predictions about the story. Continue using this pattern for the remainder of the story. The questions in the box will be helpful as you engage students in the DR-TA strategy with fictional texts.

Questions for DR-TA with Fiction

- What do you think the story will be about?
- Why do you think so?
- What do you think will happen next?
- What part of the story gave you a clue?

---

7. Tell students that when they read content material they should use DR-TA questions that are adapted for expository reading. Using an example from your content area or the following example, model how readers use questioning while reading content area texts.

8. Select a content text that students will be reading. Determine appropriate stopping places based on the content and organization of the text. Suggested stopping places for content texts are listed below.

   - Title, headings, and subheadings
   - Introduction
   - Discussion of key concepts or events
   - Discussion of final concepts or events

9. Model the strategy for students using examples from your content area or the following example.

   I will be using the Directed Reading-Thinking Activity (DR-TA) to help me understand and monitor my reading from our science book *Biology: A Human Approach* (1997). I will be reading the section "The Internal Environment of Organisms."

   First, I will read the title, and then I will look at the headings and subheadings in the section. I can ask myself the question "What do I think this section will be about?" From the title, I know it will be about the insides and inner workings of living things.

   Next, I can ask myself what clues and information I used to make my predictions. From the headings and subheadings, I saw several mentions of cells. It seems that the section will teach me about how cells work. I also used what I know about science to help me make predictions.

10. Invite students to make and support predictions about what they think they will read about in the section.

11. Next, ask students to read a portion of the text to a predetermined stopping point. Tell students that you will be discussing their initial predictions and asking them to make new predictions. Continue to use examples from your content area or use the following example.

I will read from page 79 to the top of page 82. After I finish reading, I need to ask myself "Do my predictions about the title, headings, and subheadings still make sense?" and "What other information do I think I will read about in this section?" Finally, I need to ask myself "Why do I think so?"

12. Invite students to make and support their predictions about the next section of text.

13. Continue using this pattern for the remainder of the text. The questions in the box will be helpful as you engage students in the DR-TA strategy with content texts.

Questions for DR-TA with Content Texts

- What do you think the section will be about?
- Why do you think so?
- What do you think you will read about in the next section?
- What clues did you use to make your predictions?

TEACHING STRATEGY **10**

ReQuest

ReQuest (Manzo, 1969) enhances students' comprehension by teaching them to ask their own questions about what they are reading. When students ask themselves questions while reading, they have a greater likelihood of monitoring their understanding of the text and of having better comprehension. ReQuest was originally designed for use with individual students; however, it can easily be adapted for use with a group of students.

Directions and Example

1. Select a content text your students will be reading. Choose a section that contains many new ideas that may be challenging to students.

2. Introduce the ReQuest strategy to students by modeling its use. Use examples from your content area or use the following example from the section "Heat and Temperature" in *Science Interactions* (1995). Tell students that they will be using a strategy called ReQuest to help them read, monitor, and understand the textbook passage. Begin reading the first paragraph of the text aloud. Then ask and answer questions about the contents of the passage in the following manner.

    Question: What is heat?

    Answer: Heat is the transfer of energy from something with a higher temperature to something with a lower temperature. For example, if you touch a hot surface like a stove, you feel the heat on your hand.

Question: What is temperature?

Answer: Temperature is a measurement of how much heat or thermal energy there is in an object. Temperature is used to measure the weather, or how much heat there is outside. It is also used to measure the heat in a stove or the amount of heat in our bodies.

Question: Are heat and temperature the same or different?

Answer: Heat and temperature are related, but they are not the same. Heat is the amount of thermal energy in an object, and temperature is the way we measure heat.

3. Ask students to read the next section of text. Limit this section to no more than a paragraph or two in length. Tell students that they will be taking turns asking you questions about what they read, and you will answer their questions, just like you modeled for them.

4. Ask students to read the next section of text. Inform them that you will be asking them questions about the section and they will be answering your questions.

5. Continue to alternate between student-generated questions and teacher-generated questions until the entire passage has been read.

6. Remind students to ask themselves questions as they read, because such questions will help them monitor and understand what they are reading.

TEACHING STRATEGY 11

Expectation Outline

The Expectation Outline (Spiegel, 1981) helps students ask questions about text. The focus of this strategy is for students to tell what they think they will learn from a text. Having students determine what they expect to learn from a text helps them approach text with a questioning, active stance. This stance will assist students as they monitor their reading and comprehension of the text.

Directions and Example

1. Select a text that students will be reading.

2. Model the Expectation Outline strategy for them by using examples from your content area or use the following example from "The First Americans" in *The American Nation* (1991). Tell students that as they prepare to read they should first preview the section by reading the title, headings, subheadings, and graphics.

3. After students preview the text, have them ask themselves what they think the assignment will be about. Tell them to ask this question in the form of specific questions. For example, if they think the reading assignment will be about Native American groups, a question they might ask is "What Native American groups lived in the Plains area?"

4. Invite students to generate questions that they think will be answered in the text. Write their questions on the chalkboard or an overhead transparency, or use a computer with an LCD panel.

5.   Ask students to explain how they came up with their questions. Encourage them to refer to specific clues they used in the text to generate their questions.

6.   Group similar questions together and label each group of questions. From the previous example, you might have questions grouped in the following manner.

> **Location**
> What Native Americans lived in the Plains area?
> What Native Americans lived in the North?
> What Native Americans lived in the West?
>
> **Culture**
> What traditions did different groups of Native Americans have? Why?
> What were their religions like?
> How were their families and communities organized?
>
> **Adaptations to Environment**
> How did they use the land to survive?
> How did they live in certain types of climates?
>
> **Contributions**
> What did the Mayans contribute to the world?
> What contributions did the Aztecs make?
> What contributions did Native Americans make to our culture?

7.   Engage students in discussing the major areas that they expect to learn about by reading the text. Lead them to understand that they may find gaps between their expectations and the text. For example, explain that they may find some of their questions will not be answered and that other areas may be included that were not on their Expectation Outline.

8.   Ask students to read the text to find answers to the questions they generated.

9.   After students read, discuss the answers students found to their questions. Also, discuss other sources they can use to find answers to questions that were not addressed in the text.

TEACHING STRATEGY 12

Strategy Logs

Strategy Logs (Johns & Lenski, 1997) help students monitor their reading, develop an awareness of when they are and are not comprehending, and identify appropriate strategies to improve their understanding of texts. Strategy Logs can be used in conjunction with any content text, and once students learn how to use them, they can become an ongoing activity in the classroom.

Directions and Examples

1.   Explain to students that they will be using Strategy Logs to help them monitor their comprehension and choose appropriate strategies when reading.

2. Model the steps in a Strategy Log with examples from your content area or use the following example.

   I am going to use a Strategy Log to help me monitor my understanding as I read our textbook *Mathematics in Action* (1994). I am reading the chapter "Geometry," and there are a lot of new vocabulary words and concepts. The Strategy Log will help me monitor my comprehension as I read this section.

3. Present the format for the Strategy Log to the students by displaying it on the chalkboard or an overhead transparency, or use a computer with an LCD panel. A sample Strategy Log format is shown below.

Strategy Log

Text Section _____

Page/Paragraph	Problem I Had	Strategy I Used	How It Worked

▶ Based on Johns, J.L., & Lenski, S.D. (1997). *Improving reading: A handbook of strategies* (2nd ed.). Dubuque, IA: Kendall/Hunt.

4. Model how to fill out the Strategy Log using examples from your content area or continue with the example provided below.

   As I was reading the section "Geometry," I got confused about what a line and a ray were. I used the graphics in the chapter, and I used the bold type to figure out the definitions. Then I wrote the definitions in my own words and made a drawing of a line and a ray to help me understand and remember what they were. I can fill out my Strategy Log using this information.

Strategy Log

Text Section __Geometry_____

Page/Paragraph	Problem I Had	Strategy I Used	How It Worked
page 210	Couldn't remember difference between a line and a ray.	Words in bold type. Graphics.	It worked well. I still remember it.

▶ Based on Johns, J.L., & Lenski, S.D. (1997). *Improving reading: A handbook of strategies* (2nd ed.). Dubuque, IA: Kendall/Hunt.

5.   Ask students to use Strategy Logs as they complete an assigned reading and provide time for students to share their Strategy Logs after completing the reading.

6.   General tips for implementing Strategy Logs are provided in the box below.

Tips for Implementing Strategy Logs

- Use a spiral notebook so all entries are kept together.
- Use Strategy Logs several times a week so students get comfortable with them.
- Provide sharing time for students to discuss their Strategy Logs.
- Provide credit for students who complete their Strategy Logs; do not grade entries.
- Teach new strategies based on problem areas students note in their Strategy Logs.
- Provide ongoing modeling of strategies and how to use Strategy Logs.

TEACHING STRATEGY **13**

Think Aloud for Monitoring

The Think Aloud for Monitoring strategy is helpful for teaching students the types of thought processes they should be using as they monitor their reading. Often times, students do not fully understand the types of questions and prompts that good readers use as they read. Think Aloud for Monitoring helps students understand self-questioning techniques and strategies they can use to monitor and regulate their comprehension.

Directions and Example

1.   Select a content passage that students will be reading. Look for a passage that contains difficult concepts, ambiguous information, and/or unknown words. Determine what strategy or strategies you will demonstrate during Think Aloud for Monitoring.

2.   Implement Think Aloud for Monitoring by using examples from your content area or by using the following example.

> I am going to demonstrate how you can use strategies to monitor and regulate your comprehension while you read your textbook. I will be using the section "Radiation, Energy, and Atoms" in our textbook *ChemCom: Chemistry in the Community* (1998).

> As I am reading on page 297, the book is telling me that food irradiation is being protested, but the book says it is safe. I think that all radiation comes from nuclear energy, but the book hasn't told me that yet. I wonder if that is the difference? Maybe food irradiation uses another kind of energy. I guess I will read on until the end of the page to see if the book clears up this problem.

> Now that I'm at the end of the page, I see that irradiation can be from nuclear energy, but it also can be from the sun. There is even microwave radiation that we use to cook our foods. Reading on to the end of the page really helped me understand what I was reading.

3. Encourage students to use Think Aloud for Monitoring regularly with various texts as they read independently. Suggestions for strategies to use with Think Aloud for Monitoring are provided below.

Think Aloud for Monitoring Strategies

- Making predictions
- Developing mental images
- Making analogies
- Connecting new information to background knowledge
- Self-questioning
- Using fix-up strategies to regulate comprehension

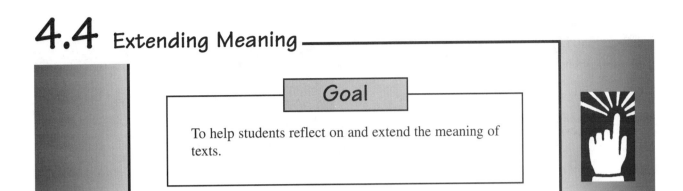

4.4 Extending Meaning

Goal

To help students reflect on and extend the meaning of texts.

Background

The reading process does not end when students have finished reading a text. In order to develop rich comprehension, readers need to reflect on and extend the meaning of the texts they have read. They need to clarify concepts and ideas from their reading, consider their responses to what they have read, share ideas and insights with others, and apply the information they have read to new situations. If you provide opportunities for your students to engage in conversations, writing, and projects after reading, they will be able to extend and deepen their understanding of what they have read.

Reading is an interactive process in which readers interact with ideas from the text, their background knowledge, and their personal experiences (Tierney & Pearson, 1994). All students will not interpret the same text in the same manner. Teaching strategies that encourage students to consider responses to open-ended questions that invite divergent responses extend and deepen students' understanding of what they have read. With this approach to comprehension instruction, emphasis is put on justifying and explaining responses rather than just producing simple factual information.

Comprehension occurs when readers build relationships among the parts of a text, their own experiences, and their own interpretations. Doctrow, Whittrock, and Marks (1978) use the term generative learning to describe how readers deepen their comprehension by creating images, summaries, inferences, elaborations, analogies, and metaphors.

Interaction with peers and teachers also helps students deepen their understanding of texts they read. Pearson and Fielding (1991) support a view of comprehension instruction that takes into account the social aspects of instruction and learning. During peer interactions, students tend to offer explanations rather than just right answers. This leads students to analyze, consider, and extend the meaning of the text.

Interaction with teachers can also help students process text more deeply, leading to richer comprehension. If teachers provide opportunities for students to initiate and lead instructional conversations rather than just engaging students in traditional question-answer exchanges that tend to focus on lower level comprehension of texts (Pearson & Fielding, 1991), richer comprehension will result.

The teaching strategies in this section focus on helping students reflect on and extend the meaning of texts they have read. The emphasis is on providing opportunities for students to process text and to think deeply about what it means, how they can use the ideas in their lives, and how they can apply the ideas to new situations.

TEACHING STRATEGY **14**

Three Level Guides

Three Level Guides help students think about texts on the literal, interpretive, and applied levels. Three Level Guides facilitate students' comprehension by moving from lower to higher levels of comprehension (Herber, 1978).

Directions and Examples

1. Select a text that students will be reading. Identify literal information that students should know after reading the text. This information should focus on explicit ideas that were clearly presented in the text.

2. Identify interpretive information you want students to understand after reading the text. Include inferences or other examples of "reading between the lines."

3. Identify applied level information that you want students to consider. These ideas go beyond what is written in the text and require students to use information, express opinions, and create new ideas.

4. Develop a Three Level Guide that presents three to six statements for each of the three levels: literal, interpretive, and applied. These statements should be written clearly and simply.

5. Present the Three Level Guide to students and model its use with examples from your content area or use the following example.

Three Level Guide for Southern Colonies

I. Literal Level
Check the items that specifically show what the author wrote in the chapter. Be prepared to support your choices.

_____ 1. Lord Baltimore founded the colony of Maryland to provide a place for Catholics to worship freely.

_____ 2. The Act of Toleration in 1649 provided religious freedom to all people.

_____ 3. The Carolinas had large estates that were worked by slaves.

II. Interpretive Level
Check the items that show what the author meant in the chapter. Be prepared to discuss supporting evidence from the chapter.

_____ 1. Wealthy tobacco planters controlled the best lands in Virginia because they arrived in the colony first.

_____ 2. Bacon's Rebellion was organized to show the colonists' lack of support for the Virginia governor.

_____ 3. Georgia was started as a place for freed debtors to get a fair, new start in life.

_____ 4. The colonies of North Carolina and South Carolina had more similarities than differences.

III. Applied Level
Check the items that you agree with and be ready to share examples from the text and your own knowledge to support your responses.

_____ 1. Religious freedom was the most important reason for starting the Southern colonies.

_____ 2. The settlers believed that they had the right to take land from the Native Americans.

_____ 3. The southern farmers worked mainly for survival.

_____ 4. England wanted military men to lead colonies because they were good leaders.

Based on *The American nation*. (1991). Englewood Cliffs, NJ: Prentice-Hall.

6. Ask students to read the assigned text selection that will be addressed by the Three Level Guide.

7. Model the process of filling out a Three Level Guide using examples from your content area or use the example provided below.

> When I fill out a Three Level Guide, I need to first think about the literal information that I read. This means I need to know about the facts that are presented in the chapter. Statement 1 says "Lord Baltimore founded the colony of Maryland to provide a place for Catholics to worship freely." I think this is what I read in the text. I see that on page 109 of the text it says just this. I will check this statement and make a note of page 109 so I can support why I checked this statement.

8. Have students read and discuss the remaining statements in the literal level section of the Three Level Guide. Remind them to locate the places in the text that support their responses.

9. Model how to respond to the interpretive level statements by using examples from your content area or continue using the example provided below.

> I need to think about the interpretive level now. This means I need to think about what the author meant. I might need to make inferences, and I will need to put together pieces of information from different parts of the chapter to respond to these statements.
>
> The first statement in the interpretive level says "Wealthy tobacco planters controlled the best lands in Virginia because they arrived in the colony first." This sounds like it might be true, but I'm not sure. I need to go back to the chapter and look for support. I see that on page 110 it says that the wealthy tobacco planters controlled the best land near the coast. The chapter doesn't say that they got there first. It does say, however, that they were wealthy and powerful and that the government told other planters to take land from the Indians. I won't check this statement because the chapter implies that the reasons the tobacco planters controlled the best lands was because they were wealthy people. I will make a few notes in the margin of the Three Level Guide to remind myself why I didn't mark this statement.

10. Have students read and discuss the remaining statements in the interpretive level section of the Three Level Guide. Remind them to make notes to support their responses.

11. Model how to respond to the applied level statements by using examples from your content area or continue using the example provided below.

> I need to think about the applied level now. This means I need to think about the statements with which I agree, and I need to be ready to share examples from the text and my own knowledge to support my responses.
>
> The first statement in the applied level says "Religious freedom was the most important reason for starting the Southern colonies." I know this was one of the important reasons, but I don't think it was always the most important reason. A lot of settlers wanted to make money, others wanted land, and still others wanted to create a buffer against Spanish Florida. I think each of these reasons was important to different groups of settlers, but I don't think that religious freedom was always the most important reason for starting the Southern colonies. I will make a few notes in the margin of the Three Level Guide so I will be ready to support my choice.

12. Help students read and discuss the remaining statements in the applied level section of the Three Level Guide. Remind them to make notes to support their responses.

13. Provide time for students to finish filling out the Three Level Guide. Engage students in discussion about the Three Level Guide. Be sure to ask them to provide support for their responses.

TEACHING STRATEGY **15**

Response Journals

Response Journals provide a forum for students to record what they are thinking and feeling as they interact with texts. Response Journals focus on students' personal responses and reactions, and they encourage students to think deeply about what they are reading. Because Response Journals focus on students' personal responses and reactions, this strategy encourages diverse responses.

Directions and Example

1. Explain to students that they will be keeping Response Journals to help them think deeply about what they are reading. Tell them that they should write about their personal responses and reactions to what they read.

2. Model how to use the Response Journal strategy using examples from your content area or use the example provided below.

    > When I write in a Response Journal, I need to concentrate on my personal responses and reactions. After I read the text, I need to think about the prompt or question that the teacher has provided. I should concentrate on what I think and feel about what I read and the prompt or question.

    > After reading our textbook *Mathematics in Action* (1994), I will write a Response Journal entry addressing a question that has been posed. The question asks me "How does algebra affect my daily life?"

    > In my Response Journal, I could write the following entry:

    > > Algebra is a part of my daily life. I never really thought about how important algebra is to me until I read this part of the text. I use proportions when I adjust the size of a recipe, when I figure out how much carpet would cost for my bedroom, and when I calculate the average fuel cost for the vacation my family is planning.

3. Ask students to write entries to specific prompts or questions related to the texts they are reading. Provide time for students to share their entries with partners or small groups of students.

4. Use various types of questions and prompts to help students get actively involved in using Response Journals. Sample questions and prompts for various content areas are provided in the box.

Math:	Math makes me feel . . . If I were a math teacher, I would explain this concept by . . .
Science:	Assume that you are a certain type of creature and explain your typical day. How does this concept apply to your daily life?
Social Studies:	Assume that you are a famous historical figure and explain a specific historical event from your perspective. Imagine you are a person living during that time and describe your experiences or reactions to . . .
English:	Assume that you are the main character and explain how you feel about . . . If you were in the character's position, what would you do and why?
Foreign Language:	If I traveled to France, I would want to know how to say . . . because . . . I think life in Germany would be . . . because . . .
Vocational Education:	Explain how you could use these ideas in a job situation. What questions would you like to ask a tradesperson about . . . ?
Fine Arts:	The music/painting makes me feel . . . I wish I could ask the composer/artist . . .

TEACHING STRATEGY 16

Text Dialogue Form

The Text Dialogue Form is an adaptation of the Book Dialogue Form (Miller, 1994). This strategy helps students process and reflect on what they have read. This strategy focuses on having students write a summary, interpretation, and evaluation of what they have read. After completing the written form, students then engage in dialogues with the teacher, a peer, or a group of peers to further extend their comprehension of the text.

TECHNOLOGY TIP

Literature Database

CD CoreWorks CD-ROM: index database and search program to access poetry, essays, drama, and short stories.

EBSCO 800-653-2726

Directions and Example

1. Select a text that students will be reading.

2. Explain to students that you will be modeling how to use a Text Dialogue Form to help them deepen their understanding of what they read. Ask students to read the text.

3. Model the Text Dialogue Form for students using examples from your content area or use the example provided below.

> I am going to use a Text Dialogue Form to help me extend my understanding of what I read in our text *Human Heritage: A World History* (1989). The top of the form asks me to fill in my name, date, the title of the text I read, and the type of text. The title of the section I read is "The Germans," and it is from our text *Human Heritage: A World History* (1989).
>
> Next, the form asks me to write a short summary of the text I just read. The form gives me a clue about what to include in the summary when it says "the most important ideas from the text." After looking back at the text, I think I should include the following main ideas in my summary: German village life, warriors, and law. I used the headings from the text to help me determine the main ideas from the section.

4. Ask students to offer other main ideas that should be included in the summary. Ask them to support their suggestions. Discuss their suggestions and include those that are appropriate.

5. Continue to model the Text Dialogue Form using examples from your content area, or use the example provided below.

> Now I need to write these ideas out as a summary. Here's a summary.
>
>> Around 400 AD, Germans lived in villages surrounded by farmlands and pastures. They had simple homes, and they worked farming grains and herding cattle. German men were warriors, and they spent time fighting, hunting, and making weapons. Young boys were trained to be warriors. Germans lived in clans which were groups based on family ties. Each clan had a military leader called a chieftain. The Germans believed that law came from the people. German rulers could not change laws without approval of the people. The German legal system did not treat all people fairly. A person's wealth often determined the penalty.

6. Model the next portion of the Text Dialogue Form for students using examples from your content area or continue with the example provided below.

> The next part of the Text Dialogue Form asks me to write my interpretation of what I just read. The form asks me to consider the following questions as I write my interpretation: "What did the text mean to you?" and "What are your thoughts and feelings related to the text?" In this section, I will tell how I interpreted the text. This will probably be somewhat different from the way that someone else might interpret the text.
>
> The text showed me how simply the Germans lived. They worked on the land, lived in simple houses, and didn't even have a written language yet. They passed on laws orally. Leadership wasn't decided by voting. The Germans admired bravery and valued warriors; therefore, they decided leadership by fighting and having a reputation as a good fighter. A lot of this information surprised

me because I know a lot about modern Germany, and this information was all pretty new to me. I thought the textbook was written clearly, and I thought the headings really helped me to know what the important information in the section was.

7. Model how to fill out the final portion of the Text Dialogue Form for students using examples from your content area or continuing with the example provided below.

> The last section of the Text Dialogue Form asks me to write an evaluation. The form gives me some clues about what I should include in the evaluation section. It says "Why was or wasn't this text meaningful to you?" and "How helpful or useful was the information in the text?" An example follows.

> I thought this section was very meaningful because I learned a lot about ancient Germany that I didn't know. A lot of the information was different from what I expected. I liked how the text included examples and stories to explain some of the main ideas. For example, the discussion of law and blood feuds really helped me understand how the Germans dealt with legal issues. I wish the section had included more information on what life was like for women and children. Most of the section just talked about the men's lives.

8. Provide time for students to fill out their own Text Dialogue Forms for this section. Ask them to follow the model you provided but encourage them to include their own ideas, especially in the interpretation and evaluation sections.

9. Divide the class into partners. Ask each team of partners to discuss their Text Dialogue Forms. Provide 10 to 15 minutes for the partners to complete this step.

10. Bring the whole class together to discuss their ideas from the Text Dialogue Forms. Use questions such as those listed below to guide this whole group discussion.

   • Were there any ideas that you and your partner disagreed on? What were they?
   • How can you support your view? What evidence can you offer?
   • Did you and your partner interpret the text in the same way? Why or why not?
   • Did you and your partner evaluate the text in the same way? Explain.
   • Did the Text Dialogue Form help you understand the text better? Explain.

11. Have students use the Text Dialogue Form for other reading assignments. Provide opportunities for students to discuss their responses with peers or with you. A blank Text Dialogue Form follows.

Text Dialogue Form

Name: _____

Title: _____

Author: _____

Type of Text: _____

Summary (What are the most important ideas from the text?):

_____

_____

_____

_____

_____

_____

Interpretation (What did the text mean to you? What are your thoughts and feelings about the text?):

_____

_____

_____

_____

_____

Evaluation (Why was or wasn't this text meaningful to you? How helpful or useful was the information in the text? Explain.):

_____

_____

_____

_____

_____

_____

Talk Throughs

Talk Throughs (Simpson, 1994) involve students in talking about what they have read by using a monologue format. As students engage in Talk Throughs, they use a variety of higher-level thinking processes such as generalizations that connect ideas across texts and students' experiences, personal or creative reactions or judgments, summaries of key ideas in the students' own words, appropriate text examples to support ideas, and personal examples or applications.

Directions and Examples

1. Select a text students will be reading and identify key ideas you will expect students to understand.

2. Explain to students that you will be modeling a strategy called the Talk Through. Use examples from your content area or the following example to demonstrate this strategy for students.

   The Talk Through strategy will help me make sure I really understand important ideas from what I read. This strategy requires me to put the ideas into my own words and to make connections to my own experiences and ideas. These are techniques that good readers use.

   I will use the Talk Through with the case study "Wolves" from our textbook *What on Earth?: Insights in Biology* (1998).

3. Ask students to read the text before you continue modeling the Talk Through strategy.

4. Continue to model the Talk Through strategy using examples from your content area or the example provided below.

   I need to think about the key ideas presented in the case study. I think I need to know about animal relocation, reintroduction of animals into an ecosystem, and prey/predator relationships. I will write each of these key ideas on an index card.

   On the back of each index card, I need to write a personal example to explain the key idea. For animal relocation, I can put school redistricting. I know a lot of people who experienced this last year when the new high school was built. I know that it had its good points and bad points, but I know that students didn't have a choice about whether they were relocated or not. That sounds a lot like the wolf situation in the case study.

   Ask students to help generate personal examples for the other two cards: reintroduction of animals into an ecosystem and prey/predator relationships. Help students generate personal examples by asking the following questions:

   - How does this key idea relate to your own experiences?
   - When will you or someone you know experience this?
   - After going back to the text and rereading the section, what new personal examples can you generate?

5. Continue to model the Talk Through for students. Ask them to think of generalizations that connect ideas from the text and their own experiences. Model this process using examples from your content area or use the example provided below.

> The next step of the Talk Through strategy asks me to make generalizations about what I read and my own ideas and experiences. For example, I might say that one generalization is that the relocation and reintroduction of living creatures in an ecosystem has benefits and costs. This idea can explain what happened to the wolves, but it can also explain what happened in our school redistricting, what has happened in parts of Africa recently, and what occurred to Native Americans in the past.

Ask students to offer other possible generalizations that explain connections between ideas in the text and their own experiences and knowledge.

6. Tell students that the Talk Through strategy requires them to explain the key ideas, personal connections, and generalizations in their own words. Model a Talk Through for students using examples from your content area or continue with the example provided below.

> I will practice my Talk Through to make sure it makes sense. I will use my index cards to help me stay focused.

> The relocation of the wolves from Yellowstone National Park caused population problems with elk, deer, mountain sheep, and antelope. On the other hand, removing the wolves saved lots of wildlife on local ranches and farms. Relocating any animal or person to a new location will have positive and negative outcomes. For example, when our school district relocated students to the new high school, the relocation had many benefits, but some students were upset that they had to travel longer distances on buses, were separated from their friends, and had to start all over in new schools.

Continue modeling the Talk Through focusing on the key points, personal associations, and generalizations that connect the text and personal ideas and experiences.

7. Ask students to use notes from the demonstration to practice the Talk Through strategy independently. Provide time for them to rehearse their Talk Throughs several times. Encourage them to ask themselves "Do these ideas make sense?" as they practice.

8. Have students practice their Talk Throughs with their partner so they can provide feedback to one another.

9. During the next class session, have students present their Talk Throughs. This can be done as a one-on-one activity with the teacher and student; it can be done with partners or in small groups; or it can be done as a whole class activity.

10. Provide continued modeling of the Talk Through strategy. Use this strategy regularly in conjunction with different types of texts so students can gain competence in applying it in different situations.

Chapter 5

Supporting Readers Who Struggle

Overview

As we enter the 21st century, teachers are facing a difficult challenge. Many students in middle and high school content area classes are unable to learn content material by reading texts. It is possible to teach content subjects without using printed material; students can learn by listening, through group discussions, by experiences, and by interacting with visual information. Reading, however, is still an important skill in today's society. From reading labels on soup cans to reading signs in an airport, we rely on accessing information from print. Therefore, it is important that you support your students' learning, based on their reading abilities and needs, in order to help them learn content material by reading.

There are two groups of students who will need additional guidance in reading content material. The first group is comprised of students who do not read well enough to be able to understand difficult text. There are various reasons why students in middle and high schools have difficulty reading textbooks. Some students are unable to read content texts because they do not have the cognitive ability to read complicated text; they may have visual processing deficits, social or emotional difficulties, or physical problems (Gunning, 1998). Some of the students who struggle with reading may have limited background knowledge in content areas, or they may have difficulty using the knowledge that they possess. Students who do not read well may pronounce words without understanding them, or they may not know which strategies to use when reading content area texts. Every student in middle and high school can benefit from instruction in reading strategies such as those presented in Chapters 2, 3, and 4. Many students need additional strategies to learn content material. Students who have difficulty reading need you to scaffold instruction for them. Scaffolding instruction means that you provide struggling readers with strategies that make textbook reading easier.

A second group that needs a modified approach when learning from textbooks is comprised of students whose native language is not English. According to recent demographic data, an estimated 3.4 million Limited English Proficiency (LEP) students will be attending American schools by the year 2000. Today, students from a variety of minority cultures make up over 42% of the total public school enrollment (Lara, 1994). Some of these students, particularly refugees, have had fragmented formal schooling and may be overwhelmed by the expectations of our schools (Igoa, 1995). Middle school and high school teachers, therefore, need to be culturally responsive teachers.

Culturally responsive teaching entails applying two principles to instruction. First, we need to recognize that education is a cultural activity (Thompson, Mixon, & Serpell, 1996). American education relies heavily on traditional American culture. When we recognize that schooling is based on cul-

ture, we use strategies that empower students to link their home cultures to content knowledge. The second principle that is crucial to culturally responsive teaching is to understand how to scaffold instruction so that students become successful in the mainstream culture. Delpit (1988) convincingly argues that when teachers do not teach nonmajority students the skills necessary for today's society, they withhold the opportunity from those students to become part of the power structure of the country. Therefore, we need to support student learning so that students who have difficulty reading texts and students for whom English is a second language can learn ways to access content information from texts.

There are many ways to support struggling readers so that students who have difficulty reading and students who have Limited English Proficiency can become successful readers. Supporting students may mean that you help students become fluent in your content area by teaching from picture books, adapted or easy-to-read texts, audiobooks, or electronic books. You can help students access information in textbooks by applying strategies that make texts more comprehensible. You can help students link their cultural experiences to your content information, help students identify which information is important, and guide them in organizing information for efficient learning. As you use the strategies presented in this chapter, you will support student learning so that readers who struggle learn from the material in your content area.

TECHNOLOGY TIP

Sources for Special Education Teachers and Limited English Proficiency Teachers

National Clearinghouse for Bilingual Education: contains articles and information about bilingual education.
http://www.ncbe.gwu.edu

Special education trends and issues Listserve
SPECED-L
listsev@uga.cc.uga.edu

Teaching English as a Second Language Listserve
TESLK-12
listserv@cunyvm.cuny.edu

5.1 Increasing Fluency in Content Areas

Goal
To provide students with language experiences in content areas that increase fluency in and knowledge of the subject.

Background

Students for whom reading is difficult need many opportunities to experience the thoughts, vocabularies, and ideas of your content area. Since content knowledge is learned through rich, meaningful language, students do not need to be proficient in English to take advantage of learning content material (Au, 1993). Struggling readers can learn from picture books, audiobooks, and easy-to-read texts. These texts scaffold instruction by making information in your content area accessible and by building background knowledge necessary for understanding new concepts.

Some of the experiences that you organize for students who cannot read the book assigned to your content area should be different from those you provide for the rest of your class. In the case of Limited English Proficiency (LEP) students, these experiences are even more important. Although English learners are able to master conversational English in approximately two years, it takes five or six years for students to be able to learn academic subjects in English (Cummins, 1994). As a result, many immigrants in the past have been unable to take advantage of educational opportunities until the second or third generation has attended school in the new country (Rothstein, 1998). The increasing numbers of LEP students and students who cannot read texts that are used at their grade level have caused a demand for different types of content materials. The materials described in this chapter can assist you in helping students build fluency in your content subject and in supporting students who struggle with reading.

TECHNOLOGY TIP

Failure Free Reading

Failure Free Reading is an interactive computer program designed to give nonreaders and lowest literacy students the opportunity to have an immediate and successful reading experience with age-appropriate materials. This talking software program contains easy-to-read stories with graphics and sound, vocabulary and spelling activities, reading comprehension questions, and assessment measures. The Adult/Adolescent Series is based on the types of life skills students need in today's society. For more information, contact JFL Enterprises at 800-542-2170.

TEACHING STRATEGY 1

Using Picture Books

Picture books can support content learning by providing a catalyst for conversations in content areas (Cassady, 1998; Miller, 1998). Picture books are books whose stories can be understood through their illustrations rather than through the text. While picture books often have words or a simple story in text, readers rely on the illustrations to tell the story. Content area teachers can use picture books to facilitate discussions about specific topics. Picture books can draw students into discussions with the language of the content area, which, in turn, develops concepts that form the groundwork for academic understanding and learning.

Directions and Example

1. Identify a topic or a concept that is central to your content area. Choose a picture book that relates to the topic. Present the picture book to the class by reading the title and asking students to form predictions about the contents of the book. You may choose to model a prediction of your own. Guide the students into a discussion about the topic you have identified, as in the following example.

> A central concept in mathematics is that math is used in many life situations, not just in math class. Jon Scieszka's book *Math Curse* (1995) gives examples of math that are found in everyday life. Think about mathematical situations that you have experienced. Here's an example.
>
> When I drove to school this morning, I had a teachers' meeting at 7:45 a.m. but wanted to stop at a convenience store for coffee before the meeting. I had to estimate whether I would have enough time to leave at my usual time of 7:00 a.m. or whether I would have to leave earlier. It usually takes me 45 minutes to drive to school, park, and get into the building. I estimated that it would take me an additional 10 minutes to stop for coffee. The mathematical formula I used in my head to figure out what time I had to leave was:
>
> X (time to leave) + 55 (minutes driving) = 7:45 a.m. (time to arrive)
>
> I decided I would have to leave the house at 6:50 a.m.
>
> What mathematical situations have you experienced in your lives?

2. Read or show the book to the class, sharing the illustrations. Several times during reading ask students to summarize the story and predict what will come next.

3. After reading, have students retell the story or create their own stories using the text illustrations. Encourage discussion about the central topic of the book. Use as many relevant vocabulary terms from your content area as possible.

4. Refer to Appendix B for sources of picture books. Selected picture books for several content areas are listed below. Of course, the picture books you select should relate to the specific topic you are teaching.

Selected Picture Books

Math and Science

Cherry, L. (1990). *The great kapok tree: A tale of the Amazon rain forest.*
Demi. (1997). *One grain of rice: A mathematical folktale.*
Jones, C. (Ed.). (1992). *Eyewitness science: Electricity.*
Parker, S. (1996). *How nature works.*
Porter, A., & Davies, E. (Eds.). (1996). *How things work.*
Romann, E. (1994). *Time flies.*
Scieszka, J. (1995). *Math curse.*
Simon, S. (1992). *Our solar system.*

Social Studies

Breckler, R. (1996). *Sweet dried apples: A Vietnamese wartime childhood.*
Bunting, E. (1990). *The wall.*
Goodall, J.S. (1986). *The story of a castle.*
Hamanaka, S. (1990). *The journey: Japanese Americans, racism and renewal.*
Jeffers, S. (1992). *Brother Eagle, Sister Sky: A message from Chief Seattle.*
Luenn, N. (1993). *The song for the ancient forest.*
Maruki, T. (1980). *Hiroshima no pika.*
Uchida, Y. (1993). *The bracelet.*

TEACHING STRATEGY 2

Using Adapted and Easy-to-Read Texts

One of the goals of your teaching is to help struggling readers learn content material. Although it is preferable that students read the texts that are commonly used at your grade level, there are many instances when students cannot read such texts. Some books are too complex, have language that is too complicated, or are too conceptually dense for students. You can choose other ways to teach content material. However, students need to be able to learn from reading books in your content area. Using adapted or easy-to-read texts is a strategy that takes into account the reading ability of students and still provides them with the opportunity to read content area material.

Adapted or easy-to-read texts are books that are of interest to middle or high school students; however, they are written at a lower reading level. (See Appendix C for information on readability formulas.) Many of the texts you use for regular classroom instruction have a readability that would approximate your grade level. For example, if you teach eighth grade, many of the textbooks in your grade level would be texts that are written at or near the eighth-grade reading level. Since some students will have difficulty reading books written at this level, consider using materials written at a lower grade level. Books written at a lower grade level usually present the type of concepts you want to teach but are written with language that is easier to read. Students who are unable to read texts assigned to your grade level can learn information in your content area from adapted or easy-to-read texts. Reading these books can increase background knowledge, fluency, and content knowledge.

Directions and Example

1. Identify topics or concepts in your subject that form the foundation of a unit of study. Choose books in that area that are adapted or written at a lower reading level. If possible, compare samples from the two texts, the original version and an adapted or easy-to-read version. Examples of passages from an original text and an adapted version follow.

"The Purloined Letter"
Original first paragraph

At Paris, just after dark one gusty evening in the autumn of 18—, I was enjoying the twofold luxury of meditation and a meerschaum, in company with my friend C. August Dupin, in his little back library, or book-closet, *au troisième,* No. 33, *Rue Dunot, Faubourg St. Germain.* For one hour at least we had maintained a profound silence; while each, to any casual observer might have seemed intently and exclusively occupied with the curling eddies of smoke that oppressed the atmosphere of the chamber. For myself, however, I was mentally discussing certain topics which had formed matter for conversation between us at an earlier period of the evening; I mean the affair of the Rue Morgue, and the mystery attending the murder of Marie Roget. I looked upon it, therefore, as something of a coincidence, when the door of our apartment was thrown open and admitted our old acquaintance, Monsieur G—, the Prefect of the Parisian police.

▶ From Poe, E.A. (1974). The purloined letter. In *The American tradition in literature* (pp. 844–860). New York: Grosset & Dunlap.

"The Purloined Letter"
Adapted version

In Paris, just after dark one gusty evening in the fall, I was enjoying a smoke with my friend, August Dupin. We were sitting silent in his little back library, busy with thought, watching the curling smoke waves.

I was thinking of that affair of the Rue Morgue, which Dupin had solved for the police. In fact, I was thinking of the Prefect of Police when the door of our apartment opened and he walked in.

▶ From Poe, E.A. (1979). The purloined letter. In *An Edgar Allan Poe reader: Adapted classic tales* (pp. 45–56). New York: Globe.

2. After reading a passage from the original version and comparing it with the sample from the adapted or easy-to-read version, determine whether the easier version would be appropriate for your instructional purposes. Some questions that might guide your decision follow.

    • Is the original version too difficult for the students to read?
    • Does the vocabulary in the original version preclude easy reading?
    • Would the language in the original version make reading difficult?
    • Are the sentences in the original version long and difficult?
    • Would students be able to read the adapted version, or is it too difficult?
    • Does the adapted version accurately represent the contents of the original version?
    • Would the adapted version accomplish my teaching goals?

3. Use comprehension strategies recommended in Sections 5.3 through 5.5 to teach the adapted or easy-to-read texts. After students have read the selection, to supplement your teaching, you might choose to

read passages from the book assigned to your subject and grade level. When students build background knowledge in a subject, they are sometimes able to read more difficult text. See the following box for sources of adapted and easy-to-read texts.

Sources for Adapted and Easy-to-Read Texts

Cobblestone
800-821-0115
Easy-to-read science and social studies materials, reading levels 4–9.

EMC Paradigm
800-328-1452
Adapted classics, reading levels 4–8.

Jamestown Publishers
800-621-1918
Easy-to-read and adapted short stories, science, and social studies materials, reading levels 2–6.

Kids In Between
800-481-2799
Easy-to-read science, math, history, life skills, and reading materials, reading levels 3–8.

Phoenix Learning Resources
800-221-1274
Easy-to-read science, math, language, reading, and social studies materials, reading levels K–6.

Rosen Publishing
800-237-9932
Easy-to-read science, life skills, and career materials, reading levels 3–8.

Steck-Vaughn
800-531-5015
Easy-to-read science, literature, social studies, math, and health materials, reading levels 3–9.

Wieser Educational
800-880-4433
Adapted classics, reading levels 3–8.

TEACHING STRATEGY 3

Using Audiobooks

Certain types of literature are more easily understood by listening to audiobooks than by reading (Baskin & Harris, 1995). Audiobooks, or books on tape, are another way to encourage fluency in content areas. When students are unable to read difficult texts, they can benefit from listening to portions of them. For example, Mark Twain's writing is entertaining and has themes that are usually of interest to middle and high school students. Twain's writing, however, is difficult to read because of his heavy use of dialect. Students who have difficulty reading the book can listen to it, learning the content in a different way. Audiobooks are especially useful for texts that have complex or archaic language, texts that are written in a dialect different from the one students speak, and texts with complicated plots. As students listen to audiobooks, they learn about the genre that you are teaching, increase their background knowledge in the subject, and increase their knowledge of the vocabulary of your content area. Students from cultures that value storytelling are likely to derive special benefit from using audiobooks.

Directions

1. Choose an audiobook that supports learning in your content area. Many publishers now produce their texts on audiotapes, videodisks, or CD-ROMs.

2. Tell students that they will be hearing a book rather than reading it. Explain that listening is an alternative means of experiencing text and will help them learn the content material.

3. Use appropriate prereading strategies that link the students' backgrounds to the text. (See Section 5.3 for prereading strategies.)

4. Play sections or chapters of the audiobook. After 10 to 15 minutes of listening, stop the tape and have students discuss what they have heard. You may continue playing the entire audiobook, or you may choose to play only a few segments. After you have finished playing the audio selection, extend comprehension by using strategies from Sections 5.4 and 5.5.

Sources for Audiobooks

Audio Bookshelf	Listening Library	Recorded Books
207-845-2100	800-243-4504	800-638-1304

5.2 Making Texts Comprehensible

Goal

To help struggling readers comprehend content material by modifying content area textbook passages.

Background

For many of the concepts that you want to teach, there will be no picture books, easy-to-read texts, or audiobooks available. For those situations, you will need to use your textbook as a basis for instruction. Books can be an important learning tool for your students, even if the books are difficult for students to read. There are strategies you can use to make the textbooks commonly used in your content area comprehensible, or readable, for your students.

One of the ways to support students who struggle with reading content area textbooks is to modify the texts. There are several reasons why modifying texts supports student learning and accomplishes your teaching goals. First, when you modify passages from content textbooks, you are able to use the same texts for students who struggle with reading as for students who are proficient readers. Using the same texts allows struggling readers to learn the same material as other students. A second reason that modifying texts supports learning is that using the same texts helps struggling readers feel more confident in their ability to read and learn through texts. A third reason for modifying texts is that you can use age-appropriate texts and modify them to fit the students' reading levels.

You can modify texts by restating the texts in the students' own words, either in English or in their home languages. Another method for modifying texts is to summarize a passage and to provide the summary as a preview for students before they read. A third strategy is to embed questions in a passage to guide students' understanding and promote self-questioning. These strategies allow students to use content area texts by making the texts comprehensible.

Electronic Texts

Electronic texts can assist students who have difficulty reading either because they do not read English or because texts are too difficult to read (McKenna & Robinson, 1997). Electronic texts contain stored digital pronunciation, audio versions of segments of the text, marginal notes created by the author or teacher, hyperlinks to other texts, and quick-time movies. Electronic texts are available on CD-ROM or online. An example of each type of electronic text follows.

Cat: The Ultimate Multimedia Guide to the World of Cats
(CD-ROM, DK Multimedia)

Living in the Americas (online, Macmillan)

TEACHING STRATEGY 4

Group Frame

A Group Frame (Brechtel, 1992) is an excellent strategy to modify content area texts in English or in students' home languages. Students who have difficulty reading selections in English may have a rich knowledge about a subject that you are teaching. A Group Frame allows students to access their background knowledge about a topic and to express that knowledge in English or in their home languages. After students have created their own passages, teachers are able to scaffold that knowledge by adding information from the content area textbook. The roles of the teacher in a Group Frame are to help students clarify their initial understandings of concepts before reading and to provide an English translation if necessary. The text is then comprehensible for students, who now should be able to read portions of the age-appropriate textbook.

Directions and Example

1. Choose a topic from a textbook about which students have some background knowledge or preliminary thoughts. Develop a question about the main topic. Explain that you will be asking a question about a chapter the students will eventually be reading. An example follows.

   > Before teaching students about the properties of a circle in *Discovering Geometry: An Inductive Approach* (1997), ask the following question:
   >
   > What is a circle?

2. Divide the class into groups of three or four students. If you have students who share a home language, group those students together. Have students read the question and write several sentences about the topic. Tell students that they can write the sentences in English or in their home languages.

3. After the students have finished, ask them to share their sentences. Write the sentences on a chalkboard or an overhead transparency, or use a computer with an LCD panel as in the following example.

Dictation from Students (English)	Dictation from Students (Spanish)
A circle is one of the shapes.	Un círculo es una de la figuras.
A circle consists of points around another point.	Un círculo consiste en puntos alrededor de otros puntos.
The middle is a point with a name.	El centro consiste de un punto nombrado.
A point from the middle to the edge is a radius.	Un punto del medio hasta el filo se conoce como un radio.

4. Explain that these initial sentences represent the knowledge that students bring to the topic. Tell students that their background knowledge is necessary for learning new information. Explain that you will revise the sentences to closer represent school learning about the subject. Revise the sentences in English or in the students' home languages as in the following example.

Revised sentences (English)	**Revised sentences (Spanish)**
A circle is a geometric shape.	Un círculo es una figura geométrica.
A circle is the set of all points in a plane at a given distance from a given point in the plane.	Un círculo es el grupo de todos los puntos en un plano que estan a una cierta distancia de un punto dado en el plano.
The given point is the center of the circle. The circle is named by its point.	El punto dado es el centro del círculo. El círculo es nombrado por su punto.
A segment from a point on the circle to the circle's center is called the radius.	Un segmento de un punto en el círculo hasta el centro del círculo es llamado el radio.

5. Have students read the revised sentences and use these sentences to learn the content information. After students have fluently read the sentences they have created, ask them to find the passage from which the ideas were taken. Read the passage aloud to the students, pointing to the areas of similarities and differences between the student-generated ideas and the ideas from the text. Note specific examples where the students' knowledge exceeded the information presented in the textbook.

6. Ask students, in partners or independently, to read selected portions of the textbook. Explain that they already know much of the material from reading the sentences they have created but that they should practice reading textbooks commonly used in class. Encourage students to read the text selection several times.

TEACHING STRATEGY 5

Listen-Read-Discuss

Listen-Read-Discuss (Manzo & Casale, 1985) is a strategy that makes texts more comprehensible by providing students with a summary of the texts to be read before they approach the texts. The summary, which is generated by the teacher, becomes an advanced organizer for reading, allowing students to be prepared for what they will encounter. When students know the gist of a text in advance, they can concentrate on some of the details. Listen-Read-Discuss supports students' reading of textbooks used in content area classrooms by giving them a head start on the content of the passage.

Directions and Example

1. Select a passage from a text that students will be reading that may be difficult for the students to comprehend. Present the information orally in a brief summary. An example follows.

Today we will be reading a section from a chapter titled "Africans in the Middle Colonies," from our text *Voices in African American History: The Colonies* (1994). On pages 22 and 23 you will find a section called "The Question of Slavery." During the mid 1600s, the Dutch West India Company transported thousands of Africans to New York. However, some of the colonists in New York did not believe in slavery. Although many Africans were slaves, others were granted their freedom and had the same rights as other Dutch citizens.

2. Have students read the textbook version independently. Allow up to 10 minutes for them to read the passage.

3. After students have read the passage, discuss the material the students have heard and read. Ask questions that pertain to the summary the students heard and also to the passage they read independently. Some general questions that you might choose to use follow.

> What were some of the things you learned about the topic?
> What did you have trouble understanding from the reading?
> What questions do you have about the topic?
> What information about the topic would you like to add to our discussion?

4. Have students summarize what they have heard and read. Write the summary on the chalkboard or an overhead transparency, or use a computer with an LCD panel. Emphasize details from the text that were not in your initial summary. Explain that students need to be able to locate details in texts by reading.

TEACHING STRATEGY **6**

Embedded Questions

Struggling readers often do not monitor their reading by asking themselves questions as they read. When students don't actively ask questions or predict during reading, they miss much of the meaning of the passage. To scaffold students' self-questioning, you can embed questions in text (Weir, 1998), or you can create texts with hyperlinks of embedded questions (Dillner, 1993/1994). Embedding questions in texts guides the students' comprehension and models the types of questions they should be asking themselves as they read. Both embedding questions and creating hyperlinks accomplish the same goal: to provide students with questions that they can use to deepen their comprehension. As students read and answer the embedded questions, the selection becomes comprehensible, and you have scaffolded instruction by modeling the reading-thinking process.

Directions and Example

1. Choose one or more short passages that students will read independently. Explain the purpose for the reading assignment, as in the following example.

> We have been studying ecosystems of the salt marsh and oak forest in the chapter "Balanced Ecosystems" in *Science for Life and Living: Balance and Decisions* (1992). Today we will be reading the section "Description of the Tropical Rain Forest" and the information from the web site http://www.ran.org/ran/rainfor.html on the internet. The purpose of reading the text and the web site will be to learn about the third ecosystem, the rain forest.

2. Write embedded questions on a chalkboard or an overhead transparency, or use a computer with an LCD panel. The questions should be embedded where you want students to emphasize important concepts, predict outcomes, focus on details, clarify vocabulary, self-question, or summarize. Have students read the texts and answer the questions as they read. They can answer the questions in writing, or they can answer them in their heads.

3. After students have finished reading the texts with the embedded questions, discuss the use of questioning to comprehend difficult texts. Explain that readers ask themselves questions to understand what they are reading and to predict what will happen next. Encourage students to think of questions they could use as they read self-selected texts. An example of questions to embed for the chapter "Balanced Ecosystems" follows.

Middle School Science Example

Embedded Questions

Central concepts

The first paragraph in the book describes walking in a rain forest as being like walking in a greenhouse. What is a greenhouse?

Prediction

What plants and animals do you think can be found in the rain forest?

Details

On the web site, go to Kid's Corner and click on rain forest animals. How many plants and animals can be found in the rain forest?

Vocabulary

The text says that the soil has few nutrients. What nutrients are needed for plant growth? Look back in your notes on plant growth for the answer.

Monitoring

What parts of this text were confusing? What more do you want to know? If you were creating a web site, what would you include?

Summary

What connections between living and nonliving things make up this ecosystem? Use the information from both texts to answer the question.

5.3 Linking Experiences to Text

Goal

To help students use their cultural experiences to understand text information.

Background

All your students, whether they have lived in your community for their entire lives or whether they are new to the area, have different background experiences. Each of us brings our own background to every learning situation. Those backgrounds shape our view of the world, our behavior, and how we interpret events. Each of us also brings assumptions about the reading process, and we bring our individual values about reading to every learning situation (Lara, 1994). Our experiences influence who we are and how we approach school learning.

Experiences and cultures vary. Some of the experiences, beliefs, and values students have will be similar to yours; others will seem to be in contrast to what you believe. To be a culturally responsive teacher, it is important to honor each student's background, even if it is very different from your own. In an essay entitled "*Buscando Su Voz en Dos Culturas*—Finding Your Voice in Two Cultures," Cline (1998), a teacher, presents a compelling argument from a parent in her school. The parent believed that keeping her daughter home from school would teach the values of the family's culture: to raise daughters to be good homemakers. This essay sensitively describes the need to honor the parent's wishes and yet provide the daughter with the opportunities that schooling can bring. We need to listen to and honor cultures that may not value schooling, while at the same time scaffolding learning for students in our classes.

As a culturally responsive teacher, you can structure opportunities for students to link their own background knowledge and cultures to the information you are teaching. Teaching school concepts does not invalidate home cultures. By asking students to discuss their cultural experiences and by connecting them to instruction, you can scaffold instruction for students who have cultural backgrounds different from your own.

TEACHING STRATEGY 7

Concept Rating Guide

A Concept Rating Guide is an adaptation of the vocabulary strategy Knowledge Rating Scale (see Teaching Strategy 3-1). A Concept Rating Guide helps students rate their knowledge of new concepts presented in texts, identify background experiences about the concepts, and relate their background to the new concepts. Many of the texts used in schools contain subtle concepts that may be unique to the cultures about which students are learning. Both expository and narrative texts will have ideas in them that may be new to students. In order for students with different backgrounds to comprehend texts, they need to link their background experiences to the new learning.

Directions and Example

1. Identify concepts in the text that may be culturally unique. Write the names of the concepts on the chalkboard or an overhead transparency, or use a computer with an LCD panel. List the concepts on the left and provide three spaces on the right for the students to rate their knowledge of the concepts. The example that follows contains concepts that have been taken from the section "Eastern Europe and Soviet Union" in *World Geography* (1992).

Concepts	Heard	Know	Can Describe
Dialects			
Religions			
Composers			

2. Read the names of the concepts and have students respond individually about their experiences. They should respond with a checkmark under the box "heard" if they have heard of the concepts, "know" if they know what the concepts mean, and "can describe" if they can describe the concepts.

3. Ask students to discuss what they know about the concepts.

4. Read the passages from the pages containing the concepts. If students have copies of the book, ask them to follow along as you read. Point out the terms used in the Concept Rating Guide.

> Over 100 languages and **dialects** are spoken in the Soviet Union.

> The major **religions** in the regions are the Eastern Orthodox and Roman Catholic branches of Christianity. Other religions practiced are Protestantism, Judaism, and Islam.

> The regions have produced many world-famous **composers**. Among them, Bach is well-known for his organ music, Chopin for piano, and Tchaikovsky for symphonies and ballets.

5. Discuss the experiences students have had with each concept. If students are from another country, have them draw upon their knowledge about their home country. Some students may have little knowledge about their home country. Students from your community with different cultural backgrounds may have some different opinions about the concept being discussed. Encourage students to share as much personal background as they can. An example follows.

> Text information: Over 100 languages and dialects are spoken in the Soviet Union.

> Questions: What languages and/or dialects are spoken in your home country? Do you know how many languages are spoken in your home country? Did you know people in your home country who speak a similar language that sounded different from your language? Do you know anyone who speaks a dialect different from yours?

> Text information: The major religions in the regions are the Eastern Orthodox and Roman Catholic branches of Christianity. Other religions practiced are Protestantism, Judaism, and Islam.

> Questions: What religions were practiced in your home country? What religions are part of your family or your culture? Are they similar to or different from the religions in Eastern Europe and the Soviet Union?

Text information: The regions have produced many world-famous composers. Among them, Bach is well-known for his organ music, Chopin for piano, and Tchaikovsky for symphonies and ballets.

Questions: What types of music are found in your home country? Can you name some of the composers? Did your home country have orchestras? What type of music do you like? What instruments are used to produce this music?

6. After students have discussed their experiences, relate the students' backgrounds to the concepts being taught in the text. If students are unfamiliar with piano music, for example, play a recording of a Chopin piece. Explain that this type of music is well-known in Eastern Europe and the Soviet Union. Discuss how the music in that part of the world is like or unlike the music from the students' home countries.

TEACHING STRATEGY 8

Concept-Text-Application

The process of reading requires students to make links between their experiences and the information found in texts. When readers are unable to relate to texts, they have limited comprehension. A strategy that promotes the relationship between students' cultural experiences and texts is Concept-Text-Application (Wong-Kam & Au, 1988). With this strategy, you are scaffolding instruction by encouraging students to use their backgrounds to understand their reading.

Directions and Example

1. Identify a central concept in a text that students will be reading. Develop a question about the topic that students can use to discuss their backgrounds. Then ask students a question about the topic. For example, say:

    Today we're going to be reading a section from the chapter "Is Married Life for You?" from our text *Married and Single Life* (1997). The topic of this section is "Sharing Responsibilities."

    How have the married couples you know divided their responsibilities?

2. Divide the class into groups of three or four students. Have students share their experiences related to the topic. Then have students discuss their background experiences with the class. Examples follow.

    My mom works and does all the housework too. She never asks my dad to help.

    Both my parents work, but mom comes home late, so dad and I do all of the cooking. Mom does the wash and the cleaning. We all take my younger brother to his soccer games. My mom tells us who should do what.

    I live with my dad, so he goes to work and I take care of the house. My grandma helps me sometimes. My dad always talks with me about what needs to be done and who has time to do it.

4. Lead a discussion that relates students' experiences to the central concepts in the text. You might say something like the following:

> Many of you have experienced different ways to share responsibilities in your families. In a marriage, responsibilities must also be shared. The text suggests ways to discuss dividing tasks.

5. Alternate text reading with discussion. Guide students to understand the text, as in the following example.

> Read the first two paragraphs. The text suggests that couples may not agree about their roles if they were raised in families that had significantly different approaches to their roles. What do you think?

> The next section suggests that couples make a list of specific jobs and, before dividing the tasks, include the amount of time each one requires. What jobs are involved in living on your own? How should these tasks be divided in a marriage?

6. Lead a discussion to make explicit the relationship between the experiences of the students and the text. For example, say:

> You all have had different experiences with sharing responsibilities in a family. In a marriage, it's important to understand what needs to be done and to discuss who should do which jobs. Otherwise, one member of the couple can become resentful toward the other.

TEACHING STRATEGY 9

Guided Writing Procedure

The Guided Writing Procedure (Smith & Bean, 1980) is a strategy that has students use their backgrounds and what they learn through writing to understand the meaning of a text. In the Guided Writing Procedure, students discuss their backgrounds and experiences with a topic and then write about these experiences. Writing can be a powerful tool in recalling and recasting prior knowledge. When students write, they can clarify their knowledge about the topic, setting the stage for learning new information. The Guided Writing Procedure works well for students from all cultural backgrounds.

Directions and Example

1. Choose a passage from the text that you want students to learn. Identify a topic of importance and create a question about the topic. An example follows.

> We have been reading about the war in the Persian Gulf in our text *Moving On: The American People Since 1945* (1994). Why did the United States and its allies take military action against Iraq?

2. Have students brainstorm ideas using their prior knowledge about the topic. Write the ideas on the chalkboard or an overhead transparency, or use a computer with an LCD panel. For example:

> The war began in 1991.

> They called the war Desert Storm.

Saddam Hussein wanted to make Iraq more powerful, so Iraq invaded Kuwait.

In 1990, Iraqi forces moved toward the Saudi Arabian border.

The United Nations boycotted Iraq.

The United States sent troops to defend Saudi Arabia. This action was called Desert Shield.

President Bush ordered an air assault.

3.   Divide the class into groups of three or four students. Have students organize the ideas from their list into a semantic web, as in the following example.

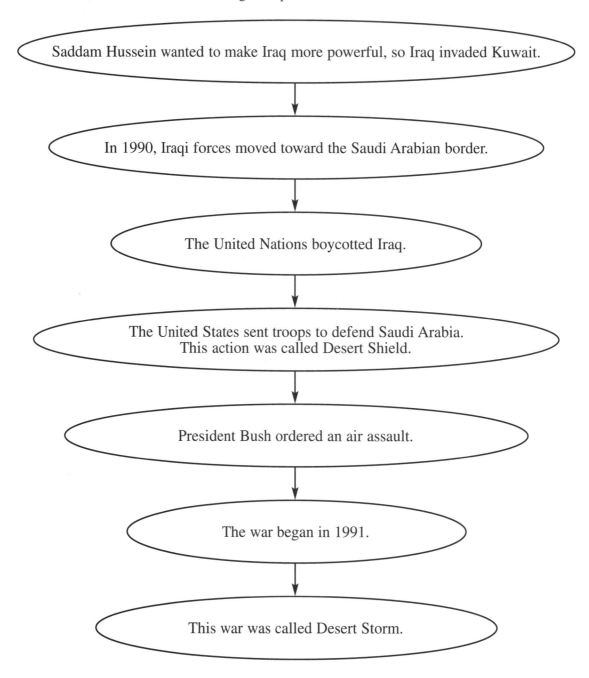

4. Ask students to write about the topic using the semantic web as a guide. Explain that they should use the semantic web to organize their ideas. If possible, students should use a computer so they can revise their writing more easily.

5. Have students read the chapter or passage from their textbooks that relates to the topic. Their brainstorming and writing should help them have a better understanding of the text.

6. Based on what they have learned from their reading, have students revise their writing.

After using the semantic web to organize their ideas, these students are ready to begin writing.

5.4 Identifying Important Information

Goal

To help students identify important information in text.

Background

When students who struggle with reading are assigned passages to read from content textbooks, they may need guidance in determining the important information in the passages. Information in content textbooks can be conceptually dense. Students who are struggling often have difficulty identifying what information is important and what information is extraneous. Content textbooks sometimes contain details that are intended to pique interest, but in reality they distract readers from the important information in the text. Anecdotes that draw students' attention away from the text are called "seductive details" (Garner, Gillingham, & White, 1989). "Seductive details," such as whether Thomas Jefferson had biracial children, are included by textbook authors to engage students' interest. However, these details tend to keep students from focusing on the important information in the text rather than helping students identify the main idea of the passage.

You can scaffold instruction by using several teaching strategies to help students identify information. Identifying important information is an essential skill for all readers, of course, but the strategies presented in this section are more teacher-directed than able readers need. Students who have little difficulty comprehending texts can benefit from independently identifying and remembering important information using strategies such as those presented in Chapter 7.

Identifying important information is an especially important learning goal for students who are using the internet to access and learn information. The strategies presented in this section—the Selective Reading Guide, Guided Notes, and Note Cue Cards—can be used for reading web sites as well as for identifying important information from textbook passages.

TEACHING STRATEGY 10

Selective Reading Guide

The amount of reading assigned to students in middle and high schools can be overwhelming. Although one goal is to have students learn content material, it is not always necessary for students to carefully read every word of the text you assign. A Selective Reading Guide (Cunningham & Shabloak, 1975) imitates the kinds of decisions mature readers make when they read. Mature readers read selectively to meet an established purpose. You can mirror this kind of reading by pointing out portions of text that do not have to be read carefully. A Selective Reading Guide can help students identify important information and can scaffold student learning by providing a model for decisions readers make.

Directions and Examples

1. Select a passage that students will read independently. Read the passage and identify the information that students need to read and the parts that students can skim or skip. Develop specific reading direc-

tions that help students select the important sections to read. Include short activities for students to follow. Below is an example of a Selective Reading Guide for the text *Today's Teens* (1994).

High School Family Living Example

Selective Reading Guide

"Caring for Clothes"

1. Read the subtitle "Routine Care" on page 333. Discuss with a classmate how you can take care of your clothes on a regular basis.
2. Read the four bulleted items from the section "Storage" on pages 334 and 335. List the suggestions the authors make for storing clothes.
3. Carefully read the paragraphs about washing clothes on pages 336–339. Discuss with a classmate the steps in washing, sorting, and prewashing clothes; choosing laundry products; and selecting a cleaning action on the washing machine.
4. Read pages 339–340 about drying clothes. Write a list of the clothes you have that you would dry in a dryer and a list of clothes that you would air dry.

---

2. Tell students that you will give them a reading assignment but that they do not have to read every word of the text. Give students a copy of the Selected Reading Guide, telling them to follow the directions while reading. Give students an appropriate amount of time to read the passages and complete the activities.

3. After students have read the text using the Selective Reading Guide, explain how mature readers select parts of texts to read. Model how readers often skim or skip parts of a text. Discuss when it is appropriate to read every word of a text and how students can select the important parts to read. (See Section 7.2 for strategies to teach students to skim and scan texts.)

TEACHING STRATEGY 11

Guided Notes

Guided Notes (Lazarus, 1988) help students identify important information by providing them with a partial outline of the passage you have asked them to read. When students read texts, they often miss important information, and sometimes they do not understand the relationships between concepts presented in the text. Guided Notes provide students with the structure of the text and some of the key terms. Students may need Guided Notes until they are able to identify information on their own. To scaffold instruction for struggling readers, you may provide more terms during the first part of your course and decrease the amount of information you give students as they learn how to access ideas from text.

Directions and Examples

1. Choose a section of a text that students will be reading independently. Develop a partial outline for the selection. Some texts are not written in a way that is conducive to a formal outline. If that is the case, you may develop a topical outline. An example of a text using a formal outline follows.

Module 4 in the text *Technology: Science and Math in Action* (1995) presents Maglev trains, a concept new to most students and an appropriate topic for close reading.

I. Definition of Maglev Trains
    A. No engine
    B.
    C.

II. Movement of Maglev Trains
    A. Suspended on magnetic field
    B.
    C.

2. Explain that you will be providing students with a partial outline to guide them in finding the important information in the text. Have students read the text independently. Then divide the class into groups of three or four students and have students add to the outline that you have developed.

3. Show students your completed outline on the chalkboard or an overhead transparency, or use a computer with an LCD panel. Have students compare their outlines to the one you present. Explain that outlines can differ, but point out what you consider to be the main ideas of the passage, as in the example below. Through modeling, help students understand how you selected the main ideas and important details.

I. Definition of Maglev Trains
    A. No engine
    B. Move at 300 mph
    C. Short for magnetic levitation

II. Movement of Maglev Trains
    A. Suspended on magnetic field
    B. Propelled by magnetic forces
    C. Glide along a guideway

4. After students have identified important information using Guided Notes, have students study the information using strategies presented in Chapter 7.

5. To scaffold instruction using Guided Notes, provide fewer items on your prepared outline each time you ask students to outline a textbook passage. When students are successful at identifying important information using Guided Notes, teach independent notetaking strategies such as those found in Section 7.3.

TEACHING STRATEGY 12

Note Cue Cards

Note Cue Cards (Manzo & Manzo, 1990b) have two instructional purposes: they help students identify important information in texts, and they facilitate discussion of key terms and concepts after reading. Note Cue Cards contain questions, answers, and comments written on note cards by the teacher about the ideas presented in a passage. When you use Note Cue Cards, you are able to guide students' attention to ideas and information as they read. After students read the text, Note Cue Cards focus the discussion on important ideas and information. Note Cue Cards scaffold learning for struggling readers by identifying key terms in the text and modeling the thinking-questioning process readers use as they learn from text.

Directions and Examples

1. Choose a passage that is important for students to read and learn. Prepare enough prereading Note Cue Cards so that each class member has at least one card. Some cards should have questions, some cards should have answers to the questions, and some cards should have comments about the topic. For example, say:

    Today we're going to read the section "The Rights of Citizens" in *Civics: Responsibilities and Citizenship* (1992). This section is important because it describes the basis for our rights in the United States.

    Question: What are some of the limits on the rights of the American people?

    Answer: The government can establish laws to restrict certain rights to protect the health, safety, security, and moral standards of a community.

    Comment: The restriction of rights must be reasonable and must apply to everyone equally.

2. Explain that you will be using Note Cue Cards to help students identify the important information in the text and to facilitate discussion and learning. Distribute the cards to students. Ask students to preview the identified passage of the text, read the cards, and think about how their cards apply to the text.

3. Ask a student to read a question card. After a student has read a question, ask students to read a card that would answer the question, and then ask for a comment card.

4. Have students read the passage of the text. After students have read the text, distribute more Note Cue Cards. You may decide to give students blank cards, so they can write their own questions, answers, and comments. For example, here are some student-generated Note Cue Cards.

    Question: How are an individual's rights limited for the common good?

    Answer: The rights of any individual may be limited to prevent interfering with the rights of others.

    Comment: Americans do not have unlimited rights.

5. Continue class discussion using Note Cue Cards. Explain that using Note Cue Cards helps students know what information to look for as they read. Discuss the ways the cards are used (i.e, questions, answers, and comments). Explain that, as they read independently, students should create self-questions similar to the questions written on the Note Cue Cards. They should ask themselves questions about the contents of texts, they should try to answer those questions, and they should make comments as they read.

6. Later, students could be invited to prepare Note Cue Cards on another section or chapter in the text.

5.5 Organizing Concepts for Understanding

Goal

To help students understand new ideas and concepts by organizing information they have read.

Background

Content learning is based on the learning of both general and specific concepts. As students learn general information, they build background knowledge and are able to comprehend content information more easily. For example, students who understand the principles of free speech in a democratic society will better understand discussions of censorship of library books or internet sites, discussions of the need for the Bill of Rights, and discussions about scientists who perform controversial research such as cloning. Students who know more general information will be able to learn more from content area textbooks.

Content learning is also based on content-specific concepts. Some of the information students will read in content area textbooks will be details that relate primarily to one discipline. For example, students who are taking a bowling class and reading the book *From Gutterballs to Strikes* (1998) learn the best foot position to approach a bowling lane. Although the approach a bowler takes may have similarities to other sports, developing a foot position to make strikes in bowling is not really generalizable to other subjects.

Textbook passages are written with both general and specific information. The general concept is written as a topic sentence, and specifics are elaborated as details. Struggling readers often have difficulty understanding the relationship between general and specific concepts in their reading. Limited English Proficiency students have an especially difficult time sifting through information in texts and understanding how to organize the information. Teachers, however, can scaffold instruction for struggling readers by providing them with instructional ideas and routines designed to organize information. When students use organizational strategies, they practice skills mature readers use as they read text.

TEACHING STRATEGY 13

Plot Relationships Chart

A Plot Relationships Chart (Schmidt & Buckley, 1991) is a strategy to organize the components of a story into a one-sentence description. Although Plot Relationships Charts were developed for narrative texts, they are also appropriate for use with textbook material in content areas. When students use the Plot Relationships Chart structure with expository texts, they are able to understand the relationships between concepts in the text.

Directions and Examples

1. For narrative texts, choose a story that has clear story elements: characters, goal, problem, and solution. For informational texts, choose a passage that has a cause-effect relationship.

2. Have students read the passage independently.

3. Explain that the passage has a structure that can be written in a single sentence. Place a blank copy of the Plot Relationships Chart on an overhead projector, or draw it on the chalkboard. Tell students that they will be using this chart to help them learn the structure of a plot or how concepts are organized in a textbook passage. A copy of the chart follows.

Plot Relationships Chart

Somebody	Wanted	But	So

4. Guide students in identifying the major elements of a narrative text: main character, goal, problem, and solution. Use the cue words *somebody, wanted, but,* and *so* to prompt students to identify the story's elements. For example, when teaching the book *Pride and Prejudice* (1998), you might ask questions such as "Who is the important *somebody* in this book?" When students answer Elizabeth, write it on the chart. To elicit the goal, present the statement, "In the story, Elizabeth *wanted . . .*" Follow this pattern of using the cues and students' responses to identify the problem and solution in the story. An example follows.

High School Literature Example

Plot Relationships Chart

Somebody	Wanted	But	So
Elizabeth	to marry Darcy	she was too proud to admit it	she needed to be humbled.

5. Have students use the statements they wrote on the Plot Relationships Chart to form a complete sentence, as in the following example.

Elizabeth wanted to marry Darcy, but she was too proud to admit it, so she needed to be humbled.

6. For expository text, have students discern the relationships between the concepts in the passage. Guide them using a Concept Relationships Chart as in the following example.

Middle School History Example

Concept Relationships Chart

Somebody	Wanted	But	So
Abraham Lincoln	to stop slavery	the South needed slavery for its economy	the Civil War began.

7. The Concept Relationships Chart can be adapted for science classes to follow the scientific method of research. Using a Concept Relationships Chart guides students to understand the relationships between the steps in the research process. For example, the term *somebody* can be changed to *problem, wanted* can become *hypothesis, but* would be *testing, so* would become *conclusion*. The following science example is based on an experiment found in the book *Human Development: How Human Beings Grow and Change* (1995).

Middle School Science Example

Concept Relationships Chart

Problem	Hypothesis	Testing	Conclusion
Is tongue rolling inherited?	When both parents can't roll their tongues, their children won't be able to roll their tongues.	Parents and children try rolling their tongues.	The hypothesis is supported. When both parents can't roll their tongues, neither can the children.

8. After completing the chart for a science experiment, have students write the results in a short paragraph, such as the following one.

> The problem was to find out if the ability to roll tongues is inherited. The hypothesis states that if both parents can't roll their tongues their children won't be able to roll their tongues either. The hypothesis is tested by having parents and children roll their tongues. The conclusion is that when both parents are unable to roll their tongues, neither can their children.

ORDER

The ORDER strategy (Scanlon, Schumaker, & Deshler, 1994) was designed to guide students in understanding how to organize information from text. ORDER is an acronym for **O**pen your mind, **R**ecognize the structure, **D**raw an organizer, **E**xplain it, and **R**euse it. You can use ORDER in two ways. You can have students use ORDER during the reading of a text as in the science example below, or you can use it on an ongoing basis as in the math example.

Directions and Examples

1. Identify an important concept that you want students to understand. Explain that when students read texts, they need to organize the information from the texts. Tell students that ORDER provides them with steps to organize and process information.

2. Provide students with a copy of the steps in the ORDER strategy. Explain each of the steps using the examples that follow.

ORDER Strategy

Open your mind and take notes.

Recognize the structure.

Draw an organizer.

Explain it.

Reuse it.

---

3. Assign students to read a passage from a textbook. Have students take notes as they read. You might have students use the notetaking strategies from Section 7.3. After students have taken notes on the passage, have them identify the structure of the information. In the textbook *Earth Science* (1997), have students take notes on the section that describes types of rocks, as in the following example.

Common Igneous Rocks

Types of Magma rocks: Basaltic, Granitic, and Andesitic

Different kinds of rocks: Gabbro, Basalt, Scoria, Granite, Ryolite, Pumice, Diorite, Andesite

4. Have students draw a graphic organizer from the information in their notes. An example follows.

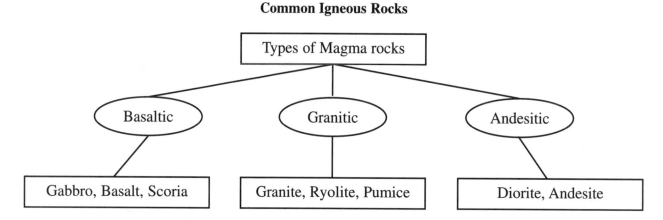

Common Igneous Rocks

5. Have students explain the information based on their graphic organizer. Their explanation may be similar to the example that follows.

> There are three types of common igneous rocks. They are basaltic, granitic, and andesitic. Each of the three types of rocks has subsets of rocks. There are three types of basaltic rocks: gabbro, basalt, and scoria. Granitic rocks also have three types: granite, ryolite, and pumice. There are two types of andesitic rocks: diorite and andesite.

6. After students have explained the information from their graphic organizers, have them keep their organizers to study for a test. (See Chapters 7 and 8 for study strategies and strategies to prepare for tests.)

7. Explain that the ORDER strategy can be used as an ongoing graphic organizer during a unit of study. Provide students with an organizer that has blanks for the concepts you will be teaching in a unit of study. As students learn about the topic, have them fill in the spaces of the organizer. When the organizer is complete, have students finish the steps in the ORDER strategy. An example using ORDER for mathematics classes using the book *Transition Mathematics* (1995) follows.

Middle School Mathematics Example

ORDER

Commutative Property of Addition   Associative Property of Addition

Formula $a + b = b + a$ _____

Example $6 + 8 = 8 + 6$ _____

    Distributive Property of Multiplication over Addition

    Formula   _____

    Example   _____

CONCEPT Diagram

A CONCEPT Diagram (Bulgren & Scanlon, 1997/1998) is a graphic representation of information related to a concept discussed in content material. The relationship between information is displayed on the CONCEPT Diagram so that students can learn how to organize concepts and related details. The CONCEPT Diagram includes an overall topic, a key concept, its characteristics, examples and nonexamples, and a summary. When students organize information using a CONCEPT Diagram, they are helped to process and organize content knowledge.

Directions and Examples

1. Tell students that a CONCEPT Diagram can help them organize information from textbooks for better learning. Provide students with the steps in the CONCEPT Diagram process and explain each of the steps using the examples that follow.

CONCEPT Diagram Steps

Convey the concept.

Offer overall concept.

Note the key words.

Classify characteristics.

Explore examples.

Practice with new examples.

Tie down a definition.

---

2. Identify a passage from the textbook that has an important topic and related information. Model how to use the steps of a CONCEPT Diagram by making a transparency of a blank CONCEPT Diagram and showing it on an overhead projector. (A copy of a blank CONCEPT Diagram follows the directions.)

3. Tell students the concept you have identified for them to discuss and learn. An example follows.

Convey the concept.

In our text *Succeeding in the World of Work* (1992), we have been learning about personal effectiveness on the job. Today we will be considering the personal traits that contribute to success.

4. Explain that the concept of personal effectiveness on the job is part of a bigger topic. Have students offer suggestions about the overall concept. If students are unable to identify the overall concept, tell them what it is as in the following example.

Offer overall concept.

Becoming personally effective is one of the elements of career success.

5. Divide the class into groups of three or four students. Have students brainstorm key words about the concept of personal effectiveness on the job. Give students five minutes to think of related terms. Ask students to volunteer the terms they have identified. Write the key words on the CONCEPT Diagram. An example follows.

Note the key words.

positive attitude	sense of humor	self-control
friendliness	dependability	showing interest in others
smiling	understanding others	making others feel important

6 Using the key words students have suggested, have them classify the characteristics into the categories always present, sometimes present, and never present. After students have classified the key words, have them suggest additional words. The following example places into categories the key terms for the concept of personal effectiveness on the job.

Classify characteristics.

Always Present	**Sometimes Present**	**Never Present**
positive attitude	making others feel important	anger
sense of humor	understanding others	dishonesty
self-control	smiling	disloyalty
friendliness	showing interest in others	
dependability		

7. Have students think of examples and nonexamples of the concept using the criteria listed above. Suggest others yourself. See the following example.

Explore examples.

Examples of characters who are effective.	Examples of characters who are less effective.
Tim Meeker (*My Brother Sam is Dead*)	Jack (*Lord of the Flies*)
Karana (*Island of the Blue Dolphins*)	Lip-lip (*White Fang*)

8. Think of additional examples and nonexamples of the concept. Write one of the examples or nonexamples on the chalkboard or an overhead transparency, or use a computer with an LCD panel. Ask students whether the word you suggest is an example or a nonexample of the concept.

Practice with new examples.

Examples of characters who are effective.	Examples of characters who are less effective.
Sal *(Walk Two Moons)*	Pinky *(A Day No Pigs Would Die)*

9. Explain that the preceding activities elaborate on the concept's meanings but that it is also useful for students to learn a short definition for the concept. Have students independently generate a definition for the concept. Have students share their definitions with the entire class. Write several definitions on the chalkboard or an overhead transparency, or use a computer with an LCD panel. After students volunteer several definitions, guide students to choose two or three of the definitions that best fit the concept. Write one of these definitions on the CONCEPT Diagram. An example follows.

Tie down a definition.

A person who is personally effective on the job is one who has positive personal traits such as friendliness and honesty and is able to positively influence others.

10. An example using a CONCEPT Diagram from *A History of Multicultural America: The New Freedom to the New Deal* (1993) and a blank CONCEPT Diagram follow.

High School Social Studies Example

CONCEPT Diagram

❸ **Key Words**

culture

heritage

native language

laws

protest

_____

_____

_____

_____

❶ **Concept**

Native American
Cultural Resistance

❷ **Overall Concept**

Discriminatory Practices

❹ **Classify Characteristics**

Always Present	Sometimes Present	Never Present
embrace heritage	keep native language	Americanization
active	keep culture	violent
protest unfairness	resist new laws	forget heritage

❺ **Explore Examples**

Examples

Protest unfair stereotyping in
textbooks in 1927

Fought Bursum
Bill in 1923

Nonexamples

Accept English
only practices

Accept American
cultural practices

❻ **New Examples**   other protests _____   write new laws _____

❼ **Definition**

During the 1920s, Native Americans used political action to preserve their native culture.

Based on Bulgren, J., & Scanlon, D. (1997/1998). Instructional routines and learning strategies that promote understanding of content area concepts. *Journal of Adolescent & Adult Literacy, 41,* 292–302.

CONCEPT Diagram

❸ Key Words

_____
_____
_____
_____
_____
_____
_____
_____

❶ Concept

❷ Overall Concept

_____

❹ Classify Characteristics

Always Present   **Sometimes Present**   **Never Present**

_____   _____   _____
_____   _____   _____
_____   _____   _____
_____   _____   _____

❺ Explore Examples

Examples   **Nonexamples**

❻ New Examples _____   _____

❼ Definition

Based on Bulgren, J., & Scanlon, D. (1997/1998). Instructional routines and learning strategies that promote understanding of content area concepts. *Journal of Adolescent & Adult Literacy, 41,* 292–302.

TEACHING STRATEGY 16

Comparison Table

A Comparison Table (Bulgren & Scanlon, 1997/1998) helps students organize the similarities and differences between concepts. Students can learn about new concepts by understanding their critical features. A Comparison Table includes the two concepts being compared, the larger topic under which the two concepts belong, characteristics of the concepts, characteristics that are alike and different, the larger categories into which the characteristics fit, and a summary. A Comparison Table graphically organizes all of this information so that students can recognize the relationships between the ideas. Comparison Tables can be used to compare concepts in expository text, or they can be adapted to compare a similar theme from two short stories.

Directions and Examples

1. Tell students that a Comparison Table can help them organize the similarities and differences between two concepts. Provide students with the steps in the Comparison Table process and explain each step using the examples that follow.

Comparison Table

Communicate the targeted concepts.

Obtain the overall concept.

Make lists of known characteristics.

Pin down like characteristics.

Assemble categories for like characteristics.

Record unlike characteristics.

Identify categories for unlike characteristics.

Nail down a summary.

Go beyond the basics.

---

2. Identify a passage from a textbook that has two concepts you want students to compare. Model how to use the steps of a Comparison Table. Make a transparency of the Comparison Table and show it on an overhead projector. (A copy of a blank Comparison Table is printed at the end of the directions.)

3. Tell students the concepts you have identified for them to discuss and learn. An example follows.

Communicate the targeted concepts.

In our textbook *Drive Right* (1993), we have been reading about safe driving. Two concepts we have read about are driving in urban areas and driving in rural areas.

4. Explain that the concepts urban and rural driving are part of a bigger topic. Have students offer suggestions about the overall topic. If students are unable to identify the overall topic, tell them what it is as in the following example.

Obtain the overall concept.

The overall concept is driving in urban and rural areas.

5. Divide the class into groups of three or four students. Have students brainstorm characteristics about the concepts urban and rural driving. Give students five minutes to think of related terms. Ask students to volunteer the terms they produced. Write the key words under each term on the Comparison Chart. An example follows.

Make lists of known characteristics.

Known Characteristics	
Urban Driving	**Rural Driving**
Higher number of hazards	Lower number of hazards
Speed limits	Speed limits
More frequent hazards	Less frequent hazards

6. Have students use the list of characteristics on the Comparison Table to identify characteristics that are similar for each term. An example follows.

Pin down like characteristics.

Like Characteristics	
Urban Driving	**Rural Driving**
Speed limits	Speed limits

7. Use the terms listed under like characteristics to discuss the categories under which they fall. Ask students to think of a broader term for each of the like characteristics. You may need to suggest ideas for this part of the strategy as in the following example.

Assemble categories for like characteristics.

Like Characteristics of Urban and Rural Driving	Categories
Speed limits	Speed of travel

8. Divide the class into groups of three or four students. Have students brainstorm unlike characteristics about the concepts urban and rural driving. Give students five minutes to think of related terms. Ask students to volunteer the terms they produced. Write the key words under each term on the Comparison Chart. An example follows.

Record unlike characteristics.

Unlike Characteristics	
Urban Driving	**Rural Driving**
Higher number of hazards	Lower number of hazards
More frequent hazards	Less frequent hazards

9. Use the terms listed under unlike characteristics to discuss the categories under which they fall. Ask students to think of a broader term for each of the unlike characteristics. You may need to suggest ideas for this part of the strategy as in the following example.

Identify categories for unlike characteristics.

Urban Driving Characteristics	Rural Driving Characteristics	Categories
Higher number of hazards	Lower number of hazards	Driving conditions
More frequent hazards	Less frequent hazards	Driving conditions

10. Explain that the preceding activities elaborate on the concepts' meanings but that it is useful for students to learn a short summary. Have students independently generate a summary. Then ask students to share their summaries with the entire class. Write several summaries on the chalkboard or an overhead transparency, or use a computer with an LCD panel. After students volunteer several different summaries, write one of them on the Comparison Table. An example follows.

Nail down a summary.

Driving in urban and rural areas has many of the same types of challenges. Although the driving conditions in urban areas are generally more dangerous, many of the same driving rules apply to both areas. Despite the number or frequency of driving hazards, drivers need to follow the speed limit and keep a safe distance between cars.

11. After students have written individual summaries, have them generate ideas that are extensions of the one already discussed. The following is an example.

Go beyond the basics.

Driving Stress

12. The Comparison Table example from the *Drive Right* (1993) textbook and a blank Comparison Table can be found on the following pages.

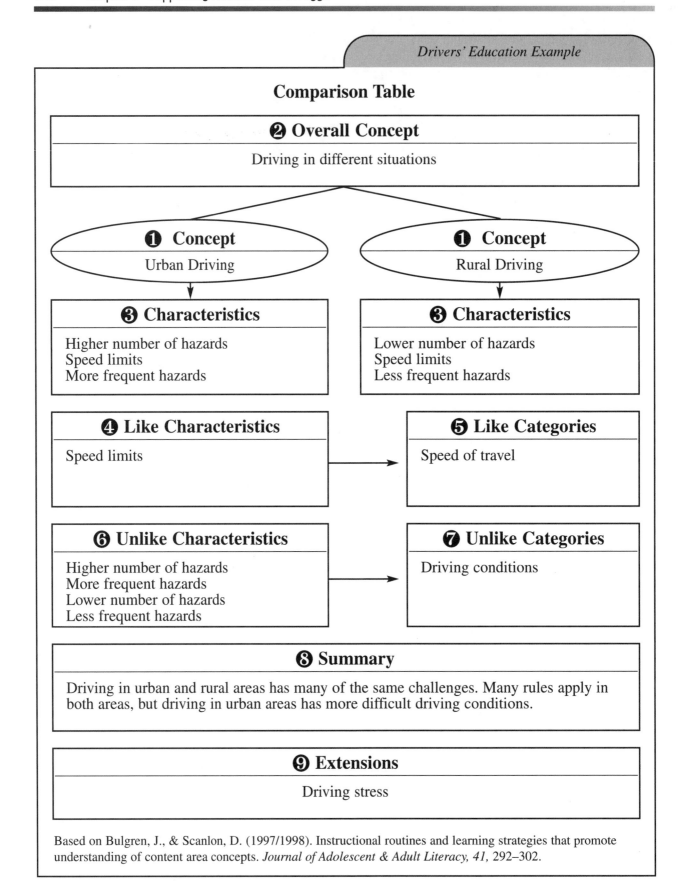

Drivers' Education Example

Comparison Table

❷ Overall Concept

Driving in different situations

❶ Concept

Urban Driving

❶ Concept

Rural Driving

❸ Characteristics

Higher number of hazards
Speed limits
More frequent hazards

❸ Characteristics

Lower number of hazards
Speed limits
Less frequent hazards

❹ Like Characteristics

Speed limits

❺ Like Categories

Speed of travel

❻ Unlike Characteristics

Higher number of hazards
More frequent hazards
Lower number of hazards
Less frequent hazards

❼ Unlike Categories

Driving conditions

❽ Summary

Driving in urban and rural areas has many of the same challenges. Many rules apply in both areas, but driving in urban areas has more difficult driving conditions.

❾ Extensions

Driving stress

Based on Bulgren, J., & Scanlon, D. (1997/1998). Instructional routines and learning strategies that promote understanding of content area concepts. *Journal of Adolescent & Adult Literacy, 41,* 292–302.

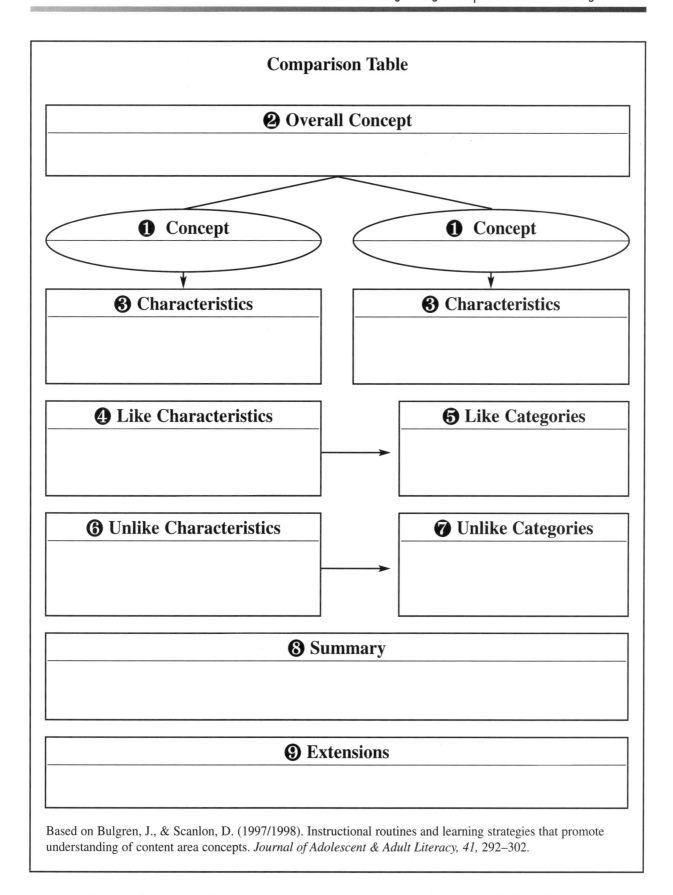

Comparison Table

❷ **Overall Concept**

❶ **Concept**

❶ **Concept**

❸ **Characteristics**

❸ **Characteristics**

❹ **Like Characteristics**

❺ **Like Categories**

❻ **Unlike Characteristics**

❼ **Unlike Categories**

❽ **Summary**

❾ **Extensions**

Based on Bulgren, J., & Scanlon, D. (1997/1998). Instructional routines and learning strategies that promote understanding of content area concepts. *Journal of Adolescent & Adult Literacy, 41,* 292–302.

Chapter 6

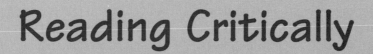

Reading Critically

Overview

In order for students to develop an understanding of your subject, they must be able to construct meaning from the texts you choose for them to read and the texts they read independently. Constructing meaning from texts is not sufficient, however, for students to be able to think critically in your content area. You also want your students to be able to look for assumptions, reasons, justifications, and implications in texts and to interpret texts fairly and accurately (Paul, 1993). In essence, you want your students to be critical readers of texts.

In recent years, there has been a new focus on critical reading in schools. Instead of students merely trying to understand an author's message, as we tra-

ditionally have thought of understanding text, we now want students to question and comment on what they read. We want students to move from constructing an initial understanding of text to thinking about text deeply and personally—taking a stand apart from a text and developing reasoned opinions. We want students to read "text in such a way as to question assumptions, explore perspectives, and critique underlying social and political values or stances" (International Reading Association & National Council of Teachers of English, 1996, p. 71).

One of the reasons why critical reading needs to have a predominant place in the curriculum is that available information is increasing at unbelievable rates, doubling every two years. We are flooded with information, much of it new. Students of the 21st century, more than any other group of students in history, will need to be able to sift through a myriad of print and electronic texts, select which texts to process, decide what information is worthwhile, and make judgments about what to believe.

Another reason why critical reading needs to have a predominant part in the curriculum is that information is more accessible to students than ever before. In 1997, there were an estimated 50 million web sites available online (Thornburg, 1997). More are available today. Many students have internet access at home, and 82% of schools are now connected to the internet (Mendels, 1998). As students access the internet, they are in contact with all sorts of information that may be inaccurate, biased, or misleading. Students need to know how to critically evaluate texts on the internet as well as texts that have been reviewed before publication.

Critical reading is important for middle school and secondary students, but many students are not yet proficient at making reasoned judgments while reading. Scores from the National Assessment of Educational Progress (NAEP) during the last decade indicated that approximately 69% of eighth-grade students and 75% of high school seniors read at a basic level. Only 2% to 4% of the high school seniors read with a critical stance (Mullis, Campbell, & Farstrup, 1993).

One of the reasons for this distressing picture about what students are able to do is that the definition and understanding of what constitutes critical reading is changing (Unrau, 1997). For years, critical reading has been identified by a discrete set of skills (e.g., determining fact and opinion). According to NAEP scores, it appears as if the skills approach has not worked very well in developing students who are critical readers.

Currently, critical reading is considered to be an activity whose outcome depends on the perspectives that a reader develops when analyzing and evaluating text (Peters, 1991). This concept is based on current views of teaching and learning. Critical reading, therefore, requires readers to do the following (Chapman, 1993):

- Draw on experiences to understand text.
- Decide what is important in the text.
- Connect current texts to past texts.
- Construct tentative hypotheses that are actively verified, modified, or abandoned.
- Infer what information is needed to fill gaps in understanding, evaluate the explicit information given and the inferences made, and integrate those that seem most important.
- Evaluate how well new information derived from the text complements previous knowledge.
- Determine which elements of the new, the old, or both may have to be abandoned or modified to create an accurate and consistent mental image.
- Store the newly constructed understandings so that they can be readily recalled in a variety of contexts and circumstances.

Although critical reading cannot be divided into a set of skills, critical readers determine authors' credibility and perspectives, make intertextual links to past texts, consider alternative views, evaluate arguments, and form judgments. The strategies in this chapter promote these more demanding types of mental processes. There is no automatic way for students to learn how to read critically, but with effective teaching, modeling, and guided practice, most of your students can learn to become critical readers of the texts and materials used in your content area.

6.1 Determining Authors' Credibility and Perspectives

Goal

To help students determine whether authors are credible sources and to evaluate the perspectives they bring to texts.

Background

The texts that you ask your students to read will vary in quality. Authors, who are fallible and have particular perspectives on issues, write texts. Therefore, some of the texts that your students read will be outdated; some will contain biased viewpoints; and others may treat issues superficially. One of the biggest legacies you can leave your students is to teach them to think about the authors of texts—to determine whether the authors are qualified and from what perspectives the authors are approaching the texts.

Writers make deliberate choices of the words, images, and information they use; they leave other information out of their texts. Critical readers become aware of the social context of writing by trying to understand something about the authors (Wray & Lewis, 1997). Readers should "consider the source" by asking questions about the authors, the purpose of the text, and the conditions under which it was published. The answers to these questions can influence the judgments the reader makes when trying to determine what parts of the text to use to develop ideas and beliefs.

After students understand something about the authors' qualifications, the publication date, and the authors' word choices, they should think more deeply about the authors' perspectives. Texts are not neutral. Authors indicate or convey their perspectives in many subtle ways. As they analyze texts, critical readers try to understand from what perspectives the authors are writing.

The internet has widened the scope of communication; students have access to millions of electronic texts. With the advent of the internet, it is even more important that students try to determine authors' credibility and perspectives. For example, Wilson (1996) describes a student and senior citizen online activity where students electronically corresponded with primary sources. Students studying the 1940s, for example, asked a woman living during that time whether she was more impressed with Eleanor Roosevelt than with the current First Lady. Students involved in these kinds of projects need to understand that their online mentors respond from a perspective. They may or may not be qualified to answer the questions; they may be biased; and their opinions may be one-sided. Since there are no current guidelines for publishing on the internet, making these determinations about authors of electronic sources is more complicated. (Section 9.3 contains strategies for evaluating electronic sources.) Learning how to critically read school texts, which are rigorously reviewed before publication, provides a good foundation for students who then will be reading electronic texts independently.

TEACHING STRATEGY 1

Consider the Source

One of the first things students need to do as they think critically about a text is to make some determination about the credibility of the source. Although most of the texts you will ask your students to read probably have been sanctioned by you, a curriculum committee, or the school board, students still will need to think about the factors in the text that could influence text credibility. A strategy you can use to initiate critical questioning of the source by your students is called Consider the Source. This strategy is a list of questions with examples for you to model with your students in order to spur questions about pertinent aspects of the text. You may want to use this activity several times during a school year with examples from your content area. Your goal, however, is for students to think independently about the credibility of sources before they read. Consider the Source can be used in various subject areas.

Directions and Examples

1. Ask students to look at the source of the passage you have asked them to read. Ask them to look for the date of publication. Discuss the importance of the copyright date. Tell students that information with a copyright date of 1999 was probably written at least a year earlier and may be considerably older than that. Explain that even when authors are discussing historical events, dates are important. New information can, at times, influence what is believed about an event. Books that are written in the near or distant past, however, are not necessarily incorrect. The date of the publication is one factor for establishing credibility, but newer is not necessarily better.

2. Use an example such as the following one to illustrate the importance of dates of publication. Discuss why the publication date is important in these examples.

    > Today Germany is two separate countries. They are different from each other in a number of ways. One of the most important differences is the form of government. East Germany has a Communist government.

    > Built in 1961, the Berlin Wall separates the city of Berlin into two sections—East Berlin, or the Communist section, and West Berlin.

    ▶ From *Exploring our world: Eastern hemisphere.* (1980). Chicago: Follett, p. 135.

3. Discuss the importance of the authors' qualifications. Many of the textbooks used in schools have a list of authors with their credentials stated at the front of the book. Look for the list of authors, read about their backgrounds, and discuss whether they appear qualified to write the book. You can use the following example for class discussion.

    > In a middle school music class using the book *Share the Music* (1995), students can look at the qualifications of the authors at the beginning of the book. Fourteen authors are listed: six middle school teachers of music, five university professors, one composer, and two choral directors.

    > Discuss how the qualifications of a middle school teacher would be different from the qualifications of a composer. Discuss whether the balance among middle school teachers, university professors, and professional musicians is appropriate for the text.

4. Discuss what seems to be the authors' primary aim in writing the book. Some books are written primarily for information, some are written for instruction, and others are aimed at persuasion. Find examples of each type of text from your content field and discuss how readers can identify the purpose of the authors. The following is an example from a world literature class.

    > In a world literature class reading *Celtic Myths* (1995), scan the Contents looking for the topics that are included in the text. The Contents of *Celtic Myths* includes introductory chapters with titles such as "The Divine Race of Ireland" and chapters with categories of myths such as "Ani-

mals in Cult and Myth." Discuss whether the the author's choice of words indicates a particular bias toward the subject.

After reading portions of the text, discuss whether the writing was informational, instructional, or persuasive. *Celtic Myths,* for example, seems to be informational, but the author appears to have a heavy bias toward the subject. Discuss whether the author's bias might detract from the informational aspects of the book.

5. Once the type of text is determined, read several passages of the text with your students to determine whether the author relies on words that may indicate a bias. Use an example from your content area or the following examples to discuss how authors can subtly steer readers toward one way of thinking.

6. Make copies of the following passages taken from an American textbook and ask students to read the two passages. Discuss how phrases such as "the harsh new British policies" lead the reader toward the colonists' viewpoint.

> By the 1760s, however, the harsh new British policies spurred the growth of an American sense of community. A growing number of colonists now began to think of themselves as Americans drawn together by their hostility to British authorities. At the same time, colonial leaders began to take political action against what they felt was British suppression.

> The concluding paragraphs [of the Declaration of Independence] contain a statement of the colonists' determination to separate from Great Britain. These paragraphs explain that the colonists' efforts to reach a peaceful solution with England had failed, leaving them no choice but to declare their freedom.

> ▶ From *Government in the United States.* (1990). New York: Glencoe/McGraw-Hill, p. 162.

7. Make copies of the following passages taken from a British history book and ask students to read the two passages. Discuss how phrases such as "the thirteen rebellious states" express the British view of the war. Ask students to identify the differences between the authors' perspectives in the American and British texts.

> King George III was a pig-headed man rather than a tyrant—but from America the distinction was not clear to the naked eye.

> And the thirteen rebellious states were recognized as the United States of America.

> ▶ From *History of England.* (1974). London: Collins, p. 287.

8. Finally, analyze several passages in the text to determine whether the author used any negative propaganda techniques. Propaganda is a one-sided statement that is used to sway the opinion of the reader. Discuss the most common types of propaganda techniques (see box on the next page) and create examples of each that fit your content area.

Propaganda Techniques

Appeal to bandwagon: Most people believe this and you should too if you want to be one of the crowd.

- Everyone in the school has a team jacket, so you should have one too.

Emotional language: Plays on connotations of words that evoke strong feeling.

- You'll be the one in power if you join the Student Council.

Appeal to prestige: Associating a product with someone important.

- Michael Jordan thinks hightop shoes are the best!

Plain-folks appeal: Typical people use this product, thereby invoking a sense of the common person.

- All of the members of the Pep Club have purchased our school shirts.

Testimonial: Use of a famous person to give credibility to a concept, idea, or product.

- Cindy Crawford studied acting here.

TEACHING STRATEGY 2

Perspective Guide

After students have considered the credibility of the author, they should think about the perspective the author may be taking. Many of the texts your students read will take a subtle perspective about a subject. Neutral texts would be bland beyond belief. It is important that students are able to identify the perspective the author is taking. A Perspective Guide presents quotations from two or more passages that have a similar theme but different perspectives. When students are able to identify an author's perspective, they are able to use what they know about the author's perspective along with the author's qualifications to make an informed decision about the topic.

Directions and Example

1. Choose two or more texts written around a central theme in which the authors have different perspectives about an issue. You can choose texts from the same medium, such as the two short stories in the example, or you can choose different types of texts. The texts, however, should have a similar theme.

2. Choose four to eight quotations from each passage that relate to the central theme. Write the quotations in random order on the chalkboard or an overhead transparency, or use a computer with an LCD panel. List the sources of the quotations at the bottom of the page.

3. Divide the class into groups of three or four students. Have students read and discuss the quotations, discussing ideas about the perspectives of the authors. Then have the students match the quotations with the sources as in the example below.

High School Literature Example

Perspective Guide

Directions: After reading the two stories "Aging in the Land of the Young" and "Woman Without Fear," match the following quotations with the stories and discuss the view of aging taken by each author. Use *a* for "Aging in the Land of the Young" and *b* for "Woman Without Fear."

1. _____ Aging paints every action gray, lies heavy on every movement, imprisons every thought.

2. _____ The world becomes narrower as friends and family die or move away.

3. _____ Although Grace was 64 years old, she was as active as a boy and worked with smooth dexterity.

4. _____ When she saw me, she hurriedly picked up the four-foot rattlesnake who had been sunning himself while his box was being cleaned and poured him into his cage.

5. _____ There is nothing to prepare you for the experience of growing old.

6. _____ I first heard of Grace Wiley when Dr. William Mann handed me a picture of a tiny woman with a gigantic king cobra draped over her shoulders like a garden hose.

7. _____ I am afraid to grow old—we're all afraid. In fact, the fear of growing old is so great that every aged person is an insult and a threat to the society.

8. _____ "Don't trip over an alligator," she added as I came forward. I noticed for the first time in the high grass a dozen or so alligators and crocodiles.

From Curtin, S. (1984). Aging in the land of the young. In *Literature* (pp. 389–391). Evanston, IL: McDougal, Littell. Mannix, D. (1984). Woman without fear. In *Literature* (pp. 325–333). Evanston, IL: McDougal, Littell.

---

4. After students complete the Perspective Guide, ask them to discuss their reasoning for their choices and guide them to identify the different perspectives of the authors. In this example, one of the authors discusses a woman's fear of aging while the other celebrates the life of a courageous older woman. Discuss reasons why perspectives about a topic may differ. Then discuss alternative perspectives on the topic. You might ask the students to write an essay or short story from a third perspective.

TEACHING STRATEGY **3**

Ask the Author

Students who understand an author's perspective can gain a deeper understanding of the text by identifying with the author. Ask the Author is an adaptation of a Creative Reasoning Guide (Jacobson, 1998) that can be tailored to provide students with the opportunity to answer questions from the author's perspective. When students are able to put themselves in the place of the author, they develop a more thorough understanding of the author's perspective.

Directions and Examples

1. Identify an event that is not fully explained in the text. For example, the text *Latin for Americans* (1997) includes Cicero's speeches for Archias. However, the text does not explain the reasons why Cicero would discuss literature with Archias.

2. Write the event as a scenario on the chalkboard or an overhead transparency, or use a computer with an LCD panel. In the scenario, direct a question to the author for reasons that caused the event. See the following example for a sample scenario.

    Earlier in this course you read stories from Pliny and Galleus and speeches from Cicero. This section contains several of Cicero's speeches for Archias, some dealing with the value of literature. With what you know about Roman culture and Cicero's character, what reasons would Cicero have to discuss literature with Archias? Give at least three reasons.

3. Divide the class into groups of three to five students. Give the students the Ask the Author scenario. Ask them to brainstorm at least three reasons that would answer the question. The reasons should be logical in light of past knowledge, but creativity should be encouraged. The following is a second example from a Latin class.

Latin Class Example

Ask the Author

Directions: After reading "The Value of Literature," in *Latin for Americans* (1997), read the following scenario and think about answers to the question.

Scenario

In further passages, Cicero discusses his views on poets. Three of the speeches are titled "Poets are Sacred," "No Fame Without Poets," and "Poets Give Immortality." What reasons would Cicero have for revering poets to such an extent? Give at least three reasons.

---

4. In a whole group setting, ask the students to share the reasons listed during the brainstorming activity. List all of the reasons on the chalkboard or an overhead transparency, or use a computer with an LCD panel. Discuss the ideas the students have generated and guide the discussion to identify characteristics and perspectives of the author.

6.2 Making Intertextual Links

Goal
To help students make intertextual links from current texts to past texts.

Background

When students read texts, they construct meaning using the texts they are reading, their prior experiences, and other texts. For example, middle school students learning about Impressionism may remember previous experiences with texts on the subject. One student may recall a trip to the Art Institute in Chicago. Another student may remember watching the video *Vincent and Theo*. Yet another student may think about an internet tour of the Louvre. A fourth student may remember reading Irving Stone's *Lust for Life* and discussing it with friends. A student's understanding of any passage, therefore, is shaped by prior experiences with texts and with life.

Students bring experiences with past texts to each reading event in your class. This process, called intertextuality, is a natural process. All of us are natural synthesizers. We learn new information by connecting it to what we already know, creating an evolving web of meaning. As readers construct meaning, they "transpose texts into other texts, absorb one text into another, and build a mosaic of intersecting texts" (Hartman, 1995, p. 526).

Texts that are stored in a reader's memory can be constructed from print or other visual or auditory sources (International Reading Association & National Council of Teachers of English, 1996). Traditionally, text has been defined as communication in print, such as a textbook or a chapter in a book. A current view, however, suggests that the term *text* has a broader interpretation. Texts do not have to be print sources; they can be any source that communicates meaning. Texts, therefore, can be print sources such as stories, textbooks, novels, poems, and essays. Texts can also be nonprint sources such as music, drama, video, art, and gesture. All of these texts are stored in a reader's memory and are available for use in developing meaning from a current text.

In order to be critical readers, students need to make intertextual links. Although making intertextual links is natural, students need to be encouraged to integrate knowledge they have from outside school with school learning. When students are guided to make intertextual links, they generally do so. The strategies in this section were designed or adapted so that you can guide students, while they are critically reading new texts, to use texts they have already experienced.

TEACHING STRATEGY 4

Text Connect

Text Connect is a strategy that guides students consciously to use past texts to learn about a concept you are teaching. The steps in Text Connect parallel the thinking processes that people use as they solve problems. The processes used in problem solving generally include identifying a problem, dividing the problem into its main components, searching through memory for past knowledge to solve the problem, selecting pertinent past knowledge, relating past knowledge to the current problem, and solving the problem.

Directions and Example

1. Model how people solve problems and answer questions using past texts and past experiences. Describe a time when you used past texts to solve a problem. The following description is the type of example that would exemplify using intertextual links to solve problems.

> I decided to refinish an old piano that had been sitting in my basement gathering dust. I had been given the piano by my mother who, in turn, had received it from my grandmother. I knew that the piano was an antique, but it had so many layers of varnish and paint that I didn't know whether the wood underneath would be worth refinishing. Before beginning the long task, I decided to find out what I could about refinishing this particular piece of furniture. To learn about the piano, I called my grandmother and mother and asked them what they had used to paint the piano when they had owned it. My grandmother told me where she had originally purchased the piano. I then called the piano factory to ask about what kind of wood was used on this particular model.

> To learn about refinishing, I talked to my father who had refinished many pieces of furniture. Then, I went to the library and checked out five books and one video on refinishing furniture. Finally, I discussed ways to refinish furniture with the local hardware store owner and was given four pamphlets on refinishing wood.

> The texts I used to solve my problem were the following:

> * interviews with my mother, grandmother, father, and hardware store owner
> * five books
> * one video
> * four pamphlets

2. Identify a topic from the text your students are reading that would have the potential for linking to past texts. After you have identified a topic, develop a question that your students could answer using past texts that they have experienced. The following is an example from a social studies class.

> After reading about the Civil Rights movement in *Our Country* (1991), ask the following question:

> In 1964, Congress passed Civil Rights laws to end segregation in public places. Why were these laws necessary?

3. Write the question on a chalkboard or an overhead projector, or use a computer with an LCD panel. Display the question for the students. Explain to the students that they will be using texts from their experiences to answer the question.

4. Explain that one way to solve a problem using past texts is to identify components of the problem. Ask students to use what they know about the topic to develop a list of selected terms that relate to the topic, as in the following example.

> Civil Rights laws
> segregation
> integration
> boycott
> Dr. Martin Luther King, Jr.
> NAACP
> nonviolent protest

5. Divide the class into mixed-ability groups. Ask the students to brainstorm past texts that relate to the listed terms. Provide students with a few examples from print and nonprint sources including movies, mathematical formulas, videos, personal experiences, music, art, fiction, and nonfiction. A list of selected fiction and nonfiction sources about Civil Rights follows.

Sources about Civil Rights

Fiction and Nonfiction Books

King, C.S. (1983). *The words of Martin Luther King, Jr.* New York: Newsmaker.

Parks, R. (1996). *Dear Mrs. Parks.* New York: Lee & Low.

Parks, R., & Reed, G. (1994). *Quiet strength: The faith, the hope and the heart of a woman who changed a nation.* Michigan: Zondervon.

Nonprint Sources

Eyes on the prize. (1986). PBS. (videos)

http://www-lelandstanford.edu/groupu/King/KingBios/briefbio.htm
    (Martin Luther King, Jr., biography)

http://www.newsavanna.com/Gravity/mlktribute
    ("I Have A Dream" speech with hyperlinks to allusions in text)

---

6. Ask students to select past texts that would answer the question. Explain that not every text about a topic that students have experienced can be used to answer this particular question. Model how you would use selected texts in an answer using an example from your content area or use the following example.

> Last year I read *Quiet Strength,* the biography of Rosa Parks (Parks & Reed, 1994) and saw *Eyes on the Prize,* the series of videos that document the Civil Rights movement. Since I knew we would be studying the Civil Rights movement in social studies, I also accessed two web sites about Martin Luther King, Jr. All of this background information reinforced my belief that the Civil Rights laws were necessary in our country.
>
> Although I was a teenager in the north during the 1960s, I did not fully realize how necessary the entire Civil Rights movement was to ensure equal rights for all people. Reading about Rosa Parks refusing to give her seat on the bus to a white person, however, reminded me how unfair life was for African Americans in the early part of the 1900s. Martin Luther King, Jr., said in his *I Have A Dream* speech that he hoped that one day his children would be judged by their character, not their color. I believe the Civil Rights laws were a necessary beginning step for that to occur.

TEACHING STRATEGY 5

Intra-Act

Intra-Act (Hoffman, 1979) is a strategy that can be adapted to encourage students to use intertextual links to reach a personal decision about a topic. The Intra-Act procedure has four phases. First, students construct meaning from a text selection. Second, they connect what they have learned about the topic with other texts. Third, students express their personal values and feelings about the topic. And fourth, they reflect on the values they have formed.

Directions and Example

1. Choose a topic or ask students to choose a topic that would be of special interest to them. The topic should be one about which students can form a personal opinion. Describe the differences between topics that lend themselves to opinions and topics that are explanatory. Provide a sample topic about which an opinion can be formed as in the following example.

    > Read "Puerto Rico—A Commonwealth of the United States" in *Exploring Our World: Latin America and Canada* (1980) to learn about the history and status of Puerto Rico. Think about whether Puerto Rico should remain a commonwealth, become the 51st state, or become an independent nation.

2. Use comprehension strategies to teach the reading selection. (See Chapter 4 for strategies that encourage students to construct meaning from text.)

3. Ask students to use contents of the text to write opinion statements that could be answered *yes* or *no*. Model examples of opinion statements that could be deduced from the text. Explain why a statement such as "Puerto Rico should become the 51st state" is an opinion and a statement such as "Puerto Rico is primarily an agricultural country" is not an opinion.

4. List on a grid four or five of the most controversial statements students generated as in the following example. Distribute copies to students.

Puerto Rico at a Crossroads

Statements				
Since the people of Puerto Rico are already United States citizens, Puerto Rico should become the 51st state if its people vote for statehood.				
Operation Bootstrap is an illustration of the way the Puerto Ricans can maintain themselves as an independent nation.				
Because the country primarily has an agricultural economy with limited natural resources, it cannot stand on its own as a nation and either should remain a commonwealth or become a state.				
Spanish is the basic language of Puerto Rico and, although many people speak English, the language barrier should prevent Puerto Rico from becoming a state.				

5. Divide the class into groups of four to six students. Students should be of mixed abilities. Assign one student from each group as the discussion leader. Then ask each student leader to conduct a discussion by summarizing the text selection. The members of each group can add details that clarify the leader's summary. Allow seven to ten minutes for discussion.

6. Ask the group leaders to brainstorm additional texts that supplement the summary of the text selection. You might list categories of texts so that students think of both print and nonprint texts. Encourage students to add categories as they think of other types of texts. List the remembered texts on a large piece of paper. An example of texts from the topic Puerto Rico follows.

Media

Newspaper articles

Segment on National Public Radio discussing Puerto Rico and statehood

The *Cobblestone* issue on Puerto Rico

Stories and Poetry

"Roberto Clemente—Bittersweet Memory" by Jerry Izenberg

Poems of Jose Antonio Davila and Luis Llorens Torres

Web Sites

http://www.puertorico51.org (discusses statehood)

http://www.tld.net/user/lucast/Puerto%20Rico.html (discusses history)

7. After the members of each group have shared texts that relate to the topic, ask them to participate in the valuation phase of the discussion. Each group leader should distribute a paper with a set of four declarative statements based on the selection's content. These value statements should reflect opinions that could be inferred from the text.

8. Have students write the names of the group's members on the top line. Then ask students to agree or disagree with the statements independently. Direct them to write *yes* or *no* under their names for each statement. Finally, ask them to predict what they think other members of the group would answer by writing *yes* or *no* in the spaces under their classmates' names as shown in the following example.

Puerto Rico at a Crossroads

Statements	Shelly	Teresa	Juan	Aaron
Since the people of Puerto Rico are already United States citizens, Puerto Rico should become the 51st state if its people vote for statehood.	yes	yes	yes	yes
Operation Bootstrap is an illustration of the way the Puerto Ricans can maintain themselves as an independent nation.	no	yes	yes	no
Because the country primarily has an agricultural economy with limited natural resources, it cannot stand on its own as a nation and either should remain a commonwealth or become a state.	yes	yes	no	yes
Spanish is the basic language of Puerto Rico and, although many people speak English, the language barrier should prevent Puerto Rico from becoming a state.	no	no	no	yes

9. Begin reflection by asking the members of each group to reveal how they each responded to the four statements. As students discuss their answers, others should check to see whether their predictions about their classmates' responses were correct.

10. Conduct a class discussion allowing students to discuss, challenge, support, and question one another's responses. Discuss how the roles of the central text and the texts from the students' memories influenced final opinions.

TEACHING STRATEGY

Wide Reading with Discussion Groups

Wide reading within a specific topic enables readers to extend their knowledge by linking information to various texts. When students read a variety of texts about a topic, they begin to understand how they can reach back to texts in their memories to make sense of a current text. Proficient readers can also predict how future texts might modify their understanding of a topic. Wide reading, therefore, can be an important component in helping students use many texts to learn.

The problem with wide reading is time. There is not enough time in our students' day to read as many texts as we would like them to read. One compromise is for the students in your class to read many different texts and share them in discussion groups. There are several reasons why reading and sharing in groups is a good combination. First, when you provide students with choices about what they will read, they are able to exercise some control over the curriculum. Students are generally more interested in reading texts they have chosen. Second, when you have a variety of texts, you can provide texts at various reading levels. (To determine reading levels and appropriateness of texts, see Appendices C and D.) As you know, many of the students in your class can read more difficult texts than those you assign, and many students are unable to read the assigned texts. When you provide a list of texts at various levels, you can guide students into reading texts closer to their reading levels. Finally, when students have the opportunity to share texts they have read, both the readers and the listeners benefit (Daniels, 1994). Discussion groups, sometimes called literature circles, are a good place for students to share texts, to discuss topics, and to make intertextual links.

Directions and Example

1. Introduce a topic to the class and explain to students why they should read books from a larger context in order to support learning.

2. Generate a list of texts. To generate a list of readings about a specific topic, you can look in your teacher's manual for related readings or use Appendix B for resources to help you locate additional texts on topics. Remember to use fiction and nonfiction texts and to include nonprint texts on your list. The sample list on the following page was developed for students in a literature class who were studying victims of WWII and were reading *Anne Frank: Diary of a Young Girl* (1995).

3. Ask students for other suggestions to add to your list of texts. Give them at least a day to gather their suggestions. Many of your students will probably have ideas about texts they have read that could be added to the master list.

4. Provide students with a complete list of books and ask them to choose one or more texts to read. (See Appendix B for sources for books.) Some texts are considerably longer and more complex than others, so some students will have more challenging and time-consuming reading. Some students will have a deeper interest in this topic; other students will not have as much interest or may not have the extra time they need to read a longer text. Allow the students' interests and time availability to guide their choices.

5. Provide plenty of time for students to read their chosen texts independently—at least one week. You may also want to give some class time for the reading. Let students know their reading deadline.

6. Provide approximately 40 minutes for discussion groups. Arrange discussion groups of four or five students, each with a different type and complexity of text. During the discussion groups, ask students to do the following:

    *   Summarize the texts.
    *   Discuss what was learned from the texts that sheds light on the topic.
    *   Chart or map the information with references in parentheses.
    *   Discuss how each reference provides insights into different aspects of the topic.

Books Related to Victims of WW II

Fiction

Choi, S.N. (1991). *Year of impossible goodbyes.* Boston: Houghton Mifflin.

Hest, A. (1991). *Love you soldier.* New York: Maxwell Maximillian International.

Lowry, L. (1996). *Number the stars.* New York: Dell.

Morpurgo, M. (1991). *Waiting for Anya.* New York: Viking.

Uchida, Y. (1992). *Journey home.* New York: Maxwell Maximillian International.

Yolen, J. (1990). *The devil's arithmetic.* New York: Puffin.

Nonfiction

Adler, D. (1989). *We remember the holocaust.* New York: Henry Holt.

Garcia, J.R., Gelo, D.J., Greenow, L.L., Kracht, J.B., & White, D.G. (1997). Internment camps (pp. 470–474). In *Our United States.* Needham, MA: Silver Burdett Ginn.

Hersey, J. (1989). *Hiroshima.* New York: Vintage Books.

Holliday, L. (1995). *Children of the holocaust and WW II: Their secret diaries.* New York: Pocket Books.

Levine, E. (1995). *A fence away from freedom: Japanese Americans and WW II.* New York: Putman.

Rogasky, B. (1988). *Smoke and ashes: The story of the holocaust.* New York: Holiday House.

Stanley, J. (1994). *I am an American: A true story of Japanese internment.* New York: Crown.

Zeinert, K. (1994). *Those incredible women of WW II.* Brookfield, CT: Millbrook.

Nonprint Sources

Anne Frank Online
http://www.annefrank.com/

Library of Congress American Memory Site
http://rs6.loc.gov/fsowhome.html

Interviews of people associated with WW II

Grolier's World War II Page
http://www.grolier.com/wwii/wwii_mainpage.html

World War II Timeline
http://www.historyplace.com/worldwar2/timeline/ww2time.htm

7. Assign students a synthesizing task that will use information from at least four of the texts. You might ask them to write a personal response or an essay, or they could give a speech about the topic that incorporates different texts. This assignment has two purposes: to learn about a topic and to become aware of knowledge from multiple sources. Here is an example of a personal response about the topic "Victims of WW II" using various sources.

Victims of WW II

I had heard about the atrocities of WW II from my grandfather who had friends in the war, but I was unaware of the kinds of things that happened in the United States. Often my grandfather talked about how the Jewish people were hunted and had to hide for their lives. He even suggested that I watch the video *The Hiding Place,* which was from the book by Corrie Ten Boom. So when we read *Anne Frank: Diary of a Young Girl,* I was prepared for more stories about the Holocaust. I didn't know, however, that we had internment camps in the United States. When Jared discussed the book he read, *A Fence Away from Freedom,* I was shocked. This happened in America? Then Jan discussed her interview with her great aunt who actually was in a Japanese internment camp in Iowa. She said that her great aunt had to leave her home in Oregon with all of her belongings and move into the camp. She lived there for almost four years. From her description, I could tell that there were also victims of the war in the United States.

One way to interest students in reading is to allow them to choose their own texts and then to share them in discussion groups.

6.3 Considering Alternative Views

Goal

To help students consider alternative views when reading.

Background

Critical readers who have determined the authors' qualifications and perspectives and have reached back into their memories for related past texts to connect with new knowledge (see Sections 6.1 and 6.2) can expand the meaning they construct by considering alternative views. One of the hallmarks of a thinking person is the ability to acknowledge new ideas and different points of view.

Students who are reading and learning in your content area need to keep their minds open as they read. Often, students who are learning about new concepts have already established ideas about those concepts. Sometimes those ideas are faulty. When students are exposed to counterintuitive concepts, or concepts that don't make inherent sense to them, they tend to resist these new ideas, even after they are proved to them (Stahl, Hynd, Glynn, & Carr, 1996). For example, students often believe that a heavier object will fall faster than a lighter one even though one of the principles of physics is that all objects fall at the same accelerating rate. Because many students resist new information if it is in conflict with previously held beliefs, some textbooks directly refute misconceptions. An example of a refutational warning in an algebra class would be the note that "2 to the third power = 8 is not the same as $2 \times 3 = 6$" (*Beginning & Intermediate Algebra: An Integrated Approach,* 1996, p. 28). Because students bring misconceptions to reading situations, an important skill for critical readers is to take into account new ideas and to try to generate alternative views as they read.

TEACHING STRATEGY 7

Alternative Views in Your Subject

All of our content subjects have examples where there are two or more viewpoints. When we teach students to be critical thinkers and readers in our content areas, we need to point out the areas where students can consider alternative perspectives. Two content examples follow that you can use to model the teaching of alternative views. Finding and using examples from your discipline will reinforce students' understanding of ways to find many views in texts.

Directions and Examples

1. Think of a situation that would be common to the lives of your students and would exemplify two or more viewpoints. An example of such a situation is the following one.

   > Currently, the legal age to obtain a driver's license in this state is 16. In some states, the legal age to drive is younger than 16. There is a movement to make the driving age consistent among the states and to raise that age to 18. What is your opinion about this matter?

2. Present the situation to the students and ask them independently to write down their views on a note card. After the students have written what they think, collect the note cards and write the viewpoints on a chalkboard or an overhead transparency. Discuss the different views the students presented.

3. Find an example in your content field that presents more than one viewpoint or adapt the following poem to fit your content area. Read the poem and discuss the alternative viewpoints the poet expresses.

High School Literature Example

Alternative Views

The Man He Killed

"Had he and I but met
By some old ancient inn,
We should have sat us down to wet
Right many a nipperkin!

"But ranged as infantry,
and staring face to face,
I shot at him as he at me,
And killed him in his place.

"I shot him dead because—
Because he was my foe,
Just so: my foe of course he was;
That's clear enough; although

"Had though he'd 'list, perhaps,
Off-hand like—just and I—
Was out of work—
had sold his traps—
No other reason why,

"Yes; quaint and curious war is!
You shot a fellow down
You'd treat if met where any bar is,
Or help to half-a-crown."

From Hardy, T. (1996). In *Literature and the language arts: The British tradition* (p. 745). St. Paul, MN: EMC/Paradigm.

---

4. Display the example on an overhead projector. Read the example to the class or ask a student to read it. Identify the alternative views present in the poem and have students elaborate on these views. You might say, "In this poem, the poet is explaining his dual attitudes toward his enemy in war; he could have befriended the man just as well as shot him. In this poem, the poet expresses two alternative views. What are the two views?"

5. Write the two views on the chalkboard or an overhead transparency. Have students highlight parts of the poem that pertain to the two viewpoints. List phrases from the poem under the appropriate viewpoint.

6. Tell students that one of the hallmarks of a critical reader is being able to identify and consider more than one point of view. Periodically, provide students with an Alternative Views application to reinforce their understanding that texts contain more than one perspective. Encourage them to identify and consider alternative views when they read.

7. An example related to mathematics follows.

High School Mathematics Example

Alternative Views

Directions: Our mathematics text *The Pit and the Pendulum: Interactive Mathematics Program* (1997) discusses the idea that time is relative. Often, we think that mathematics is a precise field of inquiry. It's not. Even when we think there is one correct answer, we find variance. Over the next few days, we will be conducting experiments which will show that one can measure the same thing twice, using the same method, and get different answers.

Procedures:

1. In a group of two students, one student watches the second hand of the clock on the wall or on a group member's watch. A second student holds a stopwatch.

2. The first student says "Start" and then says "Stop" after five seconds. The second student tries to make the stopwatch start and stop on command.

3. Record the results from the stopwatch to a tenth of a second.

4. Repeat the activity five days in a row.

5. After students have completed the experiment, have them list their stopwatch results on a chart or graph. Compile the results from each pair on a master list. Discuss the amount of variation that can be observed from a simple measurement activity.

TEACHING STRATEGY 8

Discussion Web

After you have modeled how students can find alternative views in your content area, introduce a Discussion Web (Alvermann, 1992). A Discussion Web is an organizational tool for you to use to guide discussions that present an issue and opposing points of view. Discussion Webs are designed so that, as you discuss a central question, students identify and discuss two viewpoints about the question, weigh the views, and come to a conclusion.

Directions and Examples

1. After the students have read a passage from your text, introduce a central question. The question should be one that lends itself to opposing viewpoints. Write the question on a chalkboard or an overhead transparency, or use a computer with an LCD panel. For example, ask students the following question after they read "The Man Without a Country" by Edward Everett Hale in *Enjoying Literature* (1985).

    Did Philip Nolan receive a just penalty?

2. Divide the class into groups of three or four students. Ask students to brainstorm at least three reasons for answering yes to the central question. Then have them generate at least three reasons for answering no to the central question. When students have written their reasons for answering the question in the affirmative and the negative, ask them to volunteer some of their ideas. Write the ideas in two separate columns as listed below.

Reasons why the penalty wasn't just.	Reasons why the penalty was just.
Nolan had a good background.	Nolan broke the law.
He was tricked by Aaron Burr.	He was a traitor to his country.
His words were impulsive.	He was aware of the consequences.
He was sorry.	He was part of a rebellion.

3. Discuss both sides of the question as objectively as possible. Then encourage students to take a position either for or against the issue. Some students will want to take both sides. Tell them that although they understand both sides of the issue, they need to take one position.

4. Ask students to come to conclusions independently, defending the side they have chosen and using the alternative perspective as a counterargument. Have them write their conclusions on note cards. Collect the note cards when the students are finished and use them to learn which conclusions students have chosen. An example follows.

> **Conclusion**
>
> Philip Nolan was a young, fiery man who was used by Aaron Burr. Although he deserved punishment for his wrongs, the punishment he received, banishment, was too severe for the crime.

5. An example of a completed Discussion Web based on material in the passage "Tobacco Facts" from the book *Self-Discovery: Alcohol and Other Drugs* (1984) and a blank Discussion Web follow.

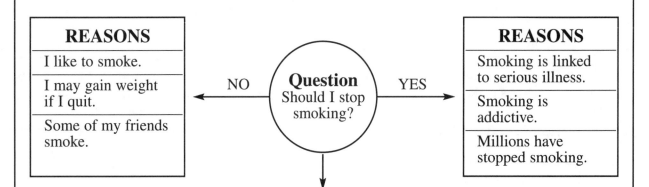

High School Health Example

Discussion Web

REASONS

I like to smoke.

I may gain weight if I quit.

Some of my friends smoke.

NO ← **Question** Should I stop smoking? → YES

REASONS

Smoking is linked to serious illness.

Smoking is addictive.

Millions have stopped smoking.

Conclusion

Although I like to smoke, I know it's not good for me. I need to find the best way to quit. I know I can stop smoking.

Based on Alvermann, D. (1992). The discussion web: A graphic aid for learning across the curriculum. *The Reading Teacher, 45,* 92–99.

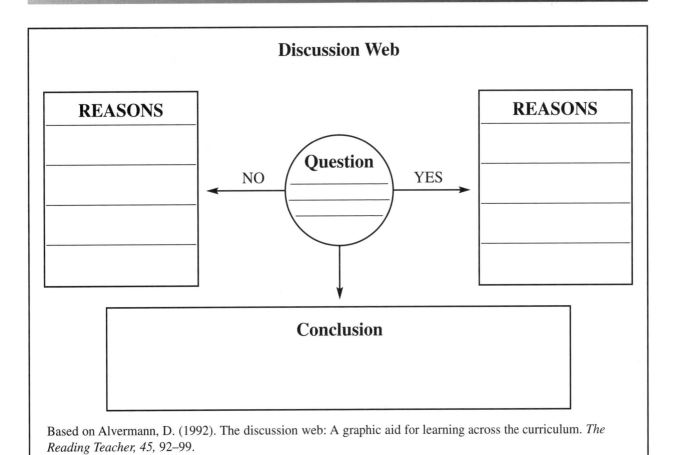

Discussion Web

REASONS

Question

NO   YES

REASONS

Conclusion

Based on Alvermann, D. (1992). The discussion web: A graphic aid for learning across the curriculum. *The Reading Teacher, 45,* 92–99.

Options Guide

Students who are able to identify and consider alternative viewpoints in their reading should begin to think about the range of views that exist about any topic. An Options Guide (Bean, Sorter, Singer, & Frazee, 1986) is a type of study guide that helps students think of predictions and possibilities about an issue from their texts. Students read up to a critical point in the passage and then stop and consider possible options and the results of the different options.

TECHNOLOGY TIP

Computer Simulations

Computer simulations are ideal for an Options Guide. While the students are engaged in the simulation, ask them to stop, generate several options, and predict how the options will influence the results. A list of selected computer simulations that could be used to help students develop critical thinking follows.

Decisions, Decisions: The Environment (Tom Snyder Productions)
Students collect and analyze data as they choose actions that affect the environment.

Lunar Greenhouse (Minnesota Educational Computing Corporation)
Students control variables for plant growth.

Oregon Trail, Gold Rush, Wagon Train 1848 (Minnesota Educational Computing Corporation)
Students play the role of pioneers crossing the country who are met with dilemmas and challenges.

Directions and Examples

1. Identify a topic and a portion of a text that would be of interest to your students. Analyze the passage for major concepts that leave events in doubt. The following example illustrates an Options Guide for a high school parenting class.

2. Have students read the section about keeping children safe in the text *The Developing Child: Understanding Children and Parenting* (1994). Develop a brief scenario that summarizes the initial reading. Develop several questions and a list of options that could result from the scenario. Write the scenario on the chalkboard or an overhead transparency, or use a computer with an LCD panel.

High School Parenting Example

Options Guide

Fifteen-year-old Nina was skipping school to spend the day with her older sister, Olivia, who was just recovering from the flu, and Olivia's month-old son, Hector. Just before noon, Nina and Olivia decided to drive to a nearby store to get some milk.

As they were getting into the car, Nina asked, "Where's Hector's car seat?"

"Oh, no," sighed Olivia. "I left it in the apartment. Well, it's only a few blocks. You just hold him. This won't take long."

Which option will Nina choose? Why do you think so? What could be the result of each option?

a. Nina will go along with Olivia and ride with the baby in her lap.
b. Nina will stay home with Hector.
c. Nina will drive to the store without a valid driver's license.
d. Nina will persuade Olivia to return to her apartment for the car seat.

Based on *The developing child: Understanding children and parenting.* (1994). New York: Glencoe/McGraw-Hill.

3. Divide the class into groups of four or five students. Ask students to discuss the possible options and the results of each option. After students have discussed options in small groups, have them share their thinking with the entire group. If necessary, guide the discussion so that students understand the cause-effect relationship for each option.

4. An Options Guide from a middle school science book follows.

Options Guide

Directions: After reading "Trees vs. People," read the scenario and answer the following questions.

Scenario

An old growth forest in the Pacific Northwest has been marked for clear cutting. The forest consists of some of the world's oldest and largest coniferous trees providing a habitat for over 600 species of wildlife. Environmentalists are arguing that this particular forest should be preserved. There is, however, a great demand for wood products in America. Timber workers want to provide lumber and save their jobs by cutting down the trees.

1.   What are some of the options open to decision makers?

2.   What are the possible results for each option?
      a.   How successful would each option be?
      b.   What would the loggers say?
      c.   What would the environmentalists say?

Based on *Biodiversity: Understanding the variety of life.* (1995). New York: Scholastic.

TEACHING STRATEGY 10

Knowledge as Design

Students who have a solid understanding of the differing viewpoints that exist in texts and in their minds can further their understanding of the complexity of knowledge by using the strategy Knowledge as Design (Perkins, 1994, 1986). Knowledge as Design not only guides students to understand alternative viewpoints; it is also a strategy that promotes critical reading by identifying the relationship between the structure of a topic and its purpose and by identifying different perspectives on the issue at hand. Knowledge as Design is a way to organize a class discussion, or it can be used as a small group assignment. Whichever you choose, you will need to model the format for your students, and you may need to give input on the more complex sections.

Directions and Examples

1.   Identify a topic that is interesting and relevant to your students. Select a topic for which students could have more than one opinion as in the following example.

> We have been reading about genetic engineering from our text *Life Science* (1993). Many of you have expressed an interest in this topic.

2. Identify the purposes of the topic. You may decide to identify one purpose as an example and ask students to identify others. If students are unable to think of purposes, direct them to the text. An example follows.

   Purpose for genetic engineering: To solve problems involving living things.

3. Share the structures, or organizing principles, of the topic. Since this is the foundation for the concept under discussion and also the most difficult part of the strategy, you may want to provide most of these answers.

   Structure: Genetic engineering is a type of biotechnology that transfers genes from one organism to another.

4. Ask students to think of examples of the topic. Have students generate examples that are written in the text as well as examples they think of themselves. If your students are unable to find all of the examples, you should provide them. List the examples on a chalkboard or an overhead transparency, or use a computer with an LCD panel.

   Examples: Development of insulin
   Creation of new strains of plants

5. Explain that many issues have at least two different sides. Discuss the idea that when there is more than one side to an issue, one is not necessarily better than the other side. It may be a matter of opinion or personal preference. For the topic at hand, have students discuss arguments for the topic. Then ask them for arguments against the topic. List the arguments for and against the topic under the examples.

   In favor: Provides needed solutions for many problems
   Opposed: Fear of abuse

6. Discuss the importance of developing individual conclusions and of respecting conclusions peers have developed. Have students independently synthesize the information and develop a conclusion. Ask students to write the conclusion on an index card. After students have written their conclusions, have several of them volunteer and share their ideas. Reinforce the importance of respectful listening by asking the other class members to listen to the conclusions offered by other students. Remind students that some of their peers will have arrived at conclusions different from their own.

   Conclusion: Genetic engineering can provide needed solutions for many problems. However, as technology advances, further guidelines for genetic engineering may need to be established.

7. An example of a middle school social studies Knowledge as Design example based on the text *Southeast Asia* (1978) follows.

Middle School Social Studies Example

Knowledge as Design

Topic

European Expansion and Colonization in Southeast Asia

Purposes

Find trade routes to Orient
Spread Christianity
Gain wealth
Protect natives from enemies

Specific Examples

Portuguese in India, Java, Spice Islands
Spanish in Philippines
Dutch in Java, Sumatra
British in India, Singapore, Burma,
    Malay Peninsula
French in Vietnam, Cambodia, Laos
Americans in Guam, Puerto Rico,
    Philippines

Structure

Established as primary ruler
Formed government
Entered world trade market
Sent colonists

Pro

Improved transportation
Improved communications
Initiated public health projects
Implemented new farming methods
Established schools
Ended enslavement for debtors

Con

Ruled by foreign culture
Natives treated as inferior
Power in foreign language
Sent natural resources abroad
Small farmers became obsolete
Increased numbers of poor

Conclusions

The improvement of the infrastructure was not worth the cost to the natives.
Greed was the primary motivation of colonization.
Powerful countries should not take advantage of those with less power.

Based on Perkins, D.N. (1986). *Knowledge as design.* Hillsdale, NJ: Erlbaum.

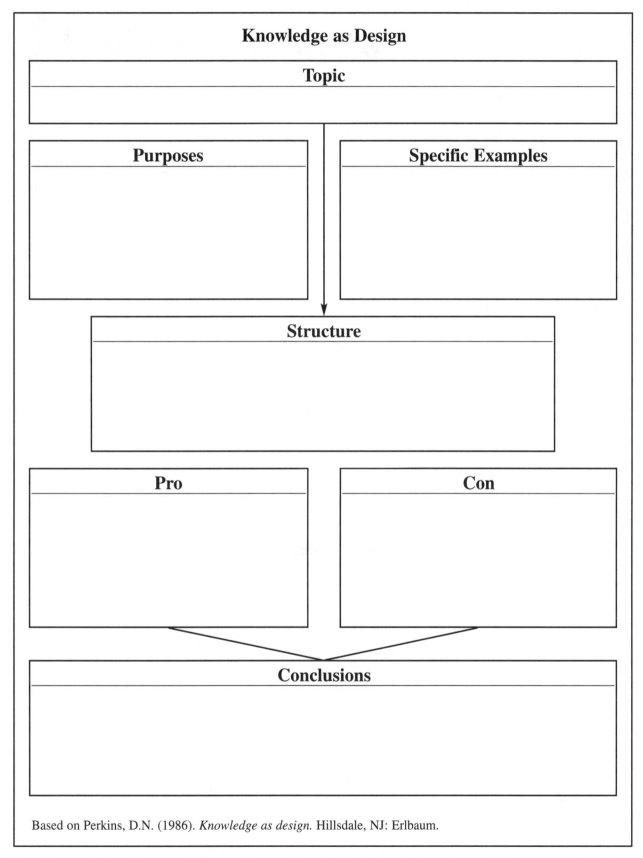

Knowledge as Design

Topic

Purposes

Specific Examples

Structure

Pro

Con

Conclusions

Based on Perkins, D.N. (1986). *Knowledge as design.* Hillsdale, NJ: Erlbaum.

Questioning Editorial Perspectives

Students need to become aware that, unless they are critical readers, the way a writer presents information can sway them toward a particular opinion. By having students consider multiple viewpoints, rather than a single perspective, you are assisting them in reading critically (Paul, 1993). Newspapers provide an excellent tool for developing students' critical thinking skills and comparative analysis skills (Laffey & Laffey, 1986).

Most newspapers publish editorials written to express a stance on a particular issue. In addition to editorials, newspapers may report news events from their particular perspectives just as authors write textbooks from a variety of perspectives. The following strategy allows students to question a newspaper's editorial stance on a controversial issue.

Directions and Example

1. Explain to students that, when they read newspapers, they need to be aware of the writer's perspectives. This is particularly true when reading editorials, as editorials provide a forum for newspaper writers to express their opinions on particular issues.

2. Discuss editorials that students may have read in the past. Ask students to share information about particular editorials they have read in which the writer presented an obvious opinion. Have copies of a variety of newspaper editorials available to facilitate the discussion.

3. Tell students that they need to ask themselves questions as they read an editorial. Write the following questions (Robinson, 1975) on the chalkboard or an overhead transparency, or use a computer with an LCD panel.

Questions for Reading Editorials

- What is the title of the editorial?
- What is the issue in this editorial?
- What stance on the issue is represented here?
- What specific evidence is given to support this side of the issue?
- Is there any evidence apparent in this editorial to suggest another viewpoint?
- Does the writer show a bias? Are there any particular words or patterns of writing used to accomplish this? If so, what are they?

4. Provide students with an editorial from a local newspaper or give students the *USA Today* (1998) example that follows. Ask students to read the editorial.

5. After students have read the editorial "Amendment Deprives Faithful of Protections" from *USA Today,* have them answer the Questions for Editorials. Answers for the *USA Today* editorial follow.

Questions for Reading Editorials

Q: What is the title of the editorial?
A: Amendment deprives faithful of protections.

Q: What is the issue in this editorial?
A: Religious freedom amendment.

Q: What stance on the issue is represented here?
A: Editorial opposes amendment.

Q: What specific evidence is given to support this side of the issue?
A: Existing law has been misinterpreted and perfectly legal religious activity has been stopped.

Q: Is there any evidence apparent in this editorial to suggest another viewpoint?
A: Editorial presents samples of distortions used by amendment supporters.

Q: How does the writer show a bias? Are there any particular words or patterns of writing used to accomplish this? If so, what are they?
A: Writer uses words such as *lies, attempt to portray,* and *religious tyranny.*

6. Divide the class into groups of three or four students. Ask students to share their responses to the questions as they discuss the writer's viewpoint.

7. Invite each group of students to write a counterargument to the published editorial. Share the students' editorials during a whole class discussion or as part of a class produced newspaper.

Today's debate: Religious freedom

Amendment deprives faithful of protections

OUR VIEW **Religious minorities would suffer; church groups could tap public funds.**

True or false:

▶ The Constitution bars children from carrying Bibles to school.

▶ The Supreme Court has banned kids from saying grace in school lunchrooms.

▶ Judges are distorting the law to drive the baby Jesus out of the town Christmas display.

All are false — just a sampling of the exaggerations, distortions and outright lies that have been used for years to mislead the public about religious rights, particularly in schools.

Today, they'll arrive on the floor of the House of Representatives, which is expected to vote on the grossly mislabeled "Religious Freedom Amendment" to the Constitution.

It's billed as a way of restoring prayer in schools. But far from protecting religious freedom, it could deprive religious minorities in any community of the protections written by the Founding Fathers. Further, it would open the public till to taxpayer subsidies for religious institutions.

In effect, the proposal would repeal the First Amendment ban on using the state to promote or finance a particular religion. It would authorize local authorities to use public events to proselytize for their own pet theologies. Those might include officially ordered sectarian devotions in schools or honored status for favored clergy. People of other religious beliefs would have little recourse.

Further, it would mandate taxpayer funding of some religious institutions, now largely prohibited under the Founders' doctrine that the state should stay out of church activities. They and their ancestors had experienced firsthand the tyranny of using the power of government to abuse religious minorities.

And all for little cause. Over the years, a few teachers, principals or other officials have misinterpreted the law and stopped perfectly legal personal religious activity. But almost all of those incidents

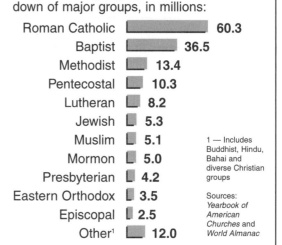

Many paths of faith

The USA comprises at least 150 denominations of 5,000 members or more, and many smaller groups. Estimated breakdown of major groups, in millions:

Roman Catholic	60.3
Baptist	36.5
Methodist	13.4
Pentecostal	10.3
Lutheran	8.2
Jewish	5.3
Muslim	5.1
Mormon	5.0
Presbyterian	4.2
Eastern Orthodox	3.5
Episcopal	2.5
Other[1]	12.0

1 — Includes Buddhist, Hindu, Bahai and diverse Christian groups

Sources: *Yearbook of American Churches* and *World Almanac*

By Genevieve Lynn, USA TODAY

have been resolved locally and the misunderstandings cleared up.

The fact that the amendment's promoters have to keep recycling the same handful of horror stories, some going back into the '80s, gives the lie to claims of widespread abuse.

They attempt to portray their opponents as hostile to religion. In fact, a broad coalition of religious and civil-rights groups stands opposed. They have a more responsible solution for incorporating religion in schools. It's a set of guidelines, *Religion in the Public Schools: A Joint Statement of Current Law,* that has been made available to every school district. President Clinton announced Saturday the Department of Education is issuing an updated version, based on recent legal developments. If followed, there would be few problems except for the folks who want to use the power of government for religious self-aggrandizement.

Down their path lies not religious freedom but religious tyranny.

6.4 Evaluating Arguments and Forming Judgments

Goal
To help students evaluate the argument, or logic, of a text and form judgments.

Background

Students are exposed to many different kinds of texts in school, from texts that are written by qualified authors with editorial review boards to texts that are written by someone with a biased viewpoint. For that reason, students need to be able to read texts in their content classes critically and to independently evaluate the logic of a passage and form a reasoned judgment.

Most of the writing that students read in our disciplines has a logical progression of ideas that lead to a conclusion. That conclusion is backed up by supporting claims. These claims can be about what the author thinks is true (knowledge claims), about what causes something (causal claims), about what is likely to happen (predictive claims), about what is good (evaluative claims), about what is right or wrong (moral claims), and about what ought to be done (policy claims). Some claims overlap into two or more categories and can be considered mixed claims (Unrau, 1997).

When students read texts, they need to be able to evaluate the worth of the author's conclusions and to evaluate whether the arguments the author makes support the conclusions without undue bias. Furthermore, students need to be able to examine the author's claims and to be able to determine what they believe about the topic. Merely challenging an author's point can lead to cynicism. Therefore, we want students to evaluate arguments in texts and come to independent conclusions about what they believe about the topic.

To assist your students in evaluating arguments and forming judgments, you can develop lessons that mirror the thinking process you do when you critically evaluate a text. This section provides four different strategies that help students begin to evaluate arguments and form judgments. As you use or adapt each of these strategies to your content area, remember that any activity that promotes the effective evaluation of an author's claims can assist students in becoming more critical readers of texts.

TECHNOLOGY TIP

Online Service

An online service that offers examples of innovative questions and solutions and welcomes the contributions of inventive thinkers.

Registry for Better Ideas
http://cctr.umkc.edu/user/rbi/Foundation.html

Guided Conversation

One of the ways students can learn to evaluate arguments is for you to model thinking through the logic of a passage. All good writing has a point and that point should be made in a reasonable manner. A strategy that you can use to model the thinking that you do to discern the logic of a passage is Guided Conversation (Gauthier, 1996). Guided Conversation is a strategy intended to teach students about ways to evaluate arguments by guiding them through the process of identifying and partitioning the problem, collecting relevant information, evaluating information, and generating solutions.

Directions and Example

1. Identify a conflicting point or problem in a text or ask students to identify one.

> After finishing Unit 1, in *Understanding Business and Personal Law* (1993), have students read the case *Lambert v. State,* 694 P.2d 791 (Alaska).
>
> Case Summary: David R. Lambert was charged with driving while intoxicated in violation of an Alaskan statute that read: "A person commits the crime of driving while intoxicated if the person operates or drives a motor vehicle . . . while under the influence of intoxicating liquor." Trooper Jeff Slamin stopped Lambert because Lambert's vehicle was weaving within its own lane and had crossed the divider and fog lines. Lambert smelled of alcohol and refused to perform sobriety tests. At trooper headquarters, Lambert was videotaped. The videotape showed that Lambert's speech was slurred and his gait unsteady. Lambert testified that for two weeks prior to his arrest he had been sick with the flu and had been taking Contac, Nyquil, and Terpin hydrate. A pharmacist testified that Nyquil is 25% alcohol which makes it 50 proof and Terpin hydrate is 41% alcohol or 82 proof.
>
> Question: What is the problem in this case?
>
> Sample answer: Whether Lambert was guilty of driving under the influence of alcohol.

2. Partition the problem into manageable segments. You may want to model this process several times before asking students to do it independently. An example follows.

   - What do we know about the parts of the problem?
   - What information is relevant to the problem?
   - What else do we need to know to construct a solution?
   - What are some possible solutions?

3. Divide the class into cooperative learning groups to solve each of the parts of the problem. Adapt the questions to fit your problem as in the following example.

   - How should the court treat a word that is not defined in a state statute?
   - What is the definition of "intoxicating liquor"?
   - Are the cough medicines intoxicating liquors?
   - How do you prove intoxication?

4. Conduct a large-group discussion to illustrate the ways a problem can be viewed and solutions sought.

    • What do we know about each of these questions?

      We know that the court interprets a word that is not defined in the statute by its commonly understood meaning.

      We know that the definition of intoxicating liquor is a substance containing alcohol.

    • What information from the case is relevant to a solution?

      The definition of intoxicating liquor.

      The officer's observations and the video.

    • What do we need to know about the law to construct a solution?

      Whether the ingestion of a lawful drug constitutes intoxication.

    • What are some possible solutions?

      Guilty of driving under the influence of intoxicating liquor.

      Not guilty, because Lambert was not proved to be intoxicated.

      Not guilty, because the ingestion of a lawful drug does not fall within the purpose of the statute prohibiting driving while intoxicated.

5. Decide on a solution.

    The jury found Lambert guilty of driving under the influence of intoxicating liquor. Lambert appealed. The appellate court affirmed the lower court's ruling.

6. Ask each student to write a convincing solution independently.

TEACHING STRATEGY 13

Opinion-Proof

Students will read and be exposed to many opinions during their schooling. Opinions can be found in their textbooks, lectures, conversations with peers, and outside reading. By middle school, students should be able to identify an opinion. Evaluating opinions is much more complex. To help students learn how to evaluate the logic of an opinion, you can use the strategy Opinion-Proof (Santa, Dailey, & Nelson, 1985). Opinion-Proof is a strategy that helps students understand how to evaluate the arguments supporting an opinion and come to a conclusion about that opinion. It takes students through the steps of forming an opinion, supporting the opinion, looking for reasoning fallacies, and writing convincingly about the opinion. Below is a list of common reasoning fallacies that you may want to develop into a chart for classroom use.

Reasoning Fallacies

Appealing to authority: Invoking authority as the last word.

Appealing to emotion: Using emotion as proof.

Appealing to force: Using threats to establish the validity of a claim.

Appealing to the people: Justifying a claim based on its popularity.

Arguing from ignorance: Arguing that a claim is justified because its opposite cannot be proved.

Begging the question: Making a claim and producing arguments that do not support the claim.

Contradiction: Presenting information that contradicts a claim.

Evading the issue: Talking around the issue rather than addressing it.

False analogy: Comparing unmatched elements.

False cause: Crediting an effect to a cause without evidence.

Hasty generalization: Drawing a conclusion from too few examples.

Poisoning the well: Overly committed to one position and explaining everything in light of that position.

Directions and Example

1. Explain, if necessary, the characteristics of an opinion statement. Invite students to generate and share opinion statements.

2. Generate an opinion statement from one or more texts students have read. You may write the opinion statement or have students write one.

   > After reading excerpts from Thoreau's book *Walden* and his essay "Civil Disobedience" in the *The American Tradition in Literature* (1974) and reading the section on Jeffersonian democracy presented in *The American Nation* (1998), present the following opinion statement:

   > Opinion statement: Thoreau believed in Jeffersonian democracy.

3. Explain that opinions need to have evidence to support them and that the weight of the evidence will assist the reader in forming a judgment. Discuss the sources from which students can find supporting evidence for the opinion statement. In this case, evidence can be found in both textbooks. Have students find and write supporting evidence for the opinion.

4. Ask students to share the evidence they found in their texts. Write the evidence on the chalkboard or an overhead transparency, or use a computer with an LCD panel.

Evidence

- Jefferson believed that there are no limits to how much the human race can improve.
- Jefferson believed that free people should follow the dictates of reason.
- Jefferson believed in minimal government.
- Jefferson said that those who labor in the earth are the chosen people of God.
- Thoreau valued his freedom above all else.
- Thoreau said that people can elevate their lives.
- Thoreau believed that government should be restricted.
- Thoreau did not believe in governmental taxation.
- Thoreau said that government gets in the way of human accomplishments.
- Thoreau lived for five years by himself at Walden Pond, doing all of the manual labor.

5. Explain that not all evidence will support the opinion. Discuss which evidence supports the opinion and which does not.

Supporting Evidence

- Jefferson believed that there are no limits to how much the human race can improve.
- Jefferson believed that free people should follow the dictates of reason.
- Jefferson believed in minimal government.
- Thoreau valued his freedom above all else.
- Thoreau said that people can elevate their lives.
- Thoreau believed that government should be restricted.
- Thoreau did not believe in governmental taxation.
- Thoreau said that government gets in the way of human accomplishments.

Evidence that Does Not Support Topic

- Jefferson said that those who labor in the earth are the chosen people of God.
- Thoreau lived by himself for five years at Walden Pond, doing all of the manual labor.

6. Write an essay as a group or have students write independently using the opinion and the evidence the students have identified. In some instances, you might introduce some reasoning fallacies. For example, the following is a section from an essay.

> The evidence from both Thoreau's *Walden* and his essay "Civil Disobedience" indicates that he was a strong believer in Jeffersonian democracy. Coming from the Age of Enlightenment, Jefferson believed that in a democracy people needed to use reason rather than government to rule themselves. Thoreau also espoused those beliefs. He did not believe that the government should tax people, for example. Instead, he thought that people should go about their own business and take care of themselves.

7. After students have written an essay, have them evaluate the persuasive power of the essay, looking for any reasoning fallacies. You might use or adapt the following rubric to evaluate the essays.

Essay Evaluation Rubric

1. Sophistication of Argument—Scope, Depth, and Clarity

    Shallow   Comprehensive
       1   2   3   4   5   6   7   8   9   10

2. Effectiveness of Supporting Claims

    Weak   Effective
       1   2   3   4   5   6   7   8   9   10

3. Effectiveness of Evidence

    Weak   Effective
       1   2   3   4   5   6   7   8   9   10

4. Effectiveness of Counterarguments

    Weak   Effective
       1   2   3   4   5   6   7   8   9   10

5. Coherence of Argument

    Disordered   Cohesive
       1   2   3   4   5   6   7   8   9   10

6. Organization

    Rudimentary   Clear
       1   2   3   4   5   6   7   8   9   10

Based on Unrau, N.J. (1997). *Thoughtful teachers, thoughtful learners: A guide to helping adolescents think critically.* Scarborough, Ontario: Pippin.

Socratic Questioning

Socratic questioning is the art of asking leading questions to stimulate the rational thinking that leads to conclusions. In Plato's dialogues, Socrates would pretend to be ignorant of a subject and would ask questions of his students and fellow citizens that probed their beliefs and assumptions in order to lead them through arguments to a conclusion. Socratic questioning is an appropriate strategy to use in schools to promote critical reading. This type of questioning helps students evaluate their own interpretations of texts by helping them think about their reasoning, by comparing their interpretations to those of others, by promoting relationships between ideas, and by forming reasoned judgments (Tanner & Casados, 1998; Paul, 1991).

Directions and Example

1. Identify the underlying concepts from a text students have read. Think about the types of responses students would give to a question and the relationships between the responses. Ask students a question relating to the concepts. The following is an example of Socratic Questioning in a middle school literature class.

> We have just finished the story "The Scribe" by Kristin Hunter from the text *Perception* (1985), and I believe you have a good understanding of the story. As you know, "The Scribe" is about a thirteen-year-old boy who lives above the Silver Dollar Check Cashing Service in an urban setting. He realizes that people who are illiterate are charged fees for having their checks cashed and their letters written or read. The boy set up a table in front of the business and told the customers that he would provide the same services free of charge. However, a town ordinance required that he purchase a business license. He then took the people in need of services to a bank and helped them with banking procedures.
>
> Now I'd like to pose a question from the theme of the story for us to discuss. Is the ability to read important in our society?

2. After posing the question, allow approximately five minutes for students to think about their answers and have students write their ideas on paper. Then play the role of Socrates and have students try to convince you that their opinions are reasonable. As students offer ideas, guide them to reasonable conclusions. Some of the questions you might use to encourage discussion follow.

   - How are your ideas like those other students have offered?
   - How is your point of view different from others that have been discussed?
   - How did you reach this point of view?
   - Where do you think your idea takes us?
   - How does your idea help us form a conclusion?
   - What reasons do you have for your opinion?
   - What evidence can you offer to support your opinion?

3. Allow at least 30 minutes for discussion. After the class has discussed the question you presented, have students answer the question independently, either in writing or by an oral presentation.

TEACHING STRATEGY **15**

Generative Writing

As students learn how to evaluate arguments and form opinions, they need to practice evaluating the arguments of their peers as well as the arguments of the texts read in school. Students are frequently exposed to (and engage in) faulty reasoning in conversations and in writing. Generative Writing (Ryder & Graves, 1998) is an activity that can help students evaluate written information from their peers. With Generative Writing, students identify a topic for which they would like to gather information from their peers, use e-mail as a tool to ask peers about a topic, evaluate the information and arguments of their peers, and draw their own conclusions.

Directions and Example

1. Identify a task or a problem from your content area that involves critical thinking. You might choose a topic that you want your class to study, or you might ask students to suggest topics. Present the topic to your students. Have students revise the topic to fit their interests.

   We have been reading about air, water, and noise pollution in *Health for Life* (1992). Do you think pollution is a problem?

2. Find several classes of students in various parts of the country or world who would be willing to engage in a dialogue about the topic. You might contact your professional organization (see Appendix A) for sources of classes that might be interested in a project of this type. Middle school students can pose the question to KIDCAFE.

TECHNOLOGY TIP

E-Mail Discussions for Middle School Students

Any young adult between the ages of 10 and 15 can send a message to KIDCAFE. Moderators will check the message for appropriateness. The moderator sends all appropriate messages to a listserv, and the listserv distributes the messages to all e-mail addresses on the KIDCAFE list.

KIDCAFE: Youth dialogue
For information, send the message GET KIDCAFE GUIDE
to listserv@vm1.nodak.edu

KIDCAFE-SCHOOL: School-organized keypal exchange
Administrative address: listserv@vm1.nodak.edu
Participation address: kidcafe-school@ vm1.nodak.edu

3. Have students outline the problem and develop questions to elicit information from other students.

    - Where do you live? Describe your community.
    - Do you have a problem with air, noise, or water pollution?
    - How serious do you believe the problem is?
    - What health issues are involved with pollution in your community?
    - Do you have any solutions to suggest?

4. Have students discuss their own answers to the questions before soliciting information from other sources. Use the text to guide your discussion. After discussing the topic, have students write their own preliminary responses to the question, providing evidence and justifications. An example follows.

    We live in a rural community with no large city within 50 miles. Most of our parents are farmers or orchard owners. Since we live in the country, we don't have much noise pollution. The nearest airport is too far away to hear. We do, however, have air and water pollution from the pesticides the farmers use on their fields. We have a crop dusting company in our area that sprays crops several times a season. They spray from small airplanes. When they spray the crops, we have to go indoors and shut the windows. The air is filled with chemicals. These chemicals eventually run into our water supply. Since we have well water, we are very concerned that the ground water stays clean.

    We have a solution to propose. We have begun a petition asking the farmers to investigate alternative ways of growing crops that would not use pesticides. We are sorry if any change would diminish the amount of business the crop duster has, but we believe it is for the good of the community.

5. E-mail the outline, question, and sample answer to other students around the country and the world. Ask that responses be returned within two weeks. After two weeks, collect the responses and duplicate them for the entire class. Divide the class into groups of four or five students to read the other students' papers and evaluate their logic. (See Teaching Strategy 6-13 for a sample rubric that could be used for evaluation.)

6. Using input from all of the groups, come to a conclusion about the original question. Write a short summary, as in the following example, and e-mail it to the participants in this project.

    Pollution seems to be a problem for students from many localities. Most of the students experience significant sources of pollution in their communities. The types of pollution vary although more students from urban areas find noise pollution to be a problem. Several solutions were suggested. Most of the solutions emphasized individual responsibility. All of the student groups felt powerless to change the biggest sources of pollution.

Chapter 7

Studying

Overview

Studying is a unique skill, different from the reading strategies presented in other chapters of this book. When students read, they focus attention on the text; then they use their ability to process print to construct meaning. While reading, students rely on textbook features and use their ability to reason in order to fulfill their reading purposes. Studying is different. When students study, they read, understand, learn, and remember information from texts for a specific task (Anderson & Armbruster, 1984).

To illustrate the difference between reading and studying, think about textbook passages you assign students to read in preparation for class discussion. You expect them to read, understand, and remember information that they can apply to a general discussion about the topic. You expect students to know some of the content information. When you assign students studying tasks, your expectations are often different. You expect students to identify the important ideas in the text, to learn and remember those ideas, to be able to understand the relationship between the information they studied and past material, and to retrieve that material in certain ways for a test or a performance.

Studying has two basic components: knowing what to study and knowing how to study. Students need to be aware of the learning task. If studying is to accomplish a specific task, students must understand the task. Generally, you will be the one who determines the studying task. For example, you might ask students to study material for a test, a performance, or a presentation. Your role is to make sure that students understand the nature of the task. Then students need to identify the subsets of the task and set study goals to accomplish each one. As students decide what to study, they may survey the materials and use flexible reading strategies to determine what information to learn and remember. They may set goals, manage their study time, and monitor their studying effectiveness. Once students have determined what they should study, they need to use study strategies to learn and remember the material for the specific study task.

Knowing what to study is not enough; students also need to know how to study. When students study to read and remember, they need to focus attention on the material, encode that information, and learn the material in such a way that they can retrieve it for the task. Students need to read the text information and form it into their own words, so that it makes sense and they are able to repeat that information in any one of a variety of forms for a test. To do this, students need to learn how to use study strategies. The following strategies are generally considered useful for most students who are studying (Wade & Reynolds, 1989):

- Preview text
- Predict
- Skim or scan text
- Read slowly and carefully
- Reread difficult sections
- Paraphrase
- Relate new information to existing knowledge
- Create mental images
- Develop questions
- Highlight, underline, or take notes
- Outline
- Create a diagram
- Summarize

Because studying is task-directed and people learn in different ways, study plans and methods tend to be idiosyncratic. For example, students who are studying the chapter "The Midwestern United States" in *World Geography Today* (1995) are faced with five new vocabulary words, eight pages to read, three charts, two graphs, and five pictures. Some students prefer to read the text in sequential order, taking detailed notes using the Cornell notetaking method. Other students prefer scanning the chapter and using the REAP strategy, taking annotative notes. Still others may use the REST strategy and take notes along with writing their own comments and questions. Because there isn't one correct way to study, you should present students with a variety of study strategies and let them choose those study strategies that work for them.

Studying in schools is often assigned so that students learn material for a culminating activity such as a test or a performance. Students should know, however, that studying is a useful life skill. Even though students are not formally graded in their everyday life in the same way they are in schools, they still have many opportunities to study: to read and learn to perform a specific task. For example, students who are learning to drive will read the driver's manual, learn driving skills from an adult, and practice driving. Students are actually studying; they are reading and learning in order to perform a specific task. Therefore, as you teach students how to study for your class, also tell them that they can use the skills they are learning for many important activities in which they will engage as adolescents and adults.

7.1 Learning to Study

Goal

To help students learn how to study.

Background

Studying is generally a self-directed activity. You can teach students a variety of study strategies, but they have to assume the responsibility for their own studying. You can assist students in learning how to take that responsibility by helping them create study plans, manage their study time, and monitor their study habits.

Helping adolescents learn how to accept the responsibility for the outcome of studying is a challenge. One of the hallmarks of adolescent thinking is the difficulty in accepting reality. Most adolescents employ "magical thinking" at times. They believe that simply because they want something to happen it will, and they don't have to work to cause it to happen. For example, many times students who are receiving a poor grade in a class will say, "I'll raise my grade next quarter." The next grading period comes and the student has earned the same grade. When confronted with the situation, the student is disbelieving. The grade was supposed to be higher simply because of wishful thinking. Adolescents frequently confuse wanting something to happen with making it happen. For that reason, you should help students learn that studying takes time and attention. Students will need to make study plans, set study goals, and use study strategies to accomplish their goals.

Even though studying is generally an individual endeavor, students should study with friends at times. Middle and high school students are social beings. Therefore, students should be encouraged to study in groups for part of their study time. Certainly, there are times when solo studying is best, but many adolescents learn better when they can share ideas with their peers. Consequently, you should encourage students to learn how to plan, manage, and monitor their individual studying, but you should also encourage students to spend some of their study time learning from each other.

Computer Software for Collaborative Studying

Realtime Writer 2.0 provides up to 40 separate discussion channels for interactive discussion. It also includes a window for composition and a window for users on an individual channel to read all of the comments that have been sent as part of the ongoing dialogue. A third window is provided for the teacher to post notices to any of the channels.

Realtime Leaning Systems 800-832-2472

TEACHING STRATEGY 1

Preplan-List-Activate-Evaluate (PLAE)

Research indicates that students who construct and implement an effective plan of study do better on tests than students who do not have a study plan (Nist & Simpson, 1989). For that reason Nist and Simpson (1989) created PLAE, a study strategy to help students create goals and plan what to do during study time. PLAE incorporates the following operations necessary for strategy control and regulation: goal setting, understanding of a variety of strategies, the ability to select appropriate study strategies, the ability to activate and monitor a plan of action, and the ability to evaluate a study plan. When students employ PLAE, they **P**replan or define their tasks and goals, **L**ist or select the strategies they will use, **A**ctivate or implement the study plan, and **E**valuate the plan's effectiveness after they receive feedback.

Directions and Example

1. Tell students that you will be demonstrating a study strategy that they can use in all subject areas to improve their learning of content material. Use examples from your content area or use the following example.

2. Write PLAE on the chalkboard or an overhead transparency, or use a computer with an LCD panel. Tell students that PLAE is an acronym for **P**replan, **L**ist, **A**ctivate, and **E**valuate.

3. Identify a study goal that students will need to accomplish in the near future. Tell students that you will be using the following example to demonstrate the **P**replan stage of PLAE.

Study Goal

For French class you will be asked to learn vocabulary and language structures associated with various foods and grocery shopping. We will have a mock grocery store with food to sell. To demonstrate your knowledge, you will be evaluated on your ability to conduct a conversation in French. Students in the fourth-year French class will play the role of the shopkeepers.

4. Divide the class into groups of three or four students. Have students create a list of tasks designed to accomplish the study goal. After students have developed lists, have them discuss their ideas with the whole group. A sample list follows.

Study Tasks

- Scan Chapter 6 in *Bienvenue* (1994), the French textbook, looking for the section that discusses the vocabulary of grocery shopping.
- Create note cards or write notes with the terms to learn.
- Memorize the vocabulary.
- Practice the new vocabulary with classmates in conversations about grocery shopping.

5. Tell students that the next step in PLAE is to list their prior knowledge of successful study strategies. Have students discuss the strategies they could use to accomplish their study tasks. This book provides students with a wide repertoire of reading and learning strategies.

6. Have groups of students discuss possible study options. Then have students brainstorm strategies that they could use to accomplish each task. Students should individually decide which study strategy to use. Ask students to write their study plan on a note card. An example of a study plan follows.

Study Plan

Skim section 1 from chapter 6.
Identify words to learn.
Memorize new words.
Practice new words in dialogue with classmates.

7. Have students activate their study plan. Each day ask students whether they were able to accomplish their study goals.

8. After students have completed their study plan and have demonstrated their learning, have them evaluate their study plan. For students to evaluate their study plan, they need to identify the outcome of the culminating event. For example, if students were being graded on their ability to use French in a grocery shopping scenario, have them list the grades they received. Then ask students to determine whether that grade was higher or lower than they expected. If the grade was lower, have students reread their study plan, think about whether they implemented the plan, and write reasons why their grade was not as high as they expected. Students should evaluate not only their final grade but also the effectiveness of their studying. If they identify a weak point, students should revise future study plans.

9. Duplicate and distribute the following description of PLAE for students to use as they study.

PLAE Study Plan

Preplan—Preplan or define study tasks and goals.

List—List or select strategies to accomplish study tasks and meet study goals.

Activate—Activate or implement the study plan using appropriate strategies.

Evaluate—Evaluate the effectiveness of the study plan.

From Nist, S.L., & Simpson, M.L. (1989). PLAE, a validated study strategy. *Journal of Reading,* 33, 182–186.

TEACHING STRATEGY **2**

Managing Studying

Teaching students all of the strategies in the world will not necessarily help them learn content information. Students also need to learn how to manage their study time. Middle and high school students often have full schedules. However, they need to make time to study and manage their study time so that they can learn the necessary material from your content area. Middle and high school students need to assume the responsibility for managing their own study time, but you can help them understand the factors involved in using time wisely.

Directions

1. Tell students that you will be discussing effective techniques for managing studying. Explain that even though many of them know how to study, unless they manage their study time they will not use their study time effectively.

2. Write the following list of Tips for Managing Study Time on the chalkboard or an overhead transparency, or use a computer with an LCD panel. Discuss each of the items on this list with the students. Tell students that if they follow these suggestions, they will have more productive study sessions.

Tips for Managing Study Time

•   Study in a comfortable environment with good lighting and minimal distractions.

•   Set study goals for each study time. List the goals and estimate the amount of time each study goal will take.

•   Determine whether short periods or long periods of study time are best.

•   Schedule study time at your best time for learning (e.g., early morning).

•   Keep a pencil or pen available when studying to summarize, underline, or write down key notes or ideas.

•   Keep a positive attitude during study time. Do not try to rush though studying. Become engaged in learning.

•   Use study questions or create self-questions while studying. Keep your mind focused.

•   Actively read and study. Monitor your attention to the task.

•   Relate what you are studying to your life.

•   Compliment yourself for productive study periods.

Based on Risko, V.J., Fairbanks, M.M., & Alvarez, M.C. (1991). Internal factors that influence study. In R.F. Flippo & D.C. Caverly (Eds.), *Teaching reading & study strategies at the college level* (pp. 237–293). Newark, DE: International Reading Association.

Monitoring Study Habits

As students study, they need to constantly monitor the effectiveness of their study time. You can teach them how to manage their study sessions (see Teaching Strategy 7-2), but students need to independently monitor their use of those management techniques as they study. Students may not be aware of the need to monitor studying. Therefore, you can teach them ways to become aware of their progress.

Directions

1. Tell students that they should become aware of the study strategies they use and should make changes so that studying is more productive. Tell students that one way to increase self-awareness is to complete a survey about study habits.

2. Duplicate and distribute the following survey. Have students answer the questions by circling the number that best describes their study habits. After students have completed the survey, have them reflect on their strengths and weaknesses and make a plan to change any habits that interfere with learning. Have students take the survey periodically so they can monitor changes in their study habits.

Study Skills Self-Assessment

	Always		Sometimes		Never
1. I read material more than once if I don't understand it the first time.	5	4	3	2	1
2. I try to identify the most important points as I read.	5	4	3	2	1
3. I preview reading assignments before reading.	5	4	3	2	1
4. I concentrate when I study.	5	4	3	2	1
5. I study with a friend when I think it will help.	5	4	3	2	1
6. I try to "overlearn" material as I study.	5	4	3	2	1
7. I take notes that help me when I study.	5	4	3	2	1
8. I study in an environment that is conducive to learning.	5	4	3	2	1
9. I set goals for each study time.	5	4	3	2	1
10. I underline or take notes as I study.	5	4	3	2	1

Based on Davis, S. J. (1990). Applying content study skills in co-listed reading classrooms. *Journal of Reading*, *33*, 277–281.

7.2 Reading Flexibly

Goal
To help students develop the ability to read flexibly.

Background

Reading flexibly is a necessary skill when studying. Flexible readers modify their reading rates and their choice of strategies to fit different kinds of texts for different purposes. Flexibility can be viewed as an aspect of metacognition (i.e., thinking about thinking). Good readers are metacognitively aware. They know when comprehension is failing and when it is time to apply fix-up strategies, including an adjustment of reading rate. The rate at which students read material is influenced by at least four factors: 1) the speaking-listening rate to which they have become accustomed; 2) prior knowledge or familiarity with the material; 3) the rate at which they can receive and think about incoming information; and 4) their purpose for reading the material (Manzo & Manzo, 1990a). Additionally, reading rate is affected by the organization of the text and the author's writing style.

According to many authors, including Crawley and Mountain (1995), there are three types of reading behaviors: skimming, scanning, and precise reading. Skimming is used to gain an overview or a general idea of text. This level of reading is appropriate for previewing a chapter in a textbook or deciding whether to choose a particular library book by skimming the book jacket. Scanning is used to locate specific information or to answer a question. For example, when looking up a phone number in the directory, we scan the page until we get close to the name we are seeking. At that time, we probably begin to do precise reading. Precise reading requires analyzing words or an author's ideas in a purposeful and deliberate manner. This type of reading is used when we read textbooks for the purpose of learning and retaining information, or when we read web sites. Internet reading requires students to incorporate the three traditional levels of reading (skimming, scanning, and precise reading) and incorporates one more: scrolling. When students read web sites, they use scrolling, scanning, skimming, and precise reading recursively. As content area teachers, teaching the following strategies can provide opportunities for your students to increase their reading flexibility while maintaining adequate comprehension.

TEACHING STRATEGY 4

Skim-Away

Skimming involves reading quickly over material in order to gain a general impression of its content. When readers skim, they preview material and start to forge links with their background knowledge as they gain a general impression of the text. According to Fry (1978), skimming is usually done at rates of about 800 to 1,000 words per minute. The following strategy is designed to develop students' ability to skim a text selection.

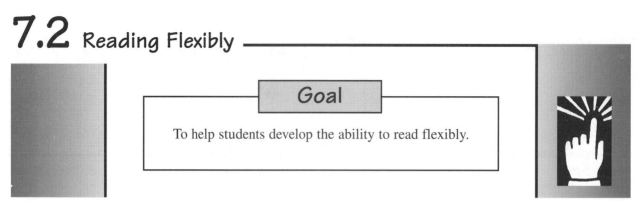

Directions and Example

1. Tell students that this reading strategy is one they can use to get an overall idea about the contents of the chapter or text. Explain that when readers skim they are reading text quickly to get a main idea. To demonstrate skimming, use an example from your content area or the following example.

2. Ask students to open their *World History* (1994) text and turn to Chapter 5 on Ancient Greece. Tell students that they are going to skim the first section of the chapter in order to get a sense of the chapter's contents and to begin to think about the main idea of the chapter. Tell students that, as they do this, they are activating their background knowledge about the chapter's subject. Allow about three minutes to complete this activity. Tell them that, as they skim, they should do the following things:

    *   Read the chapter title and glance over the headings and subheadings included in the chapter as they slowly turn the pages.
    *   Think about the focus of the chapter as they skim over the maps, charts, and illustrations.
    *   Quickly read the section review.

3. After students have completed skimming the first section of the chapter, ask them to close their books and write a paragraph that includes everything they can recall from this first section. Invite students to share their paragraphs and talk about the techniques they used as they skimmed. An example of a student's paragraph follows.

    > This section is sort of a preview about the battle between the Persians and the Athenians for the city of Athens. It looks like the chapter will focus on the geographic setting of Greece and include lots of information about the Bronze Age, the Dark Ages, and the Greek Gods. There are several photographs of Greek art works, a map of Greece during the Bronze Age, and a great photograph of the Acropolis. The section review includes some vocabulary words and questions about the contents.

4. Discuss with students the value of skimming before they read a chapter. Tell students that now that they have skimmed the first section, they have the gist, or the general idea, of the chapter and are prepared to scan it more carefully for precise information.

TEACHING STRATEGY 5

On Your Marks, Get Set, SCAN!

Scanning is used by readers to locate specific information. Readers use scanning when they look up a number in the phone book or a word in the dictionary. In scanning, readers know what information they are seeking and work at a speed of about 1,500 words per minute. This speed usually results in 100% accuracy of obtained information (Crawley & Mountain, 1995). The following strategy uses scanning as a way for students to experience finding specific information within a selection of text.

Directions and Example

1. Tell students that this reading strategy involves scanning their texts as they look for specific information. Explain that when readers scan they move their eyes quickly down the page until they locate the information they are seeking. Tell them that it is important that they read quickly and try to skip words or descriptions that do not seem pertinent to the information for which they are looking.

2. Ask students to open their *World History* (1994) text and turn to Chapter 5 on Ancient Greece or use an example from your content area. (If you have completed Teaching Strategy 7-4, your students will have a general idea of the contents of a chapter.)

3. Look over the chapter and pick out facts that students can locate as they scan. Try to pick out facts that are important to the contents. Write five to ten questions, based on text information, on the chalkboard or an overhead transparency, or use a computer with an LCD panel. Allow five minutes for completion of this activity. Tell students that they are going to scan the first section of the chapter in order to find answers to the following questions:

   - How did geography shape Greek civilization?
   - How much of Greece is covered with mountains?
   - Describe briefly the life of the Minoans.
   - What was the main business of the Bronze Age kings?
   - When did the Olympic Games begin?
   - What are myths?

4. Ask students to work as quickly as possible to locate the answers to the questions. Tell them to write down the answers but not to worry about spelling at this time. Remind them that it is not necessary to read every word in the text in order to obtain the information they need to complete the activity. Say to students, "On your marks, get set, scan!" as they begin the activity.

5. After students have completed the scanning activity, invite them to share their answers and to discuss the techniques they used as they located information. Encourage them to practice using scanning with other textbook assignments in order to increase their reading efficiency.

TEACHING STRATEGY 6

SCROL

SCROL (Grant, 1993) provides students with an opportunity to use skimming, scanning, and precise reading as they study a chapter of text. Students will scan the table of contents to locate the appropriate chapter, skim the headings of the chapter as they preview it, and carefully read the chapter in order to construct an outline of its contents. Grant (1993) has identified four advantages to using SCROL:

1. Students increase comprehension by activating their background knowledge prior to reading.
2. Students are guided in understanding the relationships among ideas in the text.
3. Students use content structure as a method for remembering text information.
4. Students' motivation for reading text is increased.

Directions and Example

1. Tell students that good readers use three levels of reading: skimming, scanning, and precise reading. Explain that all of these levels are incorporated into a strategy called SCROL.

2. Explain to students that when they scan they are looking for specific information and they should read quickly down a page. When they locate information they want to read, they may want to skim it to deter-

mine if it is information they are seeking. Then they begin to do precise reading. Model the SCROL strategy for students using examples from your content area or use the example provided below.

> Scan the table of contents in *Career Directions* (1991) and look for the page number for Chapter 10, "How to Get Jobs and Work Experience." When you find it, open your books to the appropriate page.

3. Tell students that SCROL stands for **S**urvey, **C**onnect, **R**ead, and **O**utline. As you direct students' attention to Chapter 10 in their texts, model how to use SCROL.

4. Ask students to skim the chapter and **S**urvey the headings. As they skim, they should look at the headings, subheadings and illustrations in order to get the main idea of the chapter. Tell them to consider what they already know about the topic, "How to Get Jobs and Work Experience." Tell students that when they see the heading "newspaper advertisements" they probably already know that newspaper advertisements are a good place to look for jobs. As they survey the chapter, they are skimming it for general information.

5. After students have surveyed the chapter, ask them to share some of their ideas about the chapter's contents as you write their ideas on the chalkboard or an overhead transparency. For example, one student might say, "This chapter is going to tell us about work permits. I think work permits are necessary if we want to get a job and we're under 15 or 16. I'm not sure which." Another student might say, "There's a section called Distributing a Flier. This sounds interesting. Maybe it's going to tell us how to make up our own fliers when we're looking for a job."

6. Invite students to **C**onnect the headings to one another. Ask them to look for key words in the headings to help them make the connections. As they do this, tell them that they are using scanning because they are looking for specific information.

7. Ask students to continue to scan the headings and to offer suggestions about the chapter's contents. For example, one student might say, "There are also sections about entrepreneurship and private jobs so the chapter must have some information about working on your own." At this point, students have used skimming in order to preview the text and scanning for specific text topics.

8. Now ask students to **R**ead the text looking for words and phrases that explain the headings. As they do this, explain that they are employing precise reading or reading in a purposeful manner.

9. After students have finished reading the chapter, explain that they should **O**utline the chapter by listing the headings and writing under the headings the details that they remember from their reading. An example follows.

Newspaper Advertisements

- classified advertising by employers
- help-wanted section
- read carefully before responding
- place an ad for a job in situation wanted

10. Direct students to look back at the text to determine the accuracy of their outlines. As they do, point out to them that they are, once again, scanning the chapter or looking for specific information. If they have written down incorrect information or wish to add additional information, they should revise their outlines.

Newspaper Advertisements

- Classified advertising lists available jobs.
- Help-wanted advertisements are for full-time jobs or adult skills.
- Some ads are for teenagers over the age of sixteen.
- Situation wanted ads should be brief but include essential information.

11. To conclude this strategy, review with students the different types of reading (skimming, scanning, and precise reading). Point out to them that they used all three types as they employed the SCROL strategy.

TEACHING STRATEGY **7**

Reading Flexibly on the Internet

Media literacy, defined as "the understanding and production of messages through physical devices," incorporates six components: the ability to access, analyze, synthesize, interpret, evaluate, and communicate messages (Flood & Lapp, 1995, p. 3). Successful integration of these components requires adequate comprehension and emphasizes the necessity for flexible reading. Students must be able to vary their reading rate as they navigate information sources on the internet in order to successfully determine the quality and relevancy of the information. This means that, as they scroll down the screen, sometimes they skim or scan, and often they use careful reading in order to analyze ideas and words.

Directions and Example

1. Model the use of flexible reading on the internet for students by using the following example or an example related to your content area. Use an LCD panel to project the following internet activity for the entire class or, if an LCD panel is unavailable, print a copy of a web page or several web pages for each student.

2. Tell students that they need to use various strategies when reading on the internet. They will use scrolling, skimming, scanning, and precise reading as they locate and evaluate information and determine its relevancy to their search.

3. Type the following address onto your internet address bar.

http://library.advanced.org/11163/gather/cgi-bin/wookie.cgi/

This will open up a web site titled *You Are What You Eat*. Tell students that you are researching nutrition and would like to find some information about how exercise relates to good health.

4. Show students that the web site has several sections or choices for them to skim as they scroll down the screen and look for information about the relationship between nutrition and exercise. As they skim, they read quickly and look over the topics. They will see the following choices: Introduction, Food Database, Applications, Nutrients, and Contribute. These topics give them a general idea about the information that is available through this web site. Although they have several choices of web pages, none appears to relate directly to exercise. A logical choice, at this point, will probably be the site labeled Introduction. Click on this site.

5. Tell students to scan this site in order to locate information about exercise. As they do, they will see that exercise is listed under the web link Applications. Point out to students that the type of reading they did on this page was slower and more precise as they were trying to locate a specific piece of information—the location of information about exercise.

6. Click on the word Exercise under Applications. This will take you to a page titled Exercise, with two paragraphs about the relationship between nutrition and exercise. Ask students to answer the following questions as they read this web page:

   - What effect does exercise have on your metabolic rate?
   - What are some benefits of exercise?
   - What type of information is available on the following link?

7. Point out to students that, in order to answer these questions, they need to scan the paragraphs. However, if they wish to take notes on the material or analyze some of the information, they will need to employ precise reading or study reading. This is described as slow, careful reading for the purpose of learning or studying.

8. Guide students in conducting their own internet research project. They should use flexible reading rates as they encounter web pages. (For information regarding effective research strategies, including locating and evaluating sources, see Chapter 9.)

Teachers need to be familiar with web sites that they suggest as reference sources for students.

7.3 Taking Notes

Goal

To help students learn how to take notes from textbooks.

Background

Taking notes facilitates learning in at least two ways: by the process of taking notes and by the product, or the notes themselves (McKenna & Robinson, 1997). When students take notes, they use many cognitive processes that aid learning. First, students select what information to take down as notes. Then, they condense the information into words, phrases, or sentences. Finally, they write the notes in some type of organized form. These processes are factors in learning content material.

The notes that students write are the product of the activity. These organized, selected phrases from the text help students as they review in order to learn. The product of taking notes is at least as important as the process of notetaking (Anderson & Armbruster, 1991). Therefore, students learn from the activity of taking notes and from the notes they produce.

Students will not automatically know how to take notes. If you do not teach students notetaking strategies, they may not select the most important information to write, and they may not write notes in an organized manner (Stahl, King, & Henk, 1991). It's important, therefore, that you teach students how to take notes.

There are many types of notetaking strategies, some using paper and pencil and some electronic. Taking notes is an activity that is individualistic; different students prefer different types of notes. Therefore, you should teach several types of notetaking strategies and encourage students to use the ones that are most helpful to them.

TEACHING STRATEGY 8

Read-Encode-Annotate-Ponder (REAP)

One way to take notes is to make annotations on note cards, in a learning log, or on the computer. Annotative notes are at the heart of the REAP strategy (Eanet & Manzo, 1976). When students employ REAP, they **R**ead text passages, **E**ncode the message by translating the passage into their own words, **A**nnotate or write their messages in their notes, and **P**onder the messages they have written. Annotations can take various forms. Students can write a summary annotation that condenses the main ideas of a passage into one or two concise statements. A second type of annotation is a thesis annotation that states the main point the author has tried to relate. A third type of annotation is a critical annotation. A critical annotation answers the question "So what?" Students' critical annotations first state the author's thesis and then state an opinion about that thesis. A final type of annotation is a question annotation. For this type of annotation, students write a question about a significant aspect of the passage.

TECHNOLOGY TIP

REAP Chat Corner

The Reader Exchange is an internet chat corner that uses the REAP strategy.

http://cctr.umkc.edu/user/rbi/Foundation.html

Directions and Example

1. Tell students that you will be demonstrating a study strategy that they can use as they read textbook material and learn content information. To demonstrate the REAP strategy, use an example from your content area or the following example.

2. Identify a passage that you want students to read. Tell them to read the passage independently. After they have read the passage, tell students to identify the main points and restate them in their own words. The following is an example of a textbook passage and an encoded message based on that passage. Write the passage and message on the chalkboard or an overhead transparency, or use a computer with an LCD panel.

Investing in Savings Accounts

When you invest your money in savings accounts, the money is essentially risk-free; it has the greatest safety of any investments you might choose. Even though banks might fail, as long as your investment in a bank is insured by either the Federal Deposit Insurance Corporation (FDIC) or the Federal Savings and Loan Insurance Corporation (FSLIC), your savings are risk-free. Even if the bank fails, your money is insured. Bank savings accounts are virtually risk-free investments; however, money invested in banks does not return a high rate of interest.

▶ Adapted from *Business: Stock market and investment practice set.* (1993). Englewood Cliffs, NJ: Prentice-Hall.

Encoded Message

This paragraph is about investing in savings accounts. When you invest in savings accounts your money will not accrue much interest, but it will be safe.

3. Distribute note cards to students. After students have practiced encoding, or restating, the main points of the passage, have them write their restatements on the cards. Tell students that there could be many different ways to write a summary and that one type of message is not superior to any other type.

4. Divide the class into groups of three or four students. Have students share their statements with each other. Then have them ponder, or think about, the different types of messages represented by the group.

5. Tell students that there are four main types of annotations: summary annotations, thesis annotations, critical annotations, and question annotations. Write an example of each type of annotation on the chalkboard or an overhead transparency, or use a computer with an LCD panel. Use examples from your content area or the examples that follow. Have the students identify the type of annotation they have written. Then remind students to use the REAP strategy as they study content information.

High School Business Example

REAP Annotations

Summary Annotation

Money invested in banks is insured, so it is virtually risk-free.

Thesis Annotation

Investing money in banks has low risks and low returns.

Critical Annotation

Investing money in banks has low risks and low returns. I don't think money that is not needed to pay bills should be invested in banks. The low risks don't compensate for the low returns.

Question Annotation

I thought that there was a ceiling on the amount of money that is insured by the banks. Are all savings entirely insured?

TEACHING STRATEGY **9**

Record-Edit-Synthesize-Think (REST)

Record-**E**dit-**S**ynthesize-**T**hink (REST) (Morgan, Meeks, Schollaert, & Paul, 1986) is a notetaking strategy that takes into account the integration of textbook readings, lectures, and class discussions. When students use REST, they record what they have read in the text or heard in class, edit those notes by condensing them and deleting irrelevant material, synthesize notes by recording information stressed both in class and the textbook, and think about the notes while studying and learning the content information. REST can be used when teachers assign textbook reading before class discussion, or it can be used when class discussion precedes textbook reading.

Directions and Examples

1. Tell students that you will be demonstrating a study and notetaking strategy that they can use to learn content material. Use an example from your content area or the following examples.

2. Identify a concept that will be the topic of a class discussion and will be assigned to students to read. Have students read the passage independently or in groups.

3. Have students record notes from the reading on the left half of a sheet of paper in a manner similar to the following example.

High School Science Example

REST

Notes from text (pp. 17–19)	Notes from class
• St. Paul's Island in the Bering Sea near Alaska • 41 sq. miles • 1911—25 reindeer introduced • no predators • 1937—reindeer population increased to 2,000 • by 1950 no more reindeer	
Summary	

Based on *Biology: A human approach.* (1997). Dubuque, IA: Kendall/Hunt.

4. After students have recorded notes from their reading, present a lecture or conduct a class discussion about the topic. Tell students to write notes from the lecture or class discussion on the right half of the paper as in the following example.

High School Science Example

REST

Notes from text (pp. 17–19)	Notes from class
• St. Paul's Island in the Bering Sea near Alaska • 41 sq. miles • 1911—25 reindeer introduced • no predators • 1937—reindeer population increased to 2,000 • by 1950 no more reindeer	• food capacity of island limited • interdependence involves limiting factors • no data on reindeer population in 1941–1942 • carrying capacity—maximum population of a particular species that the habitat can support

Summary

Based on *Biology: A human approach.* (1997). Dubuque, IA: Kendall/Hunt.

5. Tell students that lectures and class discussions may repeat information that students have read in their text and written in their notes. Some of the contents of lectures and class discussion, however, will be different. Tell students that both types of notes are important to study. After students have recorded notes from the class lecture or discussion, have them edit their notes and delete information that is redundant or irrelevant.

6. Explain that the next step in REST is to synthesize the information from textbook reading and class discussions. Tell students to read both columns of their notes carefully, looking for a synthesis between the information from both sources. Have students write the synthesis of the notes at the bottom of the sheet as in the following example. After students have synthesized their notes, they should think about their summary and study the content information.

REST

Notes from text (pp. 17–19)	Notes from class
• St. Paul's Island in the Bering Sea near Alaska • 41 sq. miles • 1911—25 reindeer introduced • no predators • 1937—reindeer population increased to 2,000 • by 1950 no more reindeer	• food capacity of island limited • interdependence involves limiting factors • no data on reindeer population in 1941–1942 • carrying capacity—maximum population of a particular species that the habitat can support

Summary

Reindeer were introduced to St. Paul's Island, a small island in the Bering Sea, in 1911. The reindeer population increased for 26 years but then exceeded the carrying capacity of the habitat. Reindeer were extinct by 1950 due to a lack of food.

Based on *Biology: A human approach.* (1997). Dubuque, IA: Kendall/Hunt.

7. REST can also be used as a notetaking strategy when students first hear a lecture or a class discussion. Students using REST to take notes from a class discussion should record notes on the right half of the sheet of paper. When they edit their notes, they should add questions and notes on the left half of the paper to direct their reading. After reading the textbook passage, students should synthesize both of the sources by writing a summary at the bottom of the page. The following example shows notes taken from a lecture and class discussion on the right side of the paper with notes and questions about a future reading assignment on the left side.

Middle School English Example

REST

Topic and notes to yourself	Notes from lecture and class discussion
Check textbook for examples.	The subject of a verb is in the nominative case.
Check notes for pronouns in nominative case.	A predicate nominative is in the nominative case.
That doesn't sound right. I guess I'm used to the sentence "It's me."	An objective form of a pronoun is often used in the sentence "It's me." Although that is now acceptable in speech, when writing you should use "It is I."
I need to review indirect objects.	The direct object and the indirect object of a verb are in the objective case.
I'm glad I learned the prepositions last year.	The object of a preposition is in the objective case.

Summary and main ideas

Standard English has rules that are often ignored in speech. In this lesson, I learned when to use different cases of pronouns. Pronouns used as subjects and as predicate nominatives are in the nominative case. Pronouns used as objects are in the objective case.

Based on *English: Composition and grammar.* (1988). Orlando, FL: Harcourt Brace Jovanovich.

TEACHING STRATEGY 10

Cornell Notetaking

Cornell notetaking (Pauk, 1974) is similar to the REST strategy (see Teaching Strategy 7-9) in that it is a two-column notetaking strategy. With Cornell notetaking, however, notes from textbook reading or class discussions are written on the right side of the page, and key words that organize the notes are written on the left. Cornell notetaking is an excellent strategy for topics that can be organized with main ideas and details as opposed to cause-effect and problem-solution structures.

Directions and Example

1. Tell students that you will be demonstrating a notetaking strategy that can help them study and learn content information. Use an example from your content area or use the following example to model Cornell notetaking.

2. Identify a topic that would be organized with the structure of main idea-details. Be sure students understand this type of text structure. Conduct a class discussion or have students read a passage from a textbook about the topic.

3. Distribute sheets of paper that have a vertical line drawn approximately three inches from the left side of the paper. Tell students that they should take detailed notes about the topic of the reading assignment or class discussion by writing their notes on the right side of the sheet of paper as in the following example.

High School Literature Example

Cornell Notetaking

Key Words	Notes from reading or class discussion
	• literature in early 20th century
	• depicts life as it is: brutal, difficult
	• expansion of West, after Civil War
	• growth of industry
	• books increased
	• Stephen Crane (1871–1900)
	• "An Episode of War" "The Open Boat" *The Red Badge of Courage*

Based on *Explore: A course in literature.* (1991). Circle Pines, MN: AGS.

4. Divide the class into groups of three or four students. Have students share the notes they wrote on the right half of the paper. Then ask students to generate ideas for key words to write on the left side of the paper.

5. Tell students to independently decide which key terms would be appropriate to write on the left side of their notes, as the following example illustrates.

High School Literature Example

Cornell Notetaking

Key Words	Notes from reading or class discussion
Realism in literature	• literature in early 20th century
	• depicts life as it is: brutal, difficult
Historical factors	• expansion of West, after Civil War
	• growth of industry
	• books increased
Crane's works	• Stephen Crane (1871–1900)
	• "An Episode of War" "The Open Boat" *The Red Badge of Courage*

Based on *Explore: A course in literature.* (1991). Circle Pines, MN: AGS.

Providing some class time for studying often helps students remain focused on their goals.

7.4 Summarizing Content Information

Goal
To help students learn content information by summarizing.

Background

The goal of studying is to learn content information. All of the reading strategies and skills in this book can have a positive impact on learning; however, students can go through the motions of preparing a study plan, reading flexibly, and taking notes without learning the material. To learn content material, students need to be able to translate ideas into their own words and retrieve that material to accomplish a task. When students use their background knowledge to make predictions, take notes, and summarize content material, they have a better chance of really learning (Caverly, Mandeville, & Nicholson, 1995; Armbruster, Anderson, & Ostertag, 1987).

When students study to learn content material, they need to encode the ideas in the text. One of the best ways to encode text, or paraphrase the ideas, is to write summaries of the material. Summary writing involves identifying important information, then organizing and recasting the ideas into the gist of the larger text. Summarizing is beneficial because it gives students the opportunity to rethink the content material and process that material deeply.

You can teach students to write summaries of content material and to summarize independently as they study. Teaching students to use the strategy PLAN, to write microthemes, and to use GRASP facilitates learning the skill of summarizing. Your goal, however, is to have students automatically summarize as they read. Students reading about the particles in matter in the text *How Matter Changes: Exploring the Structure of Matter* (1995), for example, first read an introduction that reviews ideas presented earlier in the text. Then the text presents a short experiment, and finally it explains a diagram of particles in solids, liquids, and gases. When students read these two pages, they should summarize each section before reading the next section. Summarizing during reading is one of the most effective strategies students can use as they learn content information.

TECHNOLOGY TIP

Computer Software that Creates Prediction Maps

Inspiration: graphically maps words, creates flow charts, and develops outlines.

Inspiration Software Inc. http://www.inspiration.com

TEACHING STRATEGY **11**

Predict-Locate-Add-Note (PLAN)

Before students can effectively summarize material, they should identify what they already know and what they do not know. **P**redict-**L**ocate-**A**dd-**N**ote (PLAN) is a strategy that can guide students in identifying what they need to learn (Caverly, Mandeville, & Nicholson, 1995). PLAN incorporates many of the important elements in reading and learning: using background knowledge to predict the content and structure of a text and to assess its potential for reading purposes, locating familiar and unfamiliar concepts, reading flexibly for information to add to what is already known, and taking note of new learning and using it to accomplish a task. PLAN is a study strategy that students can use to help them identify content information to summarize.

Directions and Example

1. Tell students that you will be demonstrating a strategy that they can use as they study to learn content information. Use your own content area example or the one that follows.

2. Identify a concept from a passage that you want students to learn. Duplicate and distribute the passage to the students. Have students predict the content and structure of the text by previewing the title, subtitles, and highlighted words. Then have students create a map or a diagram, similar to the one that follows, that describes their predictions.

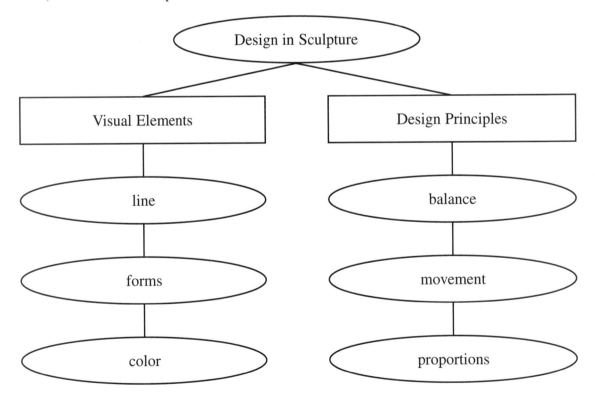

▶ Based on *Art: Images and ideas.* (1992). Worcester, MA: Davis Publications.

3. Have students locate known and unknown information on their map by placing exclamation marks (!) next to familiar concepts and question marks (?) next to unfamiliar concepts as in the following example.

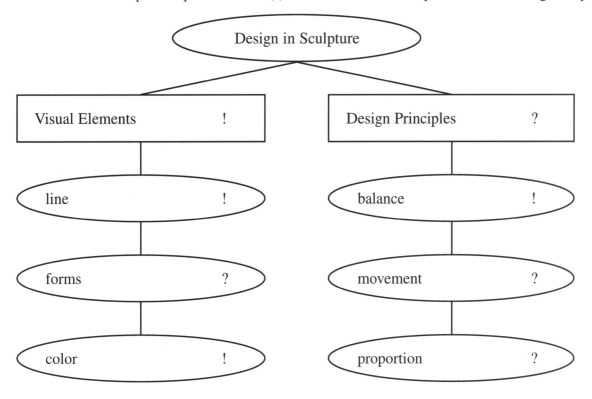

▶ Based on *Art: Images and ideas.* (1992). Worcester, MA: Davis Publications.

4. Tell students to read the passage and add words or short phrases to their map. Explain that they should use information in the passage to confirm familiar concepts and that they should add information to the areas that were not familiar. The following example shows how to add information to an existing prediction map.

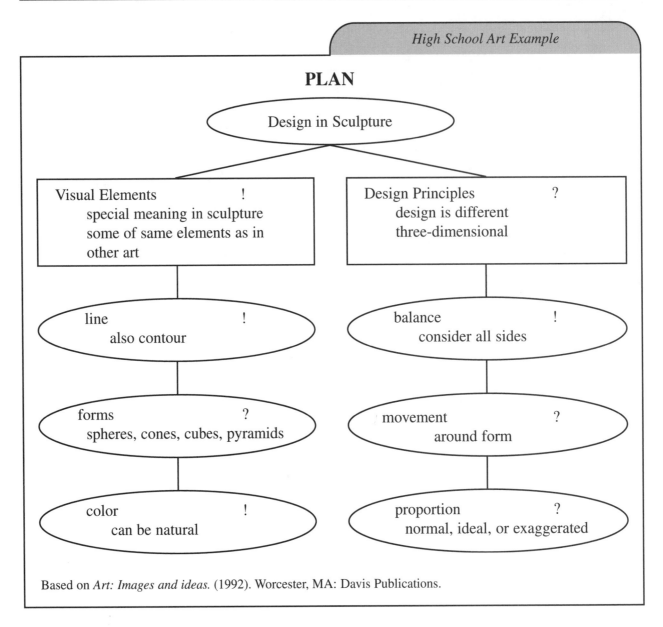

High School Art Example

PLAN

Design in Sculpture

Visual Elements   !
   special meaning in sculpture
   some of same elements as in
   other art

Design Principles   ?
   design is different
   three-dimensional

line   !
   also contour

balance   !
   consider all sides

forms   ?
   spheres, cones, cubes, pyramids

movement   ?
   around form

color   !
   can be natural

proportion   ?
   normal, ideal, or exaggerated

Based on *Art: Images and ideas.* (1992). Worcester, MA: Davis Publications.

5. Describe and demonstrate the final step in PLAN, which is for students to take note of their learning and to use it to accomplish their tasks. Students may choose to revise their prediction map using a different pattern. Then they should write a summary of the ideas. Emphasize that rereading, revising, recasting, and summarizing from their original maps can help students learn new information.

TEACHING STRATEGY 12

Summary Microtheme

In order to learn content information, students need to process that information deeply. One way to process information is to create a short summary of a passage in a textbook or a section of notes. A summary microtheme (Brozo & Simpson, 1995) is a type of summary that can be used in content area classes to help students process and learn material. A microtheme can be used in a number of ways. Teachers can assign microthemes to get a general picture about how well students understand main concepts; teachers can use microthemes to hold students accountable for learning a concept; and students can use microthemes to process information as they study.

Directions and Examples

1. Explain to students that a microtheme is a way for them to summarize a passage or concept in order to learn the material.

2. Tell students that you will be modeling an example of a microtheme. To demonstrate how to write a microtheme, use an example from your content area or use the examples that follow.

3. Identify a concept that you want students to understand. Locate a passage of text that explains the concept. Distribute copies of the passage to students. The following example is a passage about the chemical reaction that takes place when hair is curled or straightened.

> The curliness of your hair depends on how disulfide bonds are joined between parallel protein chains. When a person gets a permanent, curls are created or removed in three steps. Here's the chemical recipe. First, break the disulfide links between protein chains. Next, use a form (curlers, rollers, etc.) to curl or uncurl the hair. Third, rejoin the disulfide links between protein chains in their new orientation.

> ▶ From *ChemCom: Chemistry in the community* (3rd ed.). (1998). Dubuque, IA: Kendall/Hunt, p. 501.

4. Distribute note cards to each student. Ask students to read the passage and write a microtheme, or a short summary about the passage. After students have written a microtheme, write your own summary on the chalkboard or an overhead transparency, or use a computer with an LCD panel. Explain how you arrived at your summary by thinking aloud. Then have students compare their summary to yours. Many different summaries should be considered correct. An example of a summary microtheme about the preceding passage follows.

> A chemical reaction of breaking and reforming disulfide bonds is necessary to permanently change the curliness of hair.

5. Tell students that as they study they should stop occasionally and write a summary microtheme about the text. Tell students that by processing material they will remember it better.

6. An example of a summary microtheme based on a middle school literature story follows.

Middle School Literature Example

Summary Microtheme

Daedalus was exiled from Athens, so he sailed to Crete where he was befriended by King Minos. King Minos would not allow Daedalus to leave Crete, so Daedalus married and had a son, Icarus. Since Daedalus was homesick for Athens, he built wings for himself and Icarus. As they flew toward Athens, Icarus ignored his father's warning and soared too close to the sun. The heat melted his wings, and Icarus fell into the sea.

Based on Serraillier, I. (1995). A fall from the sky. In *Treasury of literature: Voices and reflections* (pp. 344–362). Orlando, FL: Harcourt Brace.

7.   Microthemes can be used in a number of ways. Students can use microthemes to practice identifying and summarizing information they have learned. You can use microthemes to assist students in processing information, or you may decide to evaluate or grade the microthemes that students write. A rubric is an appropriate assessment tool for the evaluation of summary microthemes. A six-point rubric that you can use or adapt to score summary microthemes follows.

Summary Microtheme
Evaluation Rubric

6   A summary that is scored a "6" meets all of the criteria for accuracy, comprehensiveness, and clear sentence structure. The main points in the text should appear correctly in the summary with all main points developed. The summary should be as comprehensive as possible and should read smoothly from beginning to end with appropriate transitions between ideas. The sentence structure should be clear and varied, without vagueness or ambiguity, and without more than one grammatical error.

5   A summary that is scored a "5" should be accurate and comprehensive, but it may lack perfect sentence structure. The summary may be clearly written but be somewhat unbalanced or less thorough than a "6" paper. It may show that the student has a minor misunderstanding of the material. A "5" summary should have no more than two grammatical errors.

4   A summary that is scored a "4" is one that is good but not excellent. It reveals a generally accurate reading of the passage with a clear sense of the main points of the material, but it will be noticeably weaker than a summary that is scored a "5" or a "6." The paper may be weak in its content, organization, or conventions but not all three.

3   A summary that is scored a "3" is strong in at least one area of competence, and it portrays a fairly clear and accurate view of the material being summarized. A "3" paper is either unbalanced or lacks the clarity and precision of a top-ranked summary. The sentence structure of a "3" paper frequently prevents inclusion of sufficient ideas for good comprehensiveness.

2   A summary that is scored a "2" is weak in all areas of competence, either because it is so poorly written that the reader cannot understand the content or because the content is inaccurate or disorganized.

1   A summary that is scored a "1" fails to meet any of the areas of competence.

Guided Reading And Summarizing Procedure (GRASP)

Summarizing text passages is a complex skill that takes guidance and practice. All too often, students are asked to summarize complex text without really understanding what a summary is or how to compress many ideas into a brief synopsis. Students can practice summarizing passages by using microthemes (see Teaching Strategy 7-12), or you can teach students how to summarize using the **G**uided **R**eading **A**nd **S**ummarizing **P**rocedure (GRASP) (Hayes, 1989). The goal of teaching GRASP is to enable students to summarize independently when they try to understand texts and when they study to learn text material.

Directions and Example

1. Provide students with a short passage of text that they can read easily. Explain that they will be writing a summary of the passage. You can use an example from your content area or the following example about Texas independence.

> In the 1820s, Americans began migrating into Mexican territory. Stephen Austin received permission from the Mexican government to found a colony of about 300 settlers in what is now east Texas. Austin led the first group of American settlers into the territory in 1822. By 1824, over 2,000 settlers lived in the area.
>
> Soon other agents arranged contracts for Americans to settle in Texas. By 1830 over 7,000 Americans lived in the area, more than twice the number of Mexicans in the territory. Worried that they were losing Texas through immigration, Mexico passed a law in 1830 prohibiting settling there.
>
> The Americans continued to move into the territory. As their numbers increased, the Americans demanded more political freedom. They declared independence for the Republic of Texas in 1836. Under the leadership of William Travis, the Americans began to fight for freedom. At the battle of the Alamo, the Mexicans routed the Americans. At a later battle, however, Sam Houston led the Americans to victory. Texans elected Sam Houston as their first president late in 1836.

> ▶ Adapted from *America: Pathways to the present.* (1998). Needham, MA: Prentice-Hall.

2. Ask students to read the passage independently with the purpose of remembering all that they can. After all students have finished reading, ask them to tell you what they remembered. List the items they volunteer on the chalkboard or an overhead transparency, or use a computer with an LCD panel. The following examples are taken from the preceding passage.

Students' first recollections

> Americans moved into Mexican territory.
> Austin was the leader of the settlers.
> Mexico began to discourage settlers.
> Americans continued to move into the area.
> Americans declared independence.
> Mexico won at the Alamo.
> The Americans won the next fight.

3. Have students reread the passage with the purpose of making additions and deletions to the list. Revise the list as needed.

Students' first recollections	Additions/corrections
Americans moved into Mexican territory.	During the 1820s, Americans moved into Mexican territory.
Austin was the leader of the settlers.	There were over 2,000 settlers by 1824.
Mexico began to discourage settlers.	Mexico passed a law prohibiting more settlers.
Americans continued to move into the area.	Americans continued to move into the area.
Americans declared independence.	In 1836 Americans declared independence.
Mexico won at the Alamo.	Mexico won at the Alamo.
The Americans won the next fight.	Under the leadership of Sam Houston, the Americans beat the Mexicans.

4. Ask students to organize the remembered information. Suggest categories for the list they generated. List the categories and ask students to divide the items on the list into categories. The following example is based on the preceding passage.

Category: Settling Mexican Territory

During the 1820s, Americans moved into Mexican territory.
There were over 2,000 settlers by 1824.
Mexico passed a law prohibiting more settlers.
Americans continued to move into the area.

Category: War for Independence

In 1836 Americans declared independence.
Mexico won at the Alamo.
Under the leadership of Sam Houston, the Americans beat the Mexicans.
In 1836 Texas elected its first president, Sam Houston.

5. Using the outline generated by categorizing the information, write a summary of the material. You might suggest that students begin with a main idea statement for the first main heading with the details as subheadings. Show students an example of a summary paragraph as in the following example.

Summary

During the 1820s Americans began settling Mexican territory, which is now east Texas. By 1824 there were over 2,000 settlers. Americans kept moving into the territory. Then Mexico passed a law prohibiting more settlers. Americans, however, continued to move into the area. By the 1830s the Americans began to want independence from Mexican authority. In 1836 the Americans declared independence. Mexico and the Americans went to war. Mexico won the famous battle of the Alamo, but the Americans won the war.

Chapter 8

Preparing for Tests

Overview

We all can remember taking tests. For some of us, it's a distant memory—perhaps the comprehensive examination that was part of our master's program. For others, test taking is a part of our lives in college courses or when we get a notice from the Secretary of State that tells us a written test will be required when we go to renew our driver's license. Still others think about the anxiety that frequently comes with the thought of taking the *Graduate Record Examination, Miller Analogies Test,* or some other test as part of the application process for graduate study.

Test taking is an ongoing occurrence for our students. Think about the types of tests you give to students. Perhaps you use mostly true-false, multiple-

choice, and essay tests. A colleague may use mostly matching and fill-in-the-blank tests. By the time students leave high school, they have probably taken a driver's license test and the SAT or ACT. The use of these latter two tests has become so widespread that the initials alone communicate identification—even on the world wide web where over 30 pages of information can be accessed for each test.

If our instruction is responsive to students' needs, there is no doubt that students will profit from the acquisition of general and specific test-preparation strategies and test-wiseness training. Such strategies and training can be useful for the tests you give to students as well as for the standardized tests students take. "The research literature supports the idea that special instruction in preparing for and taking a test can lead to higher scores" (Flippo & Caverly, 1991, p. 295).

This chapter contains a number of strategies that will be helpful to students. First, you can help students learn or review some general test-preparation strategies by showing students how to find out about tests they will be asked to take. A six-day, test-preparation plan can also be taught to students. Some of the ideas in this section will be developed in greater depth in other sections of the chapter.

Second, a number of tips and strategies for taking the four major types of objective tests (true-false, multiple-choice, fill-in-the-blank, and completion) are presented. Helping *all* students learn and use these strategies should increase test validity. For example, if all students are taught never to leave a question blank when there is no penalty for guessing, then all students will have an advantage because of this type of knowledge.

Third, we focus on essay tests and begin with a general plan to assist students in taking essay tests. Students will learn how to estimate how much they should write and how to identify the topic and task when answering essay questions. To actually prepare for essay tests, you can help students learn to use PORPE (Simpson, 1986), a powerful teaching and learning strategy. This section concludes with some strategies for answering major types of essay questions.

Fourth, a section is devoted to helping students understand scores from your tests as well as standardized tests. Because the ACT and SAT are taken by many high school students, some helpful tips for taking these tests are presented along with some electronic resources on the world wide web.

The strategies presented in this chapter should help students develop an overall study plan and learn valuable test-taking tips. Through your careful, reflective instruction, students will be better able to demonstrate their understanding of the content taught.

8.1 Preparing for Tests

Goal
To help students develop and use a plan for general test preparation.

Background

The basis for good performance on tests begins with effective strategies for reading, learning, and studying. Previous chapters in this book have provided useful information and numerous strategies. In this section, we offer ideas you can use to help students develop a plan for test preparation. As with most plans, there will probably need to be adaptations to fit your modes of assessment. Ideally, the information in this section would be presented early in your course so students can use the strategies throughout the semester or year.

TEACHING STRATEGY 1

Finding Out About the Test

Preparing for a test is made easier when numerous specifications are made available to students. In this strategy, students will learn more about some of these specifications and how to ask questions to acquire helpful information about a test.

1. Discuss important questions students want answered about a test that will be given in your class. The discussion could take place with partners or in small groups.

2. Ask students to write down their questions. Then engage in whole class sharing where the questions are written on the chalkboard or an overhead transparency. Accept all ideas, even those that are offered for a comic effect (e.g., What are the answers?).

3. Give students time to assign the various questions to logical categories. The questions might be categorized into areas such as general information (e.g., day, time, what can be used), types of test items, point values, general areas covered, and specific tips. Then the questions within each category might be prioritized through group discussion and sharing. Categories and questions will vary; nevertheless, you may want to ensure that the following questions are included.

    - When is the test (exact day)?
    - How much time do we have for the test?
    - What must we have for the test (pencil, calculator, etc.)?
    - What can we use while taking the test?
    - What kind of test is it (essay, true-false, matching, etc.)?
    - Do different types of items comprise the test?
    - If there are different types of items, how many of each type are there?

- What are the point values of the various items?
- Will a choice of questions be offered?
- What specific chapters or contents are covered on the test?
- What information is especially important to know from our reading and/or notes that might be on the test?
- What important vocabulary words or concepts should we know?
- What study strategies might be especially useful?
- Will you give us some sample items like those on the test?
- What tips do you have for studying so we can do well on the test?

4. Consider compiling tips from the foregoing discussion that are especially useful to your students and distribute them to your students. Encourage students to take responsibility and ask you questions from the list a week or so before a test is given. Consistent use of this list should help students begin to internalize the types of questions that will give them useful information for tests. Students can also be invited to use these or similar questions in their other classes where tests are used.

TEACHING STRATEGY 2

A Test-Preparation Plan

There is little doubt that students who perform well on tests have consciously or unconsciously developed a plan for study and test preparation. Other students may be uncertain or confused about what they can do to enhance their chances of doing well on a test. Although individual differences exist among students' test-preparation strategies or the lack of them, the following general plan is offered as a foundation upon which to build. The plan begins at least six days before the test is given.

Countdown: 6 Days Before the Test

1. Remind students that many of the questions in "Finding Out About the Test" (see Teaching Strategy 8-1) are useful for developing a test-preparation plan.

2. Discuss and review the important areas in which to gather information:

   - areas that will be included on the test
   - the type of test items and point values
   - general and specific tips for the test

3. Stress that students need to begin studying for the test at least six days before the test. Help students develop a study schedule with specific times for studying set aside. Tell students that the types of items on the test will influence their test preparation and, if necessary, help students make the connection between studying and types of test questions. (See Sections 8.2 and 8.3 for specific strategies for taking objective and essay tests. Teach these strategies as appropriate.)

Read, Review, Study, and Plan: 5, 4, 3, and 2 Days Before the Test

1. Have students note the assigned readings that will be included on the test. Any reading not completed should be done.

2. Tell students that they can begin reviewing immediately. Have students share ideas about what to review. Examples follow.

   - text
   - text notes
   - class notes
   - important vocabulary

   Encourage students to raise questions in class so you can explain information that is unclear or unknown.

3. Help students refine their plan for study and review. (See Chapter 7 for a number of ideas related to studying.) Stress the need for regular study periods distributed over time. Tell students to begin learning and putting into memory main ideas, important concepts, and supporting details and to review this information several times a day over a period of several days.

4. Encourage students to review their text and class notes. One way to review is to rewrite the information in briefer form. To be most effective, review should be both thoughtful and intentional. You should model this process for students.

5. Tell students to devote time to predicting questions that might be on the test and have students practice answering these questions. At first, students can refer to their text and/or notes, but later the answers should be written from memory. You may want to model the process of predicting questions by writing them on the chalkboard or an overhead transparency, or using a computer with an LCD panel.

   A science teacher, for example, might say the following: "We have been studying different types of root systems. I want to predict possible questions that might be asked about root systems. I am able to ask four different types of questions about root systems. For the test, it may be a good idea to learn the two types of root systems, be able to recall and describe them, and to know at least one example of each." Then invite students to react to the questions and share additional questions.

   True-false: There are two basic types of root systems. (T)

   Completion: The two basic types of root systems are _____ and _____. (fibrous, taproot)

   Matching: Match the two root systems with the correct characteristics or examples.

1. fibrous	__2__	carrot
2. taproot	__1__	many branching roots
	__1__	corn
	__2__	dandelions
	__2__	go deep into the soil

   Essay: Describe the two basic root systems and give an example of each.

6. Remind students that the night before the test is a time for final preparations. In addition to study and review, a good night's sleep is helpful, and such sleep is likely to occur if an intentional study plan has been initiated and executed. Students should also be reminded to gather materials needed for the test (e.g., pencils, pens, calculator, paper) before going to bed.

The Day of the Test

1. Before leaving for school, students should eat a breakfast that will give them the energy they need. They should also be sure they have the necessary supplies for the test.

2. If time exists before the test, students should be encouraged to review their course materials and notes.

3. When the test is given, students may find the following suggestions useful.

    • Take two or three deep breaths to help you relax.
    • Survey the entire test to get a general idea of what you will need to do.
    • Read the directions carefully and underline any key words.
    • Make sure you answer the questions asked.
    • Answer the easy questions first.
    • Look over your test when you have finished; double check your answers to be sure you did not omit any questions.

    The test preparation checklist on the next page may be used with students or adapted for your use.

Students often have a study period before a test to review their notes. Rereading the suggestions given in this section will provide further test-taking strategies.

Test Preparation Checklist

Here are some tips to help you organize as you get ready for a test. Answer the questions as honestly as possible. If you are able to answer "yes" to each question, then you are probably ready for the test.

		YES	NO
1.	Do I know what type of test I'll be taking (multiple-choice, essay, etc)?	———	———
2.	Do I know which general and specific areas will be covered?	———	———
3.	Have I studied a little at a time over several days, not waiting until the last minute?	———	———
4.	Have I reviewed my notes and readings carefully?	———	———
5.	Have I looked up key vocabulary words in order to understand them?	———	———
6.	Do I know important words that are printed in boldface or italics in the textbook?	———	———
7.	Have I skimmed the chapter headings to recall the overall ideas in each chapter?	———	———
8.	Can I recall the main ideas listed in the chapter summaries?	———	———
9.	Have I looked at charts, diagrams, or illustrations for important information?	———	———
10.	Can I answer the review or study questions at the end of the chapter?	———	———
11.	Have I thought of some questions that are likely to be on the test, and have I written my answers?	———	———
12.	Do I have the materials I need for the test?	———	———

Based on Lenski, S.D., Marciniec, P.V., & Johns, J.L. (1998). *Study smart and test terrific.* Normal, IL: Illinois Reading Council.

8.2 Taking Objective Tests

Goal

To help students learn strategies for taking objective tests.

Background

This section considers true-false, multiple-choice, matching, and fill-in-the-blank or completion tests. For each type of objective test, a series of tips and some ways to put the tips into practice are provided.

Ritter and Idol-Maestas (1986) have suggested the use of SCORER, a general memory device to help students take tests.

S = Schedule your time while taking the test.
C = Use clue words to help answer questions.
O = Omit difficult questions at first.
R = Read questions carefully.
E = Estimate your time.
R = Review your responses.

Share and discuss SCORER with your students. Budgeting time, reading carefully, noting key words, and reviewing thoughtfully are general test-taking strategies that can be developed within the context of your content area. Help students learn strategies for the specific types of objective tests you use. Whenever possible, the following ideas should be integrated into your content area to increase meaning and relevance. Also, remind students that even though there are some strategies for successfully completing objective tests, learning the content is key.

TECHNOLOGY TIP

Creating Tests with Software Programs

There are a number of software programs that you can use to create tests. The programs have format flexibility and may help you save significant amounts of time.

Quiz Writer Plus: a test generator that also has databases of questions in popular subject areas. Midwest Agribusiness Services, Inc. (800-523-3475).

Test Designer Supreme: used by teachers and students to create and modify tests and assignments. Super School Software (800-248-7099).

Test Quest: supports multiple-choice, true-false, completion, matching, and essay test formats. Snowflake Software (914-876-3328).

Test Quick: helps create tests in multiple-choice, true-false, question-response, and fill-in-the-blank formats. Jackson Software (800-850-1777).

True-False Tests

True-false tests are used in many content area classrooms. To help ensure that you are actually assessing content knowledge, you can share tips for taking true-false tests. The usefulness of the various tips to taking true-false tests will be made more powerful by using examples from your content area.

1.   Begin by sharing and discussing the following tips for taking true-false tests.

- Read each statement carefully. Statements that contain *never, always, all, more, impossible,* or *nothing* are usually false. Words such as *usually, generally, sometimes,* and *seldom* indicate that the statement is probably true. As a general guideline, help students understand that absolute statements (e.g., *all, none*) are usually false, while qualified statements (e.g., *usually, seldom*) are usually true.
- Assume that long statements are more likely to be true than short statements.
- Watch for negatives such as "not" or the prefix "in," because a negative can completely change the meaning of a statement.
- Simplify a statement that contains a double negative by eliminating both negatives.
- Look for statements that are partially true. If a statement is not completely true, the statement is probably false. All parts of a statement should be correct before it is marked as true.
- Assume that a statement is true unless it can be proved false.
- Never leave a true-false statement unanswered unless there is a penalty for guessing. Make a calculated guess if the answer is unknown, because there is a 50% chance of getting the answer correct.
- Assume that the statements are straightforward; do not read too much into them.
- Write T and F neatly or be sure you mark the correct space on the answer sheet.

2.   Model (think aloud) how you would put these tips into practice with several questions based on materials you have been using for instruction. The following items are based on the reading passage "Frozen in Time." The thought process is what you and students can model with specific items from your content area as in the following example.

Item 1.   Pliny wrote about the destruction of Pompeii.

Thought process for answer: I remember someone wrote about Pompeii being destroyed, but I can't remember the name. I remember he was a young boy and his writing wasn't read for many years. Pliny could be his name, but I really don't know. I won't lose anything by trying, but if I leave it blank, I'll get it wrong for sure. I know there is no penalty for guessing so I'll mark this answer true.

Item 2.   Volcanoes always erupt so quickly that people in their paths can't escape.

Thought process for answer: I think that's what happened to Pompeii, but I'm not sure it always is that way with volcanoes. I think I heard Mt. St. Helens in Washington erupted, and the people were warned in time to get off of the mountain. I don't think volcanoes always erupt that quickly, and I know that I should be cautious about answering true for a question that has the word always. I think the answer is false.

Item 3.   Pompeii was destroyed by a hurricane 2,000 years ago.

Thought process for answer: I know Pompeii was destroyed, and I remember that it was about 2,000 years ago. The reason I remember the date is because my house address is 2000. We saw pictures of Pompeii after it was discovered again, and I remember a mountain in the background. Pompeii was also by the sea, but I'm sure it wasn't destroyed by a hurricane. That means the answer is false because the part about the hurricane is false.

Item 4.   Pompeii was discovered when some workmen were digging a tunnel and found an ancient wall.

Thought process for answer: This question has a great deal of specific information and is longer than most of the questions. I remember that Pompeii was discovered by some local people, and I think the answer is true.

Item 5.   The people of Pompeii were frozen in time when they were covered by the volcanic eruption of Mt. Vesuvius.

Thought process for answer: There's part of the question that I know for sure, and that is that Pompeii was covered by the volcanic eruption of Mt. Vesuvius. I'm not sure, however, what "frozen in time" means. That might mean something about a glacier or an ice flow, but I don't see how that could have happened. Maybe it means that all of their clocks stopped. That doesn't make sense. They didn't have clocks back then. Perhaps "frozen in time" doesn't mean anything special, just that people were stopped at what they were doing. That would be the simplest answer, and I know we're not supposed to read a lot into the test question. I think I'll just answer true.

▶ Adapted from Johns, J.L., & Lenski, S.D. (1997). *Improving reading: A handbook of strategies* (2nd ed.). Dubuque, IA: Kendall/Hunt.

3. Assign groups of students to prepare true-false items on different sections of text materials or information shared in class. Information from laboratory experiences may also be used. Then mix the groups so the statements can be shared, answered, discussed, and verified. Refer, when appropriate, to the tips for answering true-false statements. You may also wish to duplicate and share a list of tips with students so they can use them in developing their questions and refer to them later when studying for a test.

TEACHING STRATEGY **4**

Multiple-Choice Tests

1. Tell students that multiple choice tests are made up of a stem and choices. Stress that students need to read the stem *before* reading the choices and try to predict a correct response. If necessary, clarify the meaning of the term *stem*. Also, tell students to read all the choices carefully before making a final choice. Sometimes a response may be partly correct, but it is not the best choice. Make a sample question based on the material being taught and model the process by "thinking aloud" as exemplified in the section on the true-false tests. The tips below are designed to be used when students do not know the correct answer.

TEACHING STRATEGY **3**

2. Remind students to note any negatives because they can choose the wrong answer by skipping an important word in the question. An example of a negative follows.

> Which of the following was not a cause of World War I?

In this example, students could eliminate causes and then select the choice that is not a cause.

3. Explain to students that they should also look for clues in the tests. Tell them that if a choice is much longer and more detailed than the others, it is usually the correct answer. If a word in a choice also appears in the statement, it is probably the correct choice. Stress that these clues are tips, and they should be applied with careful thought.

4. Encourage students to try to eliminate incorrect choices. Stress that if they eliminate an unreasonable answer, they have a greater chance of choosing a correct answer. You might model this type of thinking similar to the following example.

> The speed of sound through air is
>
> A. 3,700 feet per second.
> B. 1,085 feet per second.
> C. 2 feet per second.
> D. 186 miles per second.

Thought process for answer: My chance of selecting the correct response increases if I can eliminate one or more possible answers. If there are four choices, my chance of selecting correctly by guessing is 25%. If I can eliminate two of the choices, my chance of selecting correctly is 50%. I'm really not sure about the speed of sound. Let me see. I know it's really fast. Looking at the answers, I can tell that one answer is definitely false. There's no way C could be correct because I know sound travels more than two feet per second. I'm ruling out C, and I'm not thinking about it again.

5. Explain that when two choices are similar, they are both probably incorrect. Again, modeling the thinking behind this tip might be helpful.

> The universal donor is
>
> A. O.
> B. H_2O.
> C. AB.
> D. water.

Thought process for answer: I think I know which type of blood is the universal donor, but I'm not sure. The answers that have two types of blood, are A and C. The other two answers are the same. H_2O (answer B) is the same thing as water (answer D). I can choose only one correct answer, and neither B nor D could be correct because they both say the same thing and water is not a blood type.

6. Explain that when two of the choices are opposites, one of them is always wrong and the other is usually correct. Refer to A and B in the following example.

     A molecule is

     A. the largest part of something.
     B. the smallest part of something.
     C. always solid.
     D. invisible.

7. Remind students that the answer must be grammatically correct. If students find answer choices that do not fit grammatically with the question, they are probably incorrect. An example follows.

     The largest land animal is an

     A. whale.
     B. elephant.
     C. horse.
     D. hippopotamus.

8. Tell students that a viable choice that includes one or more of the others is likely to be correct. Use an example from material being taught and share your thought processes with students.

9. Remind students that there may be clues in the stems of other items that could be helpful in resolving a question with which they are experiencing difficulty. Then ask students to explain how these clues might be discerned. It is possible that students could remember and share a specific example from a past test.

10. Tell students to skip a difficult question and go to the next question. They should make a mark beside the skipped question so they can return to it later. This strategy has four advantages: 1) it does not waste time; 2) the correct answer may come to students while they are thinking of something else; 3) helpful clues may occur in the stems of other questions; and 4) students will not become overly frustrated about any single item.

11. Additional clues that may be useful to students are offered by Antes (1989, p. 20).

     • If the word *none* or *all* is used in a response, it is usually incorrect.
     • If *some* or *often* is used in a response, it is likely to be correct.
     • If *all of the above* is a response, determine whether at least two of the responses seem appropriate before selecting all of the above.
     • If one response is more precise or technical, it is more likely to be correct than a general response. If you are unsure about a response and the correct response for many items on the test tends to be longer, select the longer response.

12. Assign groups of students to prepare multiple-choice questions on different sections of material being used in class. The questions can be written on the chalkboard or overhead transparencies and discussed with the entire class. Have students share the tips they use to select their answers. To enhance learning opportunities, individual students can also be invited to share their thought processes by thinking aloud.

13. Duplicate and share the following tips for taking multiple-choice tests so they can be referred to by students when studying for tests.

20 Tips for Taking Multiple-Choice Tests

1. Read the stem *before* reading the choices and try to predict the answer.

2. Read all the choices carefully before making a final choice.

3. A response that is only partly correct is *probably* not the best choice.

4. Note any negatives (e.g., no, not) and be sure your choice fits the stem.

5. If a choice is much longer and more detailed than the others, it *may* be the correct answer.

6. If a word in a choice also appears in the statement, it *may* be the correct answer.

7. Improve your chances by eliminating one or more unreasonable choices.

8. When two of the choices are similar, they are both *probably* incorrect.

9. When two of the choices are opposites, one of them is always wrong, and the other choice is *usually* correct.

10. If answer choices do not fit grammatically with the question stem, they are *probably* incorrect.

11. A choice that includes one or more of the other choices is *likely* to be correct.

12. If *none* or *all* is used in a choice, it is *usually* incorrect.

13. If *some* or *often* is used in a choice, it is *likely* to be correct.

14. If *all of the above* is a choice, determine whether at least two of the other choices seem appropriate before selecting *all of the above*.

15. If one choice is more precise or technical, it is more likely to be correct than a more general choice.

16. If you are unsure about a response and the correct choice for many items on the test tends to be longer, select the longer choice.

17. For a difficult question, put a mark beside it and go to the next question. Come back to the question at the end of the test or at any time when other questions give you a helpful clue to the answer to the difficult question.

18. Be alert to clues in the stem of other questions that may be helpful with a difficult question.

19. Mark your answers or your answer sheet carefully.

20. Make a calculated guess if you are not sure of the right answer, unless there is a penalty for guessing.

Matching Tests

1. Explain to students that in a matching test items from one column are matched with those in another. If needed, provide a simple matching test related to your classroom, such as the following one.

_____	on the wall	A. chart
_____	near the chalkboard	B. clock
_____	in the front of the room	C. books
_____	on the shelf	D. desk

Spend a few minutes and demonstrate or model how you would take the test, using the process of elimination.

2. Share and discuss the following tips for taking matching tests.

   • Carefully read all of the items in both columns before answering.
   • Begin by making the easiest matches.
   • Cross out items in both columns as they are used.
   • Make all the correct matches possible before guessing at any of the other matches.
   • Make the best guesses possible for the remaining items.

3. Provide an example of a matching test from your content area and model the reasoning used to select the various answers. Try to incorporate the tips listed above. A sample is shown below (Johns & Lenski, 1997).

_C_	an animal with a backbone	A. butterfly
_D_	an amphibian	B. starfish
_B_	a spiny-skinned animal	C. snake
_A_	an animal without a backbone	D. alligator

4. Share the rationale for the above choices by saying something like the following. After reading all of the items, it seems that a spiny-skinned animal is the starfish. An amphibian can live in and out of the water. Only an alligator can do that; I know that a butterfly and starfish can't. I also know a snake and an alligator have backbones, but if I use alligator as an amphibian, that would leave snake as the animal with a backbone. I think the butterfly is the animal without a backbone. Even though I don't know if the starfish has a backbone, it is the only spiny-skinned animal.

5. Have students develop matching tests from materials used in your content area. Students can share their tests with others. Use discussion and invite students to think aloud to enhance their ability to perform well on matching tests.

TEACHING STRATEGY **6**

Completion or Fill-in-the-Blank Tests

1. Begin by sharing the tips for completion tests listed below.

    - Read the entire sentence or paragraph containing the blank line.
    - Use the length of the blank line as a clue unless all of the blank lines are similar in length.
    - Decide on the word or phrase that best fits.
    - The word or phrase must fit the blank grammatically.
    - Reread the entire sentence including your word to determine if it fits and sounds correct.
    - When a blank begins the sentence, be sure to capitalize the first word.

    Invite students to share additional ideas from their experiences.

2. Remind students that fill-in-the-blank tests are different from other types of objective tests because information for the answer must be recalled from memory. Because many true-false and multiple-choice items tap recognition, guessing is usually much easier with such items.

3. Encourage students to learn key vocabulary and important details that may be possible test items. One way to help such acquisition is to provide sentences with blanks that cover specific and key parts of a chapter. For example, the following items are based on a chapter dealing with plant support and transport.

    - Herbaceous stems are usually _____ and _____ in color.

    - Bundles of xylem and phloem in herbaceous stems are arranged _____.

    - Some examples of herbaceous stems are _____, _____, and _____.

    - The tissue that stores food in plants is known as _____.

4. Take time to discuss answers for the blanks, and stress the importance of knowing the information so it can be recalled on a test. Help students realize that "knowing the information" means that it is memorized.

5. Share some memorization techniques for recalling information that may be used for objective and essay tests. Mnemonic devices represent memory strategies that can help students retain and recall bits of information. Whenever possible, have students make a personal connection to the material. Examples of mnemonic devices that can be taught to students follow.

- *Rhyme*
  Create a rhyme or a song that includes the points you have to learn.

  Thirty days hath September . . .

- *Acronyms*
  Form words by using the first letter from each of the words to be recalled.

  HOMES (Names of the Great Lakes: Huron, Ontario, Michigan, Erie, Superior).

- *Pegwood*
  Memorize a short rhyme and then create the images that link the nouns in the rhyme with the items to be remembered.

- *Method of Loci*
  Select a spatial layout, such as your home. Mentally place the items to be recalled in each room.

- *Clustering*
  Memorize the material in categories and learn them as a pattern.

- *Silly Sentences*
  Make up a silly sentence from the first letter of each word to be remembered. Even After Dinner, Giraffes Bend Easily (guitar strings E, A, D, G, B, E).

- *Numbering*
  When you are memorizing a group of words, remember how many items there are to avoid missing any when you need to recall them.

6. Provide opportunities for students to develop fill-in-the-blank items based on their readings and/or class notes. These items can be exchanged, answered, and discussed.

8.3 Taking Essay Tests

Background

Broadly defined, essay items may be answered in a sentence, a paragraph, or a composition. In this section, the focus is on written responses, a paragraph or longer, that are completed in class.

Essay questions may be one of the best ways to assess how well students can evaluate, analyze, and synthesize course content. In addition to these higher-order thinking skills, essays also test memory. Galica (1991, p. 8) has offered seven keys to help students prepare for and write good essay examinations. We have adapted them as follows.

1. Be prepared: know your material.
2. Try to anticipate the questions and practice answering them.
3. Tell the answer to each question; show that you know the material (support or explain your answer); then end.
4. Think of your response more as an intelligent conversation; avoid the perfect draft syndrome.
5. Plan your response to fit the allocated amount of time.
6. Use simple, clear, and direct writing.
7. Integrate good information (e.g., facts, examples) with the big picture (e.g., intelligent generalizations, conclusions).

To help students achieve in these seven areas, you can first teach a broad plan to assist students with essay tests. Then teach students how to use PORPE (Simpson, 1986) to prepare for essay tests. Next, teach students how to react to the test itself. Finally, teach students strategies for organizing and writing the essay.

TEACHING STRATEGY 7

Taking Essay Tests: An Action Plan

When students receive an essay test, they need an overall plan. Although the action plan we present takes several pages to describe, it only requires a few minutes of students' time in an actual test situation. Here are the five parts of the action plan (Galica, 1991).

1. Look over the test.
2. Estimate length of responses.
3. Read the questions.
4. Choose your question (if there is a choice).
5. Decide on the order for answering.

You may wish to develop a chart that contains the five steps of the action plan. It can be used for teaching each of the five steps, and it can be posted in the classroom as a reference for students when they take essay tests.

We recommend that you model the steps below using one of your tests, highlighting specific, helpful elements. Modeling the entire process should be especially helpful to students. Do your best to use examples from previous tests, or guide students in areas that are particularly useful for your tests. Spending ample time to teach students to use the steps will enhance their performance on your essay tests.

Look over the test.

1. Tell students that their first task is to look over the test quickly and determine how many questions need to be answered. They should also read the directions. If there are several sections, students should read the directions for each one.

2. You might model with the following directions. Below are four essay questions. Choose two of the questions and answer them. Each question is worth 50 points. You have the entire period for the test.

3. Think aloud by saying something like the following:

    As I read the directions, I see that I must answer two questions so I'll circle the two. I also have a choice of questions. Because each question is worth the same number of points, I'll need to spend about the same amount of time on each. The class period is 50 minutes long, and there are now about 40 minutes left. That means I can spend about 20 minutes on each question. I'll write 20 minutes beside each question so I can remember.

4. Invite students to explain what you did. Then share some different directions and ask a student to think aloud, sharing his or her plan.

5. For those questions worth more points than others, be sure students understand that the time spent on each one should probably be proportionate to the value of the question. In addition, students should write down the estimated time to devote to each question.

6. Invite a student to summarize the important points, and write them on the chalkboard or an overhead transparency, as in the following example.

    *   Read directions.
    *   Determine the number of questions that must be answered (circle or note the number).
    *   Decide how much time to spend on each one (note the amount of time beside each question).

7. Have students make up directions for an essay test, exchange them with another student, and then think aloud with the partner. Invite whole class sharing and discussion.

Estimate length of responses.

The following activity will help students realize how much they can write in a specific amount of time. This understanding should help students visualize the amount they can write in five-minute intervals.

1. Invite students to take out a sheet of paper and write on every line at a swift pace until you say stop. Students should write legibly. The content can be whatever passes through their minds. The same sentence could also be written repeatedly. After exactly five minutes, tell students to stop.

2. Ask students to count the number of words they have written. According to Galica (1991), most people will write approximately 125 words in five minutes.

3. Have students share the number of words they wrote. If you wish, determine the class average. Then have students compare their papers. Students whose handwriting is extraordinarily large will appear to have written more; those with extraordinarily small handwriting will appear to have written less. After comparisons, have students look at the area of the page they covered. This coverage is what can be expected in five minutes of writing if the paper on the exam is similar to the paper used for this activity.

4. Help students see that if they were going to devote 10 minutes to an essay question, they could estimate writing twice as much as their samples.

5. Remind students that the amount they write on the actual test will probably be somewhat less because of the time needed for thinking, organizing, and composing. The important point is to help students see what might be a realistic estimate of length for a 10-minute essay, a 15-minute essay, and so on.

Read the questions.

1. Tell students that an essay question will always specify the two T's: a topic and a task (Galica, 1991). The topic identifies the material students have to demonstrate they know. The task is what students have to prove they can do. Often, the task will appear as a direction (discuss, compare, contrast, summarize, etc.).

2. Use a question from your content area and demonstrate how students can identify the topic (underline it) and task (circle it). For example, a mathematics teacher might share the following:

   (Define) the term relation.

   In this example, the topic is the term relation and the task is to define it.

3. Note that the above question has only one topic and one task. Help students realize that while other essay questions may be longer and more complex, they can be marked up (circles and underlines) in a manner similar to the one-topic, one-task example.

4. Present more complex examples on the chalkboard or an overhead transparency and invite students to circle the task and underline the topic. Assist students as necessary. Although examples from your content area or other classes students are taking will be the most relevant and helpful, several questions from the science area are provided below.

   (Compare) the two common kinds of wetlands, and give an example of each.
   (Identify) and (describe) the five layers of woody stems.
   (Compare) and (contrast) bacterial cells and human cells.

Choose your questions.

1. Remind students that sometimes they may be able to choose among several questions. Invite students to share their ideas for how they will choose the questions they want to answer and those they want to omit.

2. Write students' ideas on the chalkboard under the categories Reasons to Choose and Reasons to Omit. Discuss their responses.

3.   Invite students to share how they could choose among questions they are not sure about. Fuse their ideas with the questions and tips listed below.

- Do I know enough about the topic to develop a suitable answer? (You could jot down any information that seems relevant.)
- Is the question broad or narrow? (Decide if you're a "big-picture person" or a "detail person.")
- How do the details fit into the big picture? (You could connect the main ideas by creating a concept map.)
- Which question may be more like others I have answered in the past? (You may have answered compare and contrast questions in the past and may feel comfortable with the basic way to respond. Or you may be able to take a position and support it.)

4.   Tell students that once they have made their decisions they should circle the numeral beside their selected questions.

Decide on the order for answering.

1.   Invite students to share their ideas for the order in which to answer questions. Because of individual differences, it is likely that students will have different response patterns.

2.   Honor their patterns of responding, but suggest the following tips.

- Begin with the short-answer questions. They may be the types of questions that help you activate other bits of knowledge and information that can be used in longer questions. Also, you won't get bogged down initially in a longer essay question.
- For the longer essay questions, begin with the question you feel most prepared to answer.
- Do not begin with a question just to get it out of the way.
- Remember that in the process of answering questions you may recall some information that would apply to a question you have not yet answered. Jot down a word or phrase next to that question to help you recall the information when needed.

TEACHING STRATEGY 8

Preparing for Essay Tests: PORPE

To help students become adept at taking essay tests and learning important course concepts, a metacognitive strategy called PORPE (Simpson, 1986) can be taught. PORPE stands for **P**redict, **O**rganize, **R**ehearse, **P**ractice, and **E**valuate. The keys to teaching PORPE successfully are to share the specific steps, provide extensive modeling, give repeated practice in concrete and realistic contexts, and tell students why these five areas are important to their learning (Simpson, 1986). You can readily see that teaching this strategy will take some time, but the result will be that students "learn how to behave as effective and mature readers" (Simpson, 1986, p. 408).

An overview of PORPE is given in the box on the next page; it may be shared with students or developed into a chart to be placed in the classroom.

> **Preparing for Essay Tests**
> **PORPE Strategy**
>
> 1. **P**redict possible essay questions from your reading.
>
> 2. **O**rganize the information to answer the questions.
>
> 3. **R**ehearse and memorize the information so it can be recalled from long-term memory.
>
> 4. **P**ractice recalling the answers to the questions by writing the answers.
>
> 5. **E**valuate the quality of your practice essay answer.

Predict

1. Introduce the language used for writing essay tests by sharing and discussing a list such as the following one.

Key Word	Meaning
enumerate	to name one at a time
illustrate	to explain with examples
trace	to tell the history or development
compare	to point out similarities and differences
contrast	to discuss the differences
summarize	to give a brief description of important points
evaluate	to discuss the merits of
justify	to give reasons for
critique	to summarize and evaluate
apply	to put into action
analyze	to separate into parts or basic principles
criticize	to judge the merits or faults of
explain	to make plain; expound

2. Model the procedures you use to predict possible essay questions from a chapter of your text or a particular unit of instruction. Write the questions on the chalkboard or an overhead transparency, or use a computer with an LCD panel. Then discuss how and why they were selected. Help students realize that important aspects of the chapter or unit are the basis for most essay questions.

3. Continue to model the process of formulating questions. Then gradually guide students to provide the stems for potential essay questions relating to a specific topic. For example, if part of a text chapter discussed bacterial cells and human cells, you could have students begin their predicted questions with the words *compare* and *contrast* or possibly *explain the difference between.*

4. When you believe students are getting the knack of formulating questions, have them develop their own questions for a specific chapter or unit. Often, boldface headings and chapter summaries provide possible topics for essay questions and reduce the common tendency for students to focus on details instead of key ideas.

5. Have students share their questions with partners or in small groups. Then use whole group discussion and sharing to arrive at the most plausible questions for the essay test.

Organize

1. Organize means to summarize and synthesize the key ideas from the chapter, unit, or area of study. Students are asked to organize their answers to one of the plausible essay questions using a graphic map, chart, outline, or other suitable scheme.

2. Model this process for students from your own map, chart, or outline. Show students how this aid can be used to rehearse and practice for the essay test.

3. Have students work in small groups to brainstorm possible questions and organize possible answers. Invite a student from each group to share the predicted questions and organizational structure (probably a map, chart, or outline).

4. Discuss the work of various groups and possibly have students develop their own map or outline for a different essay question. Provide written or oral feedback to the students. Feedback can focus on the areas shown in the following chart, or you can adapt the chart to fit your particular situation.

Unit/Chapter _____ Name _____

Area for Evaluation	Improve	OK	Good
Accuracy of information			
Completeness of information			
Organization of information			
Examples (if appropriate)			

Rehearse

1. Stress that the goal of rehearsal is to help students place the organization, key ideas, examples, etc. of the chapter or unit into their long-term memory so they can be recalled during the essay test. Remind students that to rehearse means to perfect by repetition.

2. Help students recognize that recall is different from recognition, a skill often used in multiple-choice tests (see Section 8.2). Recall demands memorization and is best accomplished over several days of study.

3. Share the following guide with students to help them with their rehearsal and memorization. Remind students that the rehearsal time necessary to memorize information will vary. Stress, however, the need to rehearse the material over several days.

Tips for Rehearsal and Memorization

What You Can Do	Check (✓) Times Practiced								
1. Recite aloud the overall structure of your map, chart, or outline.									
2. Test yourself by repeating the structure orally or by writing it.									
3. Add key ideas and examples one section at a time. Test yourself as in 2.									
4. Add other sections and test yourself as in 2.									
5. Test yourself several times over a few days to ensure the information is in your memory. Go back to previous steps as needed.									

Based on Simpson, M.L. (1986). PORPE: A writing strategy for studying and learning in the content areas. *Journal of Reading, 29,* 407–414.

4. Have students work with a partner or in a group to talk-through (Simpson, 1993) their map, chart, or outline. After a specified amount of time, have students discuss and evaluate each talk-through. If desired, a chart similar to that provided under "organize" may be used.

Practice

1. In this step, students practice writing, from memory, the answers to their predicted essay questions. Prior to actual practice, it is helpful to provide numerous examples of essay answers of varying quality. A clear and focused discussion of the strengths and weaknesses of the answers should help students acquire more knowledge about what makes a good essay.

2. Model the process of answering an essay question through the use of a talk-through. Specific tips are contained in An Action Plan (see Teaching Strategy 8-7) and Writing an Answer found later in this section.

Evaluate

1. In this step, students evaluate the quality of the practice essays they have written for their self-predicted questions.

2. Share an evaluation sheet similar to the following one on the next page and have students evaluate their answers.

Practice Essay Answer Evaluation

Directions: Evaluate the quality of your answer by using this checklist. If you score above average in the six areas, you are probably ready for the test. If, however, you find some of your answers to the predicted essay questions to be below average or average, go back to your notes, map, chart, or outline. Examine your organization again—did you leave out some key ideas or details? Review these ideas and details; then go through the steps again—**O**rganize, **R**ehearse, **P**ractice, and **E**valuate.

Evaluating Practice Essay Answers

	Below Average	Average	Above Average
1. I directly answered the question that was asked.	1	2	3
2. I had an introductory sentence that restated the essay.	1	2	3
3. I organized the essay answer with key ideas or points that were obvious.	1	2	3
4. I included in the answer relevant details or examples to prove and clarify each idea.	1	2	3
5. I used transitions in the answer to cue the reader (e.g., first, finally).	1	2	3
6. My answer made sense and demonstrated a knowledge of the content.	1	2	3

Adapted from Brozo, W.G., & Simpson, M.L. (1995). *Readers, teachers, learners: Expanding literacy in secondary schools* (2nd ed.). Columbus, OH: Merrill.

3. Distribute other sample essay answers and have small groups of students use the checklist to rank the various essays. Be sure to spend time discussing reasons for the rankings. After sufficient practice, students can complete similar tasks in pairs to evaluate each other's practice essays. Ultimately, each student should acquire the critical stance necessary to evaluate his or her practice questions in an objective manner so necessary review and rehearsal will be the natural outcome.

TEACHING STRATEGY 9

Writing an Essay

Every essay answer has three parts: an introduction or beginning, a middle or body, and a conclusion or end. These three parts of an essay answer are the foundation upon which responses are developed, although there are some special challenges for various types of essay questions. Galica (1991) has identified four types of essay questions.

1. single-topic questions
2. explicit multiple-part questions
3. implicit multiple-part questions
4. multiple-topic questions (such as compare-contrast)

Decide which type of questions you use and then model the appropriate strategies shown below. Whenever possible, use questions from your content area.

Single-Topic Questions

1.   Provide a sample question. For example, describe the environments in which the three types of archaebacteria exist.

2.   Help students to see that in a question of this type they will probably use a straight-line pattern. In other words, they will discuss a number of points one after another.

     • Hot environments
     • High salt concentrations
     • Lack of free oxygen

3.   Show students, by writing on the chalkboard or using an overhead transparency, how they might compose their answer. An example follows.

> There are three types of environments where archaebacteria can exist. One type of archaebacteria lives in hot environments that are acidic. An example of an environment would be hot sulfur springs.
> Another environment requires a high concentration of salt in order for the archaebacteria to exist. They can be found in salty areas along ocean borders and in places like the Great Salt Lake.
> The third place where archaebacteria exist is in areas where there is no free oxygen. They can be found in sewage treatment plants and even in the digestive tracts of some animals—including us!
> In summary, archaebacteria can live in environments that are hot and acidic, that contain lots of salt, and where there is no free oxygen.

4.   Invite students to evaluate the quality of the answer. Show how the straight-line pattern was used to answer the question.

Explicit Multiple-Part Questions/Implicit Multiple-Part Questions

1.   Write the words *explicit* and *implicit* on the chalkboard. Ask students to share their knowledge of the two words.

2.   Develop the idea that *explicit* means that something is clearly defined or carefully spelled out. *Implicit,* on the other hand, means not directly expressed or readily apparent.

3.   Relate these two words to answering essay questions. Develop the understanding that explicit questions divide the question into component parts in a fairly straightforward manner. The task is stated quite directly. Implicit questions have more than one part, but the parts are not as clear. Students need to break the question into smaller questions or tasks in order to answer it fully.

4.   Show students a sample of an explicit question with several parts and model how an answer would be formulated. The following example can be used.

> 1) What major causes led to the <u>beginning</u> of World War II? 2) What were several of the significant results of the war?

> After reading the question, make the following remarks. I can see that this essay has two major parts so I'll number them 1 and 2. For the first part, I need to list the major causes of the beginning of the war. I'll list causes, and then I'll write about them. Then I can do the same for the results of the war.

	Causes		**Results**
	1. the treaty of World War I	1.	massive destruction
	2. economic problems	2.	new power struggles
	3. rise of dictatorships	3.	many displaced persons
		4.	fear of powerful weapons
		5.	birth of the United Nations

Now I'll use these lists to answer the questions with two mini-essays. One mini-essay will contain a list and discussion of the three causes; the other mini-essay will focus on the five results.

5. Explain to students that this same basic strategy can be used with implicit multiple-part questions. However, there is a major difference: students will need to identify the parts of the question. Write the following question on the chalkboard and invite students to come up with ideas for breaking the question into parts.

> Think about the beginning and end of World War II and discuss important causes and significant outcomes of the war.

6. Guide students to realize that the approach to this question would be very similar to the explicit question presented earlier. Then ask a student to think aloud how he or she would rephrase the question into other questions. Be sure students come to understand that these rephrased questions (e.g., What are important causes of the war? What are significant outcomes of the war?) make the question more manageable and create a plan for writing the essay.

7. Provide several essay questions related to your content area (both explicit and implicit), and have students identify whether they are explicit or implicit. For implicit questions, direct students to rephrase questions to clarify the writing task. Students should also circle the task and underline the topic.

Multiple-Topic Questions (especially compare-contrast)

1. Write compare-contrast on the chalkboard and tell students that such words are a common part of essay tests. Share the meanings of the words with students.

> compare—to examine in order to note similarities or differences
> contrast—to discuss the differences

2. Suggest topics from daily life that students could compare and contrast and have students brainstorm ideas. Possible topics could include the following ones.

> • your class with another class
> • a school day and a Saturday
> • surfing the internet and playing video games
> • watching TV and reading a book

3. Write the students' ideas on the chalkboard or an overhead transparency. For example, if the example is comparing your class (e.g., English) with another class (e.g., science), a list may look like the following one.

English	**Science**
read novels and short stories	read textbook
discuss readings	do experiments
class lasts 43 minutes	class lasts 43 minutes
take three tests each grading period	take six tests each grading period
meets on first floor	meets on second floor
male teacher	female teacher

4. Help students organize a response to the essay question "Compare and contrast your English class with your science class." Students might be asked to place the material into a Venn diagram to help with organization and visualization. Responses to compare-contrast questions usually follow one of the patterns listed below (Galica, 1991).

Pattern 1: Straight-Line	**Pattern 2: Zigzag**
(subject-by-subject)	(point-by-point)
Subject A	Point 1
Point 1	Subject A
Point 2, etc.	Subject B
Subject B	A and B Compared
Point 1	
Point 2, etc.	Point 2
Comparison Comments	Subject A
Similarity or Difference 1	Subject B
Similarity or Difference 2	A and B Compared
	(and so on)

A chart containing the two patterns may be developed for the lesson or future reference.

5. Invite students to think about which pattern may work best for the questions about the two classes. Encourage discussion and help students see that the zigzag pattern works best when the topics can be matched exactly. The straight-line pattern is easier to control and may more closely match the way students have studied. In the case of the two courses, the zigzag pattern may be the best to use because the topics match up very well.

6. Using the chalkboard or an overhead transparency, model how to answer the questions for one of the points (perhaps the types of readings done). Then invite students to write the next part of the answer. Have them share their responses. Continue this process until the answer is completed.

7. Transfer learning to your content area in two ways. First, point out to students how certain topics being studied may lend themselves to compare-contrast essay questions. Second, provide sample questions to students, guide them through the writing process, and provide additional opportunities for practice. By carefully teaching and practicing the above strategies within the context of your content area, students will improve their ability to answer compare-contrast essay questions and demonstrate knowledge they have gained.

8.4 Understanding Test Scores

Goal

To help students understand test scores.

Background

There are two major classifications of tests: teacher-made and standardized. The scores on most teacher-made tests are often reported in raw scores and percentages. These scores can also be converted into grades using a grading scale. Standardized tests have numerous scores (e.g., percentiles and stanines) that can be derived from the raw score. In addition, most of these tests use the concept of score bands or standard error of measurement (SEM).

As you consider the teaching strategies in this section, adapt the ideas to your specific classes using examples that are a regular component of your assessment procedures. For the information on standardized tests, if possible, use examples of scores from standardized tests students take (e.g., a state test, a group standardized achievement test, the ACT, the SAT). Additional easy-to-understand information on test scores can be found in Lyman (1986).

TEACHING STRATEGY 10

Understanding Teacher-Made Test Scores

1. Reflect on the types of scores used for your classroom tests. Review your grading scale. Use actual examples from your classroom so they are meaningful to students. This example will use raw scores and percentages.

2. Tell students that the raw score refers to the number correct in relationship to the total number of possible questions or items. Perhaps it is getting 8 out of 10 correct on a math quiz or 18 out of 20 on a social studies test. The raw scores are 8 and 18.

3. Show students how these same scores can be converted into percentages. A score of 8 out of 10 would be the same as 80%. Percentages are figured by dividing the number correct (8) by the total number of questions (10) and then multiplying by 100. If appropriate, model the process for students.

4. Relate the scores to your grading scale. Two common types of grading scales are those based on total points or percentages. Share your grading scale. For example, 90% or greater may indicate a grade of A, 80% to 89% may be a B, etc. If you use points, share how your points relate to grades. Be sure students also understand how grades are determined for the grading period, semester, and course.

5. Consider sharing a grade record sheet so students can keep an ongoing record of their performance in your class.

TEACHING STRATEGY **11**

Understanding Standardized Test Scores

1. Identify a standardized test taken by students. Explain to students that their raw scores on such a test are compared to other students throughout the nation using a norm or comparison group.

2. Tell students that two types of scores commonly derived from raw scores are percentiles and stanines.

3. Explain that both percentiles and stanines show how a student's score compares to the norm group. A percentile rank of 50 is considered an average score. If a student achieves a percentile rank of 58, it means that the student scored better than or equal to 58% of the norming group. This score is slightly above average. Be sure that students do not confuse percentiles with percentages, although percentiles are based on the idea of percent.

4. Tell students that stanines are derived scores that divide all possible scores into a "standard nine" scale. Scores in stanines 1, 2, and 3 are classified as below average; stanines 4, 5, and 6 are average; and stanines 7, 8, and 9 are considered above average. Stanines are very broad scores. Because of these broad categories, scores can be misleading. An example may help students understand this idea.

> Let's say Samantha has a percentile rank of 23 and Brad has a percentile rank of 22. Samantha's score could be a stanine of 4, which is considered in the average range of stanines. Brad's score could be a stanine of 3, which falls into the below-average range of stanine scores. There is only 1 percentile rank difference between Samantha and Brad. But, as these scores are converted to stanines, Samantha may be ranked as an average student, while Brad may be seen as below average. Stanines, therefore, give a very broad picture of achievement.

TEACHING STRATEGY **12**

Standard Error of Measurement

1 Tell students that test scores often give an incorrect impression of exactness. Invite students to share some of the variables that may have influenced their performances on tests taken over the years.

2. Write their ideas on the chalkboard or an overhead transparency and discuss them. Some variables students might offer are listed below.

stayed up late	family emergency
lost my notes and couldn't study	overslept and had to rush
didn't feel well	didn't study

3 Tell students that test publishers calculate a standard error of measurement (SEM) for each test. The SEM helps guard against putting too much importance on a single score. The SEM is used to create a score band or confidence interval. For example, suppose the publishers of an achievement test have calculated the SEM on the science subtest to be 4. If a student's percentile rank were 71, it would be

reported as a score band of 67 to 75. That means that the test publishers have added to and subtracted from the student's score the SEM of 4 to take error into account.

4. Show students how this score band might look in printed form.

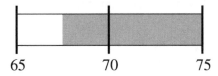

Relate the concept of score bands to meaningful differences in test results. Tell students that when scoring bands for two or more tests overlap, there are no meaningful differences between these scores. If two scoring bands do not overlap, there is a meaningful (significant) difference between the two scores.

8.5 Preparing for the ACT and SAT

Goal
To help students gain tips for the ACT and SAT assessments.

Background

Although extensive discussion about the ACT and SAT is beyond the scope of this chapter, a visit to cyberspace provides web sites for both tests (www.act.org and www.sat.org) and many pages of information. Some of those pages contain useful tips that are also relevant to many classroom tests. For more specific information about the ACT or SAT, visit their web sites or look over the wide variety of ACT/SAT test-preparation booklets that can be found in bookstores and libraries. Below are some tips that may be shared with students who are likely to take one or both of these tests.

Preparing for the Tests

1. Take a variety of classes in high school in order to broaden your knowledge base.
2. Identify the content areas you have not studied lately and study them.
3. Refresh your knowledge and skills in all content areas that are tested.
4. Know what to expect on the test day by reading all the information in your registration packet and following all directions carefully.
5. Get plenty of rest the night before the test.
6. On the day of the test, eat a breakfast that will give you the energy you need for over three hours of intense concentration.
7. Dress comfortably and in layers. You never know what the temperature in the testing room will be.

Taking the Tests

1. Know how the test is scored. Answer every question. There is no penalty for guessing on the ACT. There is a penalty on the SAT.
2. Pace yourself.
3. Read the directions for each question carefully.
4. Read each question carefully.
5. Make sure you answer the question asked.
6. Make sure your answer is reasonable.
7. Answer the easy questions first.
8. Use logic to answer difficult questions.
9. Guess smart. By ruling out one or more choices for a multiple-choice question as definitely wrong, your chances of guessing the right answer improve.
10. Review your work.

Reading Test

1. Read passages carefully.
2. Refer to the passages when answering questions.

Math Test

1. Check the restrictions on calculator use for the math test in your registration packet.
2. If you do not regularly use a calculator in math class, do not use one the day of the test.
3. Use your test book to do scratch work.

Answer Sheets

1. Mark your answers neatly. Avoid extra marks on your answer sheet.
2. Mark only one answer for each question.
3. Check periodically during the test to make sure you are marking the correct oval on the answer sheet.
4. If you erase an answer, erase it completely.

Chapter 9

Conducting Research

Overview

Conducting research is not merely a school activity; it is an integral part of life. All of us respond to our natural curiosity by asking questions, forming hypotheses, gathering data, and drawing conclusions. We conduct research in many areas of our lives. One of the reasons we research is to learn about new situations. For example, when we are planning a trip to a new place, many of us investigate the options available to us. We look into travel arrangements, places to stay, restaurants, and things to do once we are there. We research by gathering information, weighing the various options, and making decisions. Another type of research we conduct is to solve problems. When we encounter a problem such as deciding what make of car to buy, we learn about the different cars, decide which car we want, and

make a decision. These practical types of research are part of our everyday lives.

Middle and high school students also conduct research regularly. They may investigate career and college options; they may find out about sports teams and players; or they may learn about musicians and movie stars. All of these activities that students do on a regular basis are research activities. Researching is a natural part of life for middle and high school students, just as it is for adults.

Although researching is an activity in which all of us participate from time to time, there are skills and strategies that make researching more efficient and productive. Researching is usually comprised of the following strategies: generating a research question; locating and evaluating information; selecting, organizing, and synthesizing information; and conveying the findings to the appropriate audience. The steps in researching are individual, just as the steps in the writing process are individual. Students may go through the steps in the research process in a linear manner, they may spiral back through the research stages, or they may move through the research stages recursively (Lenski & Johns, 1997). Each researching situation is different, and the context of the research and students' preferences influence the manner in which students proceed through the stages of research.

There are two main purposes for having students conduct research in middle and high schools. First, learning how to research is an important life skill. Because students will be conducting informal research during their lives, it is important for you to help them learn the strategies that will allow them to ask and answer pertinent questions. Even though students naturally draw on multiple knowledge sources to learn, guiding them in the research process is an important function of schooling (Stotsky, 1991). Learning how to research and practicing research in a school setting can help students develop skills that will be an important part of their lives.

A second reason for having students research is so they can personalize their learning by conducting research about content area topics. For example, students who are learning about space in science class will learn more deeply about one aspect of the subject if they conduct research. Some students may be interested in learning about individual planets; others may want to learn about the stars; and others may be more interested in space flight. Allowing students to research topics from your content area provides them with the opportunity to learn about topics that interest them.

Teaching students to conduct research has been a traditional school assignment that has been in favor at times and out of favor at other times. Now, however, it is essential that we teach students how to research. Researching is required by employers in our information society. Mendrinos (1997) reports the results of a survey given to a sample of employers about their expectations for employees. Employers expected their employees to have the following research skills:

- Recognize the need for information.
- Formulate questions based on information needs.
- Identify potential sources of information.
- Develop successful search strategies.
- Access sources of information including computer-based and other technologies.
- Analyze information critically.
- Evaluate information.
- Organize and manipulate information for practical application.
- Make decisions based on accurate and complete information.

Our society thrives on information; we are glutted with it. In order to make sense of our world, we need to know when we need more information; we need to be able to ask the right questions; we need to have the ability to sift through abundant sources of material; we need to have the ability to evaluate what we find; and we need to have the ability to organize data so that a reasonable conclusion can be drawn or a decision can be reached. These steps in the research process can be taught in your content area classes. As you teach students to conduct research, they will derive dual benefits: students will learn more about topics in your content area, and they will be able to obtain and evaluate information for work and for leisure.

9.1 Generating a Research Question

Goal

To help students generate a question to research.

Background

Generating a question to research is the first step in the research process. Students may have a vague idea of a topic that they want to research, but refining their questions so that they can actually find answers is a difficult strategy for novice researchers. Many times students generate research questions that are either so broad that they find too many sources or so narrow that they find too few sources. Students need guidance in order to generate research questions that can actually be answered.

You can help students pose research questions by assisting them in accessing their background knowledge. When students remember what they already know about a topic, they can identify what they want to learn through researching. While students are accessing their prior knowledge, they should read general source texts such as encyclopedias. As students remember what they know about the topic, they should also build their background knowledge so that they can ask a research question that will be sufficiently narrow and not overly broad. Students need practice in generating a question that would be appropriate for school research.

Many of the research assignments you give your students will be linked to your content area. Since students learn from researching, giving them opportunities to research in your discipline will help them become more interested in your subject and will help them learn about topics that you believe are important. These research assignments are valid and useful for students. You may also decide to give students authentic research assignments, or research assignments that provide information for real-life situations. When students research a problem that is authentic, they become more highly motivated to answer the research question. For that reason, you might consider incorporating Problem-Centered Research into your curriculum. (See Teaching Strategy 9-4.) Giving students practice generating research questions that stem from your content area and assisting them in identifying questions for real problems are both important ways to help students learn to conduct research.

TECHNOLOGY TIP

References on CD-ROM

Multimedia reference texts are now available on CD-ROM. Selected references available on CD-ROM from DK Publishing (888-342-5357) are listed below.

Eyewitness Encyclopedia of Science 2.0
Eyewitness History of the World 2.0
The Ultimate Human Body 2.0
Earth Quest

TEACHING STRATEGY 1

Factstorming

When students begin to think about the topic they want to research, they first need to identify what they know about the subject. Factstorming, a strategy adapted from the cooperative learning activity Fact Storm (Klemp, Hon, & Short, 1993), encourages students to access their background knowledge so that they can begin to identify topics that would be appropriate for researching. Factstorming is similar to brainstorming but with an important difference. When students participate in Factstorming, they think about facts and associations that are pertinent to the topic. When they brainstorm, they generate ideas to solve a problem or answer a question. Factstorming is an excellent strategy to generate ideas that will eventually form a research question.

Directions and Example

1. Explain that before students research they need to access their background knowledge and identify what they know about the topic. Tell students that Factstorming allows them to call up facts and associations about a topic.

2. Divide the class into groups of three or four students of mixed abilities and interests. When students Factstorm with others who have different backgrounds and interests, they are able to generate more ideas.

3. Tell students that they will be researching a topic related to what they are learning in class. Have them Factstorm what they know about the topic by writing all of their ideas in a list. An example follows.

    > We have been reading about cardiovascular fitness in our text *Fitness for Life* (1993). Your next assignment will be to write a research paper on ways you can participate in a cardiovascular fitness program to improve your fitness level. List as many types of cardiovascular fitness activities as you can. If other related issues come to mind, such as experiences, add them to the list.

4. Give students 10 minutes to complete the Factstorming activity. After 10 minutes, have students share their ideas with the entire group. Write the ideas on the chalkboard or an overhead transparency, or use a computer with an LCD panel. Encourage students to share other ideas that come to mind during this time. Some examples follow.

aerobic dancing	speed swimming	karate	bicycling
in-line skating	baseball	horseback riding	racquetball
rowing	skiing	tennis	hiking
soccer	ballet	basketball	walking

5. Have students think about the entire list of ideas. Then have them individually choose two or three ideas that appeal to them for further thought. Explain that when researchers select a topic about which to write research questions, they process many initial ideas. Tell students that they are generating ideas from which their research questions can be developed.

6. Encourage students to use a similar process when they identify or generate topics for research.

TEACHING STRATEGY 2

Quick Writes

Students who are thinking about the topic they want to research need to briefly explore several topics before deciding which topic is of interest to them. Quick Writes are short writing assignments that help students access their background knowledge about a topic and clarify their interest in the topic. During Quick Writes, students write about a topic for five minutes. Their writing should be a conscious stream of ideas rather than an organized essay. As students write, they should not be concerned about spelling or punctuation; rather, they should write as much about the topic as they can in the time allotted. Students should then use their Quick Writes to decide which topic is of most interest to them as they generate research questions.

Directions and Example

1. Explain that when researchers generate a topic they probably have several ideas from which to choose. Tell students that as researchers ponder their topics they think about the information they know about each topic. As they access their background knowledge, researchers decide which topic is of most interest at that time. (See Section 4.1 for additional ideas on accessing background knowledge.)

2. Have students reread the list of topics that they produced during the Factstorming activity (see Teaching Strategy 9-1). As students read the list, have them think about what they know about each topic. Give students several minutes to think about each topic.

3. Explain that when researchers choose a topic they make a choice among several possible options. Tell students that they need to make a preliminary decision about their topic of research. Even though several topics may be appealing, students must limit their choice to one topic for the present assignment. Explain that there probably will be opportunities to research other topics of interest in the future.

4. After students have chosen their topics, divide the class into groups of two or three students. Have students discuss their topics with the group. Give the class 10 minutes to talk about their topics.

5. Explain that ideas are often clarified through discussion and through writing. Tell students that they will be writing about their topics as a basis for generating a research question using the strategy Quick Write. Explain that they should write anything that comes to mind about the topics and that they should not worry about writing in an organized fashion. Give students five minutes to write about their topics. Encourage students to write about what they have learned from their textbook, in class, and from other sources (e.g., background knowledge).

6. During the next class meeting, have students reread their Quick Writes. Tell students that they can add to their writing if they choose, or they can choose other topics about which to write. Give students five minutes to write more about their topics or to choose other topics. An example of a Quick Write from a science class follows.

Middle School Science Example

Quick Write

Directions: We just finished reading "Investigating Weather and Climate" in our science text *Science Anytime* (1995). We also joined the Weather Around the World project at http://www.galaxyconnect.com where we e-mailed our weather reports to other schools and read their weather reports. Choose one aspect of weather to research.

Topics chosen from Factstorming list:

hurricanes, tornadoes, electrical storms

Quick Write

I am really interested in hurricanes and other storms outside of the control of humans. As I read the weather reports around the world on our online project, I became most interested in the weather from New Zealand. We got information from The Whangamata Area School, which is in a coastal resort on the east coast of the North Island of New Zealand, about 150 km from Auckland. The students reported that they rarely have hurricanes. My grandparents in Florida said that they have lived through at least 8 hurricanes in the last 20 years. I know from our science class about Hurricane Andrew and the destruction it caused in 1992. What interests me most is how hurricanes form and why they hit certain areas.

TEACHING STRATEGY 3

Poster Questions

After students have generated topics for research, they need to develop researchable questions. Poster Questions (Moore, Moore, Cunningham, & Cunningham, 1998) guide students' thinking as they turn their topics into questions. The topic is turned into a question by having students brainstorm questions using the words who, what, when, where, why, and how as an inquiry base. After questions are generated, they are posted for further deliberation. Questions that seem to be too narrow or too broad are eliminated, and questions that seem to be appropriate for research are posted as possibilities for student research.

Directions and Example

1. Explain that once students have generated topics they need to think of research questions from those topics. Tell students that you will be modeling the process researchers use as they develop their research questions. For example, think aloud by saying the following.

   We have been reading "Trends in Communication Technology" in our text *Technology: Today & Tomorrow* (1993). We know that any text about technology becomes quickly dated, so we are researching new information for the various topics we have studied. One of the topics we have

studied is biotechnology. In that section, we learned about the advances made in developing prostheses, or the area of medicine that is developing artificial devices to replace body parts. One research topic, therefore, is to find out more about prostheses, or the artificial devices that have been developed.

2. Write the name of a topic on the chalkboard or an overhead transparency, or use a computer with an LCD panel. Place the topic in the center of the page.

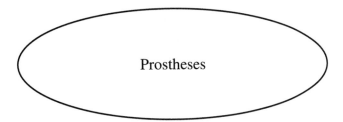

3. Ask students to generate questions that begin with each of the following words: who, what, when, where, why, and how. Write the questions so they radiate out from the center term.

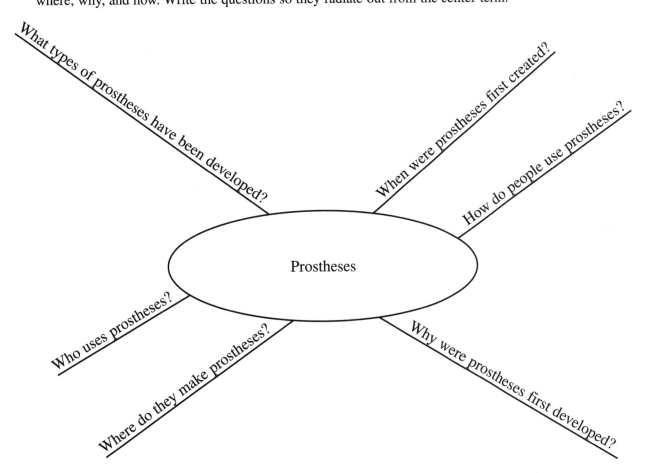

4. Ask students whether they think the questions are too narrow or too broad. You might need to model this type of thinking for students. Delete the questions that you consider to be too narrow or too broad for their research assignments. Use the following example to model how to make decisions about research questions. Write the questions on the chalkboard or an overhead transparency, or use a computer with an LCD panel. Explain why you would keep the question or delete it, as is illustrated in the examples below.

Who uses prostheses?

Although this subject is interesting to me, I don't think I will be able to learn much more than I already know about prostheses. I could search the internet for names of people who have prostheses, but I don't want to offend anyone with my questions. I don't think this question is going to work for my research.

What types of prostheses have been developed?

I would like to learn the answer to this question. We learned mostly about the myoelectric hand in class, and I would like to find out about more types of prostheses. I think there would be plenty of information, but because the topic is fairly limited, I think it would be good for a research question.

When were prostheses first created?

I'm interested in the development of prostheses, but I don't think that question is broad enough for a research paper. I will delete it.

Where do they make prostheses?

Although this question would be appropriate for a research study, it really does not interest me. If I were interested in how they make prostheses and where, it would be a good question. I think I'll delete it.

Why were prostheses first developed?

I am very interested in the reasons why people create new ways of coping with physical difficulties, so this question really interests me. I think there would be some interesting things to learn, so I will leave this question as a possibility.

How do people use prostheses?

This is a really broad question. I think there would be as many ways to use prostheses as there are different types of prostheses. I think I'll delete this question because it is too broad for a research paper.

5. Explain that the questions left on the display are possible questions for research. Post the questions on a display as examples of research questions about a specific topic.

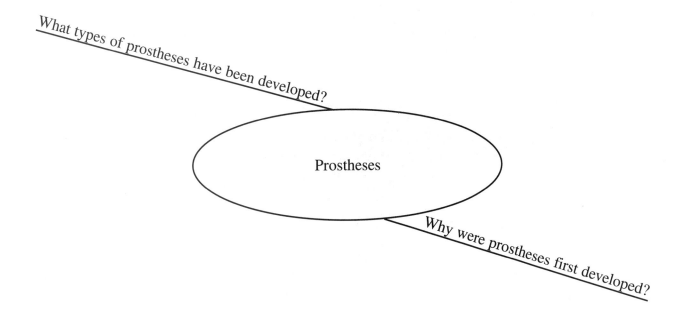

6.   Have students use the same process to develop their own research questions. Divide the class into groups of two or three students. In each group, have one student select a topic and then ask all of the students to generate questions about that topic. After preliminary questions are generated, have students discuss which ones would be too broad and which ones too narrow. Delete those questions. The remaining questions would be appropriate for research. Repeat the procedure for each student in the group.

TEACHING STRATEGY 4

Problem-Centered Research

When students conduct research using Problem-Centered Research, they generate a research question based on a real-life problem. Problem-Centered Research is the type of research that is most often used by people to solve everyday problems or to find out about important issues. For example, consider the following problem. You have moved to a new house that does not have a fenced-in yard. You have two dogs that will wander off if left to themselves. You have a "problem." How should you keep the dogs in the yard? Of course, there are many solutions to that problem. You can build a fence; you can put in an invisible fence; or you can put the dogs on tethers. To solve the problem, you would need to conduct research to determine your options, collect facts about each option, consider the advantages and disadvantages of each option, and come to an informed conclusion. Usually real problems have many solutions, not one correct answer. Using Problem-Centered Research in the classroom is an excellent way for your students to understand how research is used to solve problems that exist in real life.

Directions and Examples

1.   Identify a real problem that exists in your school, in your community, or in the lives of your students. To decide what problem to research, ask students to think about issues that are important to them.

2. Divide the class into groups of three or four students. Have students generate a list of ideas that could be used for a Problem-Centered Research project. Tell them the criteria for a Problem-Centered Research question are listed below.

- Solutions to the problem exist.
- There are many solutions.
- There is not one correct solution.
- The research could be done in the allotted time.
- There is an authentic audience for the solution to the problem.

3. Ask members of the groups to share their ideas. As students volunteer ideas, write their ideas on the chalkboard or an overhead transparency, or use a computer with an LCD panel. Help students frame the ideas as real problems, as in the following example.

One of the problems generated by the class is that there aren't enough parking spaces for students. Many students have to park their cars on the side streets which are quite narrow. Last year 12 cars were sideswiped. The problem expressed is the lack of student parking.

4. Using the entire list of ideas, discuss which problems are possible to research and solve given time and money constraints. For example, you make the following comments.

Parking is one of the biggest problems students report on their yearly survey. The parking issue is currently being discussed by the Board of Education. Perhaps we should wait for them to make recommendations before we act on that particular problem.

Another problem that was raised was that our town has no Sister City. Of course, the lack of a Sister City is more of a situation than a problem, but it does meet our criteria: the situation has a solution; there is more than one possible solution; there is not one correct solution; the research could be done in the allotted time; and there is an authentic audience for the solution to the problem.

5. Create a modified list of problems that the class could actually research and solve. Have the class vote on a problem to be solved.

6. Have students conduct research to solve the problem using ideas from Sections 9.2 through 9.4 or adapt the example that follows.

Problem-Centered Research

Problem

A group of students petitioned the Student Council for their school to sponsor a trip to Mexico to study Spanish. The Student Council President discussed the request at a faculty meeting. The faculty members decided that the request for foreign travel would be an excellent topic for research.

Research Question

Should the school sponsor trips to foreign countries?

Procedures

1. In class, have students brainstorm different subtopics for research. For example, the following might be subtopics for this research question.

Insurance	Opinions of parents
Faculty interest in sponsoring	Connection to school curriculum
Funding	Student interest
Destinations	Existing travel programs
Safety	Red tape (passports, visas)

2. Tell students that each subtopic will be the task of an expert group. Have students apply to these groups for membership.

3. After expert groups have been formed, have groups develop mission statements, goals, and timelines. This material should be shared with the entire class.

4. Guide students toward information and resources that will accomplish their goals. Students may need to develop and distribute surveys, conduct an internet search, interview people, telephone or write to a country's embassy, read books, or find information in other ways.

5. Have students decide on a way to disseminate their information to the entire class. Then have students share the information they found.

6. Invite students to use information from all of the groups to develop an answer to the research problem. Discuss different forms this final report could take.

7. Have students present their findings to the audience for which it was intended. In this case, the findings would be presented to the faculty of the school.

9.2 Locating and Evaluating Sources

Goal

To help students locate and evaluate sources that answer their research questions.

Background

Finding enough information to answer a research question is rarely a problem anymore. Quick clips of information frequently bombard us. When we watch television, 10-second commercials try to persuade us to buy a product. When we log onto the internet, advertisements clutter the web sites. At the web sites, we can link to a wide variety of additional sources. When we access a CD-ROM reference, we have the option of accessing links, photos, and video clips. We are truly living in the information age.

Students who are conducting research need different types of skills than were needed even a few years ago. Because of the abundance of information that is readily available, students now need help in learning how to make decisions about which information to access. Locating information has taken on a new meaning. Although we do need to teach students how to use search tools and conduct Boolean searches, we also need to teach students how to decide which information they should locate at different points in their research process. Students need to decide whether to locate sources through the library, the internet, or on CD-ROMs. They need to decide whether to use primary or secondary sources. They also need to learn when to use general information and when to use specific information. These decisions for locating sources can be taught through Self-Questioning (see Teaching Strategy 9-5).

Once students locate information, they need to determine the authors' qualifications and purposes for writing the texts. Texts sometimes contain errors. Students need to learn how to verify the information they find in the sources they read. Chapter 6, Reading Critically, contains many strategies students can use to evaluate their research sources. Students, however, also need to be able to evaluate web sites. Teaching Strategies 9-6 and 9-7 provide strategies that teach students to evaluate the appropriateness of web sites for their research. These strategies can help students as they locate and evaluate sources that answer their research questions.

TECHNOLOGY TIP

Online Reader

The Online Reader provides full-text magazine articles that are assigned a reading level. The Online Reader also provides teaching suggestions and student activities for the articles.

EBSCO Curriculum Materials 800-633-8623

Self-Questioning

Researching is a recursive process. Even though students have generated research questions and subtopics, they need to continue to revise their questions as they interact with sources. As students locate sources that they believe will provide information to answer their research questions, they need to ask themselves questions about the sources and about their research questions. There are several types of questions students should ask themselves as they research. First, students need to ask themselves when to use the library, CD-ROMs, and the internet. Many different types of resources are available to students. Most students have library print sources available. Many students also have nonprint sources at their disposal, such as reference texts on CD-ROMs and the internet. Even though the internet is new and appealing for most students, conducting a search on the internet may not be the most efficient way to locate sources.

A second question students should ask as they research is whether they need primary or secondary sources. The internet has provided easy access to many primary sources that were difficult for students to locate in the past. At times, primary sources are the most appropriate choice for research. At other times, however, secondary sources provide better information. Students have to ask themselves which kinds of sources they need at different points in the research process. Finally, students need to ask themselves whether the information they are reading is of interest to them. Researchers need to balance the time they can devote to the research project with their interest in the topic. Students need to continually monitor their levels of interest in their research topics and revise their research to sustain their interest. Teaching students how to use Self-Questioning can help them make informed decisions about which sources to use, locate sources efficiently, and monitor their interest in their topics.

TECHNOLOGY TIP

Selected Internet Sites of Primary Sources

Newslink: over 2,000 newspapers, broadcasts, and web resources.
http://www.newslink.org

FedWorld: United States government resources including government reports.
http://www.fedworld.gov

Index of History
http://kuhttp.cc.ukans.edu/history/index.html

Internet Public Library
http://ipl.sils.umich.edu

Library of Congress
http://lcweb.loc.gov/homepage/lchp.html

Directions and Examples

1. Tell students that even though they have decided on preliminary research questions they need to continue to revise their questions as they locate and evaluate sources. Write the following questions on the chalkboard or an overhead transparency, or use a computer with an LCD panel. Tell students that the following questions are typical questions researchers ask themselves as they locate source texts.

    *   What is my research question? Do I need to revise the question?
    *   What do I know about my topic? How does that influence the sources I am locating?
    *   How interested am I in my topic? Can I sustain my interest for the length of this project? If not, how can I revise my question to promote interest?
    *   Where is the best place to search for sources: the internet, CD-ROMs, or the library?
    *   Do I need primary sources, secondary sources, or both?
    *   Are the sources I have located appropriate for my purposes? Is the information too broad, too specific, or just right?
    *   Is the text too difficult for me to read with good understanding?

2. Ask students to generate other questions that they think will be useful as they locate and evaluate sources for researching. Compile and duplicate a complete list of questions to distribute to students to use as they research.

3. Model how researchers answer questions about sources. Use a research topic from your content area or use the following example. The following is an example of Self-Questioning to determine a research question from a high school literature class.

    *   What is my research question? Do I need to revise the question?

        I want to know what the members of the Bloomsbury Group thought about the challenges women writers faced during the early 20th century. I think the question is fine for now.

    *   What do I know about my topic? How does that knowledge influence the sources I am locating?

        From my reading of the text *Literature and the Language Arts: The British Tradition* (1996), I know that Virginia Woolf was one of the founding members of the Bloomsbury Group. I know that Virginia Woolf wrote the book *A Room of One's Own,* which deals with the topic of obstacles women writers faced.

    *   How interested am I in my topic? Can I sustain my interest for the length of this project? If not, how can I revise my question to promote interest?

        I am mildly interested in the topic. I think I really want to learn more about Virginia Woolf's views. I was really intrigued by the portion of her book *A Room of One's Own* in which she discussed a hypothetical sister of Shakespeare who was as talented a writer as he was. I never thought how difficult it would be for a girl who was as talented as a boy to be brought up in the same house but with different treatment. I think if I changed my research question to learning about Woolf's views rather than the views of all of the members of the Bloomsbury Group, I would enjoy my research more.

    *   Where is the best place to search for sources: the internet, CD-ROMs, or the library?

TEACHING STRATEGY 5

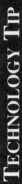

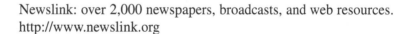

I have a *Grolier's Encyclopedia* on CD-ROM at home. I think I'll start with that source. After I read the encyclopedia entry under Virginia Woolf, I'll go to the library to find books written about Woolf's life. After I find books in the library, I'll log onto the internet to see what else is available.

- Do I need primary sources, secondary sources, or both?

  I need to start with secondary sources. I need to learn more about Virginia Woolf before I try to read primary sources such as her letters.

- Are the sources I have located appropriate for my purposes? Is the information too broad, too specific, or just right?

  The encyclopedia entry told about Woolf's life. It seemed as if she was influenced by her father, Sir Leslie Stephen, and his friends. I wonder if she really wished she were a man, so that she could have had the same opportunities her father and his friends had. This information gave me some valuable insights into Woolf's views about women. The information was general, but I needed general information at the time. I think I'll read at least one more general source before I try to read anything specific.

- Is the text too difficult for me to read with good understanding?

  The encyclopedia was easy to read. It was a synthesis of Woolf's life and was written in language that I could understand. I think when I read some of the primary sources, however, I will have difficulty with the texts. Some of the writing from that time period is hard for me to understand.

4. Ask students to discuss other issues that may arise when they research. After the discussion, have students begin to locate and evaluate their sources using Self-Questioning. As students research, ask them to write down any other issues, questions, or decisions they face as they research. Use the students' questions to revise your list of Self-Questions.

5. The following page is a list of Self-Questions that can be duplicated and distributed to students.

Self-Questions During Researching

Directions: Answer the following questions as you are locating sources to use to answer your research question.

1. What is my research question? Do I need to revise the question?

   _____

   _____

2. What do I know about my topic? How does that influence the sources I am locating?

   _____

   _____

3. How interested am I in my topic? Can I sustain my interest for the length of this project? If not, how can I revise my question to promote interest?

   _____

   _____

4. Where is the best place to search for sources: the internet, CD-ROMs, or the library?

   _____

   _____

5. Do I need primary sources, secondary sources, or both?

   _____

   _____

6. Are the sources I have located appropriate for my purposes? Is the information too broad, too specific, or just right?

   _____

   _____

7. Is the text too difficult for me to read with good understanding?

   _____

   _____

TEACHING STRATEGY 6

Web Winnowing

Gathering information has changed substantially with the advent of the internet. Students conducting research have great amounts of information available to them simply by conducting a search on the internet. The internet provides access to numerous sources including texts, graphics, photos, and moving images. Sources for this information can include libraries, governmental agencies, private agencies, businesses, and individuals (Ryder & Graves, 1996/1997). Since anyone can publish information on the internet, the sources students locate may or may not have accurate and unbiased information in them. The address of the web site, however, provides readers with a general category of the sponsoring agency or author. As students locate web sites, they should be able to identify the type of site before they decide to read it. They need to winnow out the web sites that are sponsored by sources that may not give the information fair treatment. To guide students in winnowing out inappropriate web sites, use the strategy Web Winnowing.

Directions and Examples

1. Explain that when students are researching they need to carefully locate and evaluate sources, especially when using the internet. Tell students that before they read a web site they need to know who authored the site so that they can evaluate whether the web site is an appropriate source of information.

2. Explain that web addresses have identifying Uniform Resource Locator (URL) addresses and that students can make an initial decision about the site based on the URL address. Duplicate and distribute the Web Site Identification resource page for information on the types of URLs.

3. Discuss each type of web site. If you have a computer with an LCD panel and have online access, locate an example of each of the types of web sites. You can use the examples on the Web Site Identification page, or you can locate other sites that are related to your content area.

4. Have students read their lists of web site sources. Have students locate news sites, personal sites, and sites that are sponsored by organizations, businesses, and governmental or educational agencies.

5. After students have identified and classified their web sites, have them winnow out any sites that may be inappropriate for their current research. Have students winnow their web lists to a manageable number of sites before they continue their research projects.

6. Model the process that students should use as they make decisions about their sources. Use an example from your content area or use the following example.

Middle or High School History Example

Web Winnowing

I am going to research the causes of the Vietnam War. When I logged onto the computer with the search terms "Vietnam War," I got 1,009,008 hits. I scanned the top five hits, looking for the kinds of web sites that would best provide me a balanced treatment of the war.

The first web site I looked at was the Vietnam Veterans Home Page, a web site developed by veterans to describe their experiences. The web address was http://grunt.space.swri.edu/index.htm. I noticed that this web site is an .edu site. That means it must be an informational page, and although some of the information may be personal opinion, I think I'll access it.

The second web site that I found was Jay's Veterans' Resource Links, a database of links to other resources about the Vietnam War. The web address was http://www.nerawt.com/left/veterans.htm. This site has a .com address, so I guess it's a news web page or a business web page. Since the information is a list of resources, I would assume this web site is a news site. I will keep this one and scan through the links.

The third site I found was the Vietnam Helicopter Flight Crew Network at http://www.vhfcn.org/. This web site has a .org address so it must be an advocacy page. The synopsis describes the web site as one that discusses the experiences of the helicopter pilots. I don't know which organization sponsored this web site, but I don't think I'm interested in it.

The fourth site I found was the web site Vietnam War with the address http://www.home.gil.com.au/~tomumac/main.html. This site describes Australia's role in the war and must be a Personal Home Page. I don't think it will fit my research.

The final site I found was the Vietnam War History Page at http://www.bev.net/computer/htmlhelp/Vietnam.html. The site description sounds like it's an overview of the war. I can't tell from the URL address what type of site it is, but I think I'll access it and see what happens.

Original Web Site List

1. http://grunt.space.swri.edu/index.htm
2. http://www.nerawt.com/left/verterans.htm
3. http://www.vhfcn.org/
4. http://www.home.gil.com.au/~tomumac/main.html
5. http://www.bev.net/computer/htmlhelp/Vietnam.html

Web Winnowed List

1. http:grunt.space.swri.edu/index.htm
2. http://www.nerawt.com/left/verterans.htm
3. http://www.bev.net/computer/htmlhelp/Vietnam.html

Web Site Identification

Advocacy Web Page

An Advocacy Web Page is one sponsored by an organization attempting to influence public opinion. The URL address of the page usually ends in .org (organization).

Example: http://www.c-span.org (provides companion materials to C-SPAN programs).

Business/Marketing Web Page

A Business/Marketing Web Page is one sponsored by a commercial business usually trying to promote a product. The URL address of the page usually ends in .com (commercial).

Example: gopher://futureinfo.com (organization to restore the Puget Sound region).

Informational Web Page

An Informational Web Page is one whose purpose is to present factual information. Many of these Web Pages are sponsored by educational institutions or governmental agencies. The URL address usually ends in .edu or .gov.

Examples: http://forum.swarthmore.edu/ (a program at which students can discuss mathematics with a group of students and professors at Swarthmore College).

http://www.whitehouse.gov/ (official White House web site).

News Web Page

A News Web Page is one whose primary purpose is to provide current information. The URL address of the page usually ends in .com (commercial).

Example: http://www.cnn.com (CNN Interactive offers headlines and news stories).

Personal Home Page

A Personal Home Page is one published by an individual who may or may not be affiliated with a larger institution. The URL address of the page may have a variety of endings. The tilde (~) is usually present in the address, or the address may end with .html (hypertext markup language).

Example: http://curry.edschool.virginia.edu/~insttech/frog (interactive frog dissection tutorial).

http://coe.ilstu.edu/jabraun/socialstudies/coalmining/welcome.html (social studies web site about coal mining).

Adapted from Alexander, J., & Tate, M. (1998, April 8). *The web as a research tool: Evaluation techniques* [On-line]. Available: http://www.science.widener.edu/~withers/advoc.htm

Web Site Evaluator

After students have located web sites to read and before they decide whether their sources are appropriate for research, students should evaluate their web sites. Even web sites that have been published by authorities in their fields need to be evaluated to determine how appropriate they are for a particular research project. The internet is a different type of publishing system. Typically, publishers claim responsibility for the materials they publish. No one, however, is responsible for the resources found on the internet. Because many web sites have not been subject to review boards or external editors, they may be inaccurate, unreliable, misleading, or false. Students, therefore, need to evaluate web sites before they use them as a source for research.

TECHNOLOGY TIP

Internet Source Validation Project

The Internet Source Validation Project is a web site that provides students with a tutorial on evaluating web sites. The primary objective of this site is to have students use concrete and context validity to read web site examples and determine their validity. Examples of web sites to be evaluated are on this site. The HTTP address follows.

http://www.stemnet.nf.ca/Curriculum/Validate/validate.html

Directions and Example

1. Explain that the internet is a huge network of computers from which a great deal of information can be accessed. Tell students that the sponsoring agency or individual for each web site is responsible for the contents of its site. Explain that some sources have a vested interest in presenting information that is incomplete or not wholly accurate. Tell students that the texts they read on the internet need to be evaluated before being used and that they need to become skilled consumers of information on the internet.

2. Duplicate and distribute copies of the Web Site Evaluation Questionnaire that follows. Explain that students should fill out the Questionnaire for each of the sites they decide to read for their research.

3. Model how to evaluate a web site by choosing a site that applies to your discipline and by answering the questions posed by the Web Site Evaluation Questionnaire, or use the example that follows for the web site GlobaLearn at http://www.globalearn.org/.

4. Make a transparency of the Questionnaire, display it on an overhead projector, and discuss each of the sections with your students or duplicate the Questionnaire and distribute it to your students. Explain that there are five categories of questions students must consider as they evaluate web sites: the authority of the author, the accuracy of the contents, the objectivity of the sponsoring organization or individual, the recency of the material, and the coverage of the contents.

5.   Explain that researchers must determine whether the authors of the site are credible. To determine credibility, students should find out the authors of the web site, the authors' qualifications, and the authors' reasons for producing the site. Listed below are questions and answers about the authority of a web site.

Authority

- Who is the author or producer of the page?

  I accessed the section of the web page that described the organization. GlobaLearn is a nonprofit company founded in 1993 by Murat Armbruster. The page is sponsored by the company.

- What are the author's qualifications for the information written on the site?

  The author of the site is unknown, but the staff and Board of Directors of GlobaLearn are listed. Several of the staff members are associated with Yale University.

- If the web site is sponsored by an organization or business, is the sponsoring organization clearly stated? Who is the sponsor?

  Yes, the sponsoring agent is listed and described. GlobaLearn is a company that sponsors live expeditions around the world. Students can become involved by interacting with the explorers through the internet.

- Can the legitimacy of the organization be verified? If so, how? If not, why not?

  The existence of GlobaLearn can be verified by looking at an index for nonprofit companies.

- What is the purpose of the web site?

  The purpose of the web site is to educate people about the company.

6.   Explain that it is also important to determine whether the contents of the site are accurate. In general, information should not be taken at face value unless it can be verified by at least one other qualified source. Since information on the internet usually is not verified by an editor, researchers should use information on web sites cautiously unless other informed sources verify the contents of the site. Tell students that traditional print information is read by several reviewers and at least one editor who prepares the manuscript for publication by reading it for grammatical errors. When reading a web site, students should evaluate the accuracy of the language. If the site has numerous errors, students can conclude that the authors of the site either do not have an adequate command of the language or that the site was hastily written. In either case, a site that has many grammatical errors may also have errors in its contents and should be read with that in mind. Listed below are questions and answers about the accuracy of a web site.

Accuracy

- Can information on the site be verified by another source? If so, how?

  After one becomes involved in GlobaLearn, the site can be verified by other participants.

- Is the page relatively free of grammatical errors? If not, what conclusions can you draw?

  Yes, it is well written.

- Who has the responsibility for the accuracy of the contents of the site?

  It doesn't say.

7. Explain that all authors take a personal interest in their subjects. At times, however, authors can distort information, thereby making it biased. Tell students that they must be especially aware that the materials they read on the internet are objective. Although students may not be able to determine whether an author of a web site is completely honest, several questions can make students aware of blatant subjectivity. Listed below are questions and answers about the objectivity of a web site.

Objectivity

- Is any sort of bias evident? If so, what seems to be the author's bias?

  No bias seems to be evident.

- Is the author's motivation for writing the web site clear? What do you think it was?

  I think the author wants more students to learn about this project.

- If there is advertising on the page, is it clearly differentiated from the contents?

  There is no advertising on the site.

8. Information on web sites may be more current than print sources, but that is not always true. Some web sites may be several years old and contain information that is just as dated as a print source. To guard against the thinking that all electronic information is current, tell students that they need to determine when the web site was developed. One of the benefits of electronic publishing is that it is easier to update information on the internet than it is for print sources. Tell students also to look for a note saying whether the site has been revised. When web sites are updated, links that were once operational may no longer work. Explain that when students evaluate web sites, they also need to check whether the links are working. Listed below are questions and answers about the recency of a web site.

Recency

- When was the web site produced?

  The site was copyrighted in 1997.

- Has the web site been updated? If so, when? If not, are the contents out of date?

  I didn't find any updates, but it seems to be current.

- Are the links in operation? Are the links accurate? If not, which links are not in operation or are inaccurate?

  There were several links, all of them in operation.

9. Tell students that web sites are frequently on the internet while they are being constructed. A web source title may sound perfect for research, but that site may be under construction. As students evaluate web sites, have them look for parts of web sites that are unfinished. Also have students survey the entire web site before deciding whether it will be a good source for their research projects. Explain that they need to know what contents are covered on the site and that they should survey the site just as they would scan a table of contents in a textbook. Listed below are questions and answers about the coverage of a web site.

Coverage

- Has the web site been completed, or is it under construction? If it is under construction, is there an indication of when it will be finished?

  The site is complete.

- Are the topics of the web site clearly stated? If not, what is unclear?

  Yes, the topics are clear.

- Does the page address the topics stated? If not, what is missing?

  Yes, all of the topics are addressed.

10. Have students independently evaluate the web sites on their research lists using the Web Site Evaluation Form.

11. Divide the class into groups of three or four students. Ask students to share what they have learned about their web site evaluations. Have students discuss which sites are appropriate for their research projects and which are not. Encourage students to discuss the reasons the sites they deemed inappropriate do not apply to their research.

These teachers are reviewing students' *Web Site Evaluation Forms* to determine appropriateness of web sites.

Web Site Evaluation

Part I

Authority

1. Who is the author or producer of the page? _____

2. What are the author's qualifications for the information written on the site? _____
   _____

3. If the web site is sponsored by an organization or business, is the sponsoring organization
   clearly stated?   Yes _____   No _____
   Who is the sponsor? _____

4. Can the legitimacy of the organization be verified?   Yes _____   No _____
   If so, how? If not, why not? _____
   _____

5. What is the purpose of the web site? _____
   _____

Accuracy

6. Can information on the site be verified by another source?
   Yes _____   No _____   If so, how? _____
   _____

7. Is the page relatively free of grammatical errors?   Yes _____   No _____
   If not, what conclusions can you draw? _____
   _____

8. Who has the responsibility for the accuracy of the contents of the site?
   _____

Adapted from Alexander, J., & Tate, M. (1998, April 8). *The web as a research tool: Evaluation techniques* [On-line].
Available: http://www.science.widener.edu/~withers/advoc.htm

Web Site Evaluation

Part II

Objectivity

9. Is any sort of bias evident?   Yes _____   No _____   If so, what seems to be the author's bias? _____

10. Is the author's motivation for writing the web site clear?   Yes _____   No _____ What do you think it was? _____

11. If there is advertising on the page, is it clearly differentiated from the contents?

_____

Recency

12. When was the web site produced? _____

13. Has the web site been updated?   Yes _____   No _____   If so, when? If not, are the contents out of date? _____

14. Are the links in operation?   Yes _____   No _____   Are the links accurate? Yes _____   No _____   If not, which links are not in operation or are inaccurate?

_____

Coverage

15. Has the web site been completed?   Yes _____   No _____   If it is under construction, is there an indication of when it will be finished? _____

16. Are the topics of the web site clearly stated?   Yes _____   No _____   If not, what is unclear? _____

17. Does the page address the topics stated?   Yes _____   No _____   If not, what is missing? _____

Adapted from Alexander, J., & Tate, M. (1998, April 8). *The web as a research tool: Evaluation techniques* [On-line]. Available: http://www.science.widener.edu/~withers/advoc.htm

9.3 Selecting and Organizing Information

Goal

To help students select and organize information that answers their research questions.

Background

Once students have located and evaluated source texts, they are ready to begin reading the texts and looking for information that will answer their research questions. As students read, they need to select information to write down as notes, and then they need to organize that information. While reading, students make complex cognitive decisions about what to select for their notes and what not to select. Readers of source texts look for the organizational patterns of the texts they are reading, select what parts to read and remember, and connect that information to their background knowledge (Spivey, 1997). Students use many strategies to accomplish this difficult task. They need to identify the structure of the text they are reading. Then they need to decide whether to skim the selection, scan for information, or read the passage carefully. Finally, students need to connect what they have read to the information they already know about the topic. Finally, students need to write their findings as notes. Selecting information to answer research questions involves the use of many reading strategies.

As students select information, they need to monitor all of the strategies they are using. Questioning the Author (QtA) is one strategy that helps students monitor their reading. QtA is a useful strategy for students who are selecting information from texts while researching.

Students can take notes as they select information, but then they need to organize their notes for easy access. Two popular ways to organize information are using databases and using I-Charts. When students have a great deal of discrete data, databases are an ideal organizational tool. If the information that students have selected is conceptual, I-Charts are a good choice. Selecting and organizing information that answers research questions is possibly the most difficult of the steps in the research process. Students will need much practice and guidance as they decide what information to select and how the material should be organized.

TECHNOLOGY TIP

Computer Software to Organize Information

The Research Helper: stores and sorts information, writes bibliographic entries.

Harcourt Brace 800-237-2665

TEACHING STRATEGY **8**

Questioning the Author (QtA)

After students have located sources for their research and evaluated the appropriateness of those sources, they need to read the texts for information that will answer their research questions. The selection process entails making determinations about which information would be helpful in accomplishing the students' goals and which information is not useful. To facilitate the thought processes necessary in selecting information, the strategy Questioning the Author (QtA) (Beck, McKeown, Hamilton, & Kucan, 1997) can be used. QtA is a comprehension strategy designed to increase students' active understanding of texts. When using the QtA strategy, students step back from the text and ask pertinent questions to help them understand what the authors are expressing. As they make decisions about what the authors are saying, students can also take an additional step and ask questions about whether that information answers their research questions.

Directions and Example

1. Tell students that they will be reading their source texts using a strategy that is different from the usual strategies they use as they read. Explain that as they read to select information they need to think that authors are real people who may or may not have been successful in communicating their ideas. Help students realize that they need to actively discern what the authors are trying to communicate and how texts answer students' research questions.

2. Tell students that you will be demonstrating a strategy that promotes active thinking about texts during reading and that guides them in ways to select information that answers a research question. Begin modeling the QtA strategy by choosing a text from your content area or by using the following example.

   > We have been reading about fungi in our text *Biology* (1994) and are answering the following research question: In what ways do we encounter fungi in everyday life? To begin researching, we decided that it would be appropriate to read the section from our biology book to develop general knowledge before reading more specific sources. Therefore, I will use the QtA strategy using material from Chapter 20 in our biology text.

3. Explain that before they begin reading their source texts students should remind themselves of their research questions. Rereading their research questions will help students focus on the pertinent information from the text. Then as they begin reading, they should ask the following questions.

   What are the authors trying to say?
   What are the authors' messages?
   How do the authors' messages answer my research question?

4. Choose a passage of text from your content area or use the following example to demonstrate how a reader would Question the Author. To use the example, make a transparency of the text and display it on an overhead projector.

Fungi are important in many ways. For example, mushrooms are a type of fungus, and bread-making requires another type of fungus. Yeasts are used to make bread rise. Molds that spoil food are fungi. Mushrooms are part of the recycling of nutrients of decaying matter that is released back into the ecosystem. A few fungi cause diseases in plants and animals. Other fungi are used for food, to make medicine, and to give flavor to cheese. Fungi are essential organisms.

▶ Adapted from *Biology*. (1994). Menlo Park, CA: Addison-Wesley.

5. Demonstrate questions you could ask about the meaning of the text. An example follows.

What do the authors mean when they write "fungi are important?" Does that mean they are an important part of everyday life? What does the term "important" imply? Are fungi so important they are essential, or do fungi exist to accomplish many purposes. Later, the author states that "fungi are essential organisms," but I'm not sure whether they are essential for food and medicine, or whether they are essential for life. I need to find out more about how and why fungi are important.

6. Demonstrate questions you could ask that help students select information from the text, as in the following example.

My research topic is about ways fungi are used in everyday life. This paragraph has many different ideas that would fit my research topic. The paragraph mentions several different ways fungi are important: mushrooms are fungi, fungi are used to make bread rise, they cause food to spoil and wood to rot, and they are used in food, medicine, and cheese. I think I will concentrate on a few of these items. I can't research them all. I think I'll focus on the ways fungi help humans. Therefore, I will only select the facts that fit this idea. I will write that fungi are used in making bread, cheese, and medicine.

7. Tell students that each time they select information their decisions influence which information they will select in the future. Demonstrate how researchers make decisions about future selections. Use your own content area example or use the following example.

Since I have decided that I will only select information about the uses of fungi for humans, I will need to read the portions of text that discuss mushrooms, yeast, cheese, and medicine. While I read, I will also look for other ways fungi are useful to people. When I see sections of text that discuss ways fungi help the ecosystem, I will skim over those parts. Although that topic is of interest to me, I will not be using it for this project, so I will not read those sections carefully.

8. Provide students with a list of QtA questions to use as a prompt as they read sources and select information. Copy the following page and distribute it to your students.

Questioning the Author (QtA)

Directions: Ask the following questions as you read source texts and select information to write as notes. If you think of additional questions that would be useful to you, write them on the blank lines.

1. What are the authors trying to say here?

2. What are the authors' messages?

3. What are the authors talking about?

4. Did the authors explain this clearly?

5. Is this passage consistent with other passages?

6. How does this passage connect with previous passages?

7. Do the authors adequately explain things?

8. Why are the authors telling us this now?

9. Are the authors giving me information that will answer my research question?

10. Does what the authors say change my research question? If so, how?

11. _____

12. _____

13. _____

14. _____

Adapted from Beck, I.L., McKeown, M.G., Hamilton, R.L., & Kucan, L. (1997). *Questioning the author: An approach for enhancing student engagement with text.* Newark, DE: International Reading Association.

TEACHING STRATEGY **9**

Organizing with Databases

Using a database is an excellent way to organize information when researching information that was collected from multiple sources. A database is a collection of information that can be organized for searching and retrieving information in a variety of ways. According to Braun, Fernlund, and White (1998), a telephone book is a type of database. Of course, it is difficult to organize or reorganize data using a print source such as a telephone book. An electronic database, on the other hand, allows data to be sorted according to a variety of categories. Students can design and build their own databases to access and manipulate the data they have gathered for researching. As part of a curriculum unit on weather, for example, a group of students collected data daily from the school's rooftop weather station. Then they pooled the information into a common database accessible to all networked students through Local Area Networks (LANs). Students from other schools then added information about the weather in their community to the database. Eventually, the students had a large data set of recorded weather that was used for a variety of research projects.

Sofware to Build Databases

Students can build databases using programs such as ClarisWorks (Apple), FoxPro (Microsoft), and FilMaker Pro (Claris).

Directions and Example

1. Tell students that, even though they have collected a great deal of information from reading their sources, they need to organize it before they can write a report. Explain that data can be organized in many ways and that students need to decide how they want their data organized.

2. Model how a researcher would read data and decide on categories for inputting the data in a database. Use an example from your content area or use the example that follows.

   One of the research questions we have been considering based on our textbook *Exploring Careers* (1990) is careers in health occupations. Several sources, both print and nonprint, were used to find the information. A partial list of the information is contained in the following chart.

Health Careers

Medical Practitioners	Medical Records Personnel	Rehabilitation Occupations
Treat patients	Keep records	Work with patients
Diagnose illness	Office job	Hands-on work
Work in office or hospital	Work in office or hospital	Work in hospital or homes
Need M.D.	Various positions	Need special training

3. Discuss ways these data could be organized into a database. In this example, one of the categories could be the education needed for a career. Another might be the location of the job.

4. Tell students that data in a database can be accessed in many different ways. Have students read their data, thinking of ways their data could be categorized. Then have the students input their data into a database.

5. Explain that the way data are retrieved from a database depends on the research question that is asked. Have students think about their research questions and manipulate their data so that their questions can be answered.

TEACHING STRATEGY 10

Information Charts

An Information Chart (I-Chart) is a strategy developed by Hoffman (1992) that has been adapted by Randall (1996) to help students select and organize relevant information from multiple sources as they conduct research. An I-Chart has three components: the preparation of the charts, research and notetaking using the charts, and the completion of a final product using the information organized within the charts. Teachers can use I-Charts as an instructional tool to explicitly teach the processes students need to use during research. As students become proficient researchers, teachers should guide students to use I-Charts independently.

Directions and Examples

1. Guide students in choosing topics and developing general research questions (see Section 9.1). After students have chosen topics, have them develop lists of sources from which they can find information (see Section 9.2).

2. Explain that once researchers have identified general research questions they need to develop additional questions that are more specific. These additional questions will be subtopics of their general research questions.

3. Divide the class into groups of three or four students. Have students read their research questions to the group. Then have students discuss subtopics of the questions that they intend to research. Model an example for the students before they begin by writing your research question and subtopics on the chalkboard or an overhead transparency, or use a computer with an LCD panel. See the following example.

We have been learning about the Harlem Renaissance in our text *The African American Experience: A History* (1992). Several of you have developed research questions that center around the African American artists and musicians who were popular during the 1920s. The following is a general research question about that topic.

Who were the driving forces behind the Harlem Renaissance?

From the general research question, we can think of specific questions that we need to answer before we can answer the general question. The following are some subtopics of our general research question.

- Who were some of the popular African American writers of the 1920s?
- Who were some of the popular African American artists of the 1920s?
- Who were some of the popular African American musicians and performing artists of the 1920s?
- Why were these people so influential?

4. Make a transparency of a blank I-Chart to display on an overhead projector. Write one of the subtopics of the research question in the blank as in the following example.

Subtopic: Who were some of the popular African American musicians and performing artists of the 1920s?

5. Distribute several copies of blank I-Charts to all students. Have them write each of their subtopics on a different chart.

6. Explain that students have a great deal of background knowledge about each of their subtopics but that reading other sources will provide them with more information. Tell students that part of researching is to identify what the researcher knows about the topic. Then have students write on the next line a brief statement about what they know about the subtopic.

What I already know: I know that Louis Armstrong (Satchmo) was a cornet player who was well-known for his jazz playing. I also know that Duke Ellington was a composer and conductor. I think he is known for the song *Mood Indigo*.

7. Have students write what they know about each subtopic on their charts under the section "What I already know."

8. Ask students to begin reading their source texts. Tell them that as they read their first source they should write the name on the line next to Source #1. If the source has information that answers the subtopic question, they should record that information on the Source #1 line. An example follows.

Source # 1 *Microsoft Encarta Encyclopedia* (CD-ROM)

Rose McClendon was one of the most popular American actresses early in the 1900s. McClendon acted in the play *Deep River* and later in *Porgy*, a play about African American life in South Carolina. McClendon was one of the founders of the Negro People's Theater in Harlem.

9. After students have taken notes from several sources and written the notes on the I-Charts, invite them to write in the blank labeled "Interesting related facts" that information that does not answer their

research question. Tell them that, even though this information will not be used for their current research, it is additional knowledge that they have gained by researching.

10. Explain that if students read any words that are new to them, they should note those words under the section "Key words." Finally, explain that as students read they should be considering additional research questions. Tell students that when they have new questions they should write them in the section "New questions to research."

11. A blank copy of an I-Chart follows.

While doing research, students often uncover interesting facts about unrelated topics.

Information Chart

Name _____ Topic _____

Subtopic _____

What I already know _____

_____

Source # 1 _____

_____

_____

_____

_____

_____

Source # 2 _____

_____

_____

_____

_____

_____

Interesting related facts _____

_____

_____

Key words _____

New questions to research _____

_____

_____

Adapted from Randall, S. N. (1996). Information charts: A strategy for organizing student research. *Journal of Adolescent & Adult Literacy, 39*, 536–542.

9.4 Synthesizing and Writing Information

Goal

To help students synthesize and write information gathered from research.

Background

When students conduct research, they find information from multiple sources that answers their research questions. This information is carefully selected and organized. Then students need to synthesize the information they have selected into a logical progression of thought. As they synthesize their material, they need to transform their texts into their own thoughts and words.

Synthesizing information from multiple sources is a complex undertaking. As researchers synthesize information from texts, they look for patterns in their material and weave together their knowledge to form new patterns of thought. This integration of information into something new is what makes researching different from paraphrasing or summarizing. Researchers take thoughts and ideas from outside sources and state them in new ways, thereby transforming ideas from many sources into their own words.

The paper or presentation that results from student research should be an integration of what the student knew about the topic before researching, what the student has learned from reading multiple sources, and how the student has transformed the material into new knowledge. Student research should be original in the sense that the products of research projects should indicate that students have learned from their research. Student research does not have to present ideas that no one else has thought of before, but the product of student research should be new learning.

TECHNOLOGY TIP

Writing Assistance Web Site

The Paradigm Online Writing Assistance is an interactive, menu-driven, online writers' guide distributed over the web. The main menu offers advice on the ways to organize writing.

Paradigm Online Writing Assistance
http://www.idbsu.edu/english/cguilfor/paradigm/

TEACHING STRATEGY **11**

Writing Frames

Once students have generated a research question, gathered information, and organized that information, they need to synthesize the information into a coherent whole. Students may present their information in a number of ways: they may decide to write a report; they may give an oral presentation; or they may present the material visually. No matter how students choose to present their research, the research needs to be organized so that an audience can follow the relationships among the ideas. To promote a logical flow of ideas, Ryder (1994) suggests using Writing Frames to organize ideas gathered from multiple sources. Writing Frames are grids with categories to organize material into patterns. The patterns that are most commonly used are descriptive, goal, and problem-solution. Teaching students to organize their thoughts into Writing Frames can help them synthesize and write their research findings.

Directions and Examples

1. Tell students that they need to look for relationships among their thoughts, ideas, and information and that they need to organize that information into a logical progression of thought. Explain that when students read or hear ideas that are clearly related, they can more easily understand what the author is saying. Tell students that there are three types of organizational patterns that are commonly used in writing: descriptive, goal, and problem-solution. Have students read their research questions and their notes and decide which type of pattern best fits their purposes. Model how a researcher would make those decisions. Use an example from your content area or use the following example.

    We have been reading about desert regions in our text *States and Regions* (1997) and have asked the following research question: How should the water in the Colorado River be allocated?

    Some of the information we found is that the Colorado River is the main source of water for much of Arizona, California, and Nevada. Over 30 years ago, representatives from the three states agreed on the amount of water each state would use. As these states became more inhabited, however, they began to need greater amounts of water. California needed additional water first. That wasn't a problem because there was plenty of water available, and Arizona and Nevada weren't using their shares. Now Arizona and Nevada need their shares of the water.

    To solve the problem, some people in California think that less water should be kept in Lake Mead. A group from Nevada thinks a commission should be created to determine how the water should be used. People in Arizona want to keep their supply of water in a water bank to be used as needed. So far the three groups do not agree on ways the water should be allocated.

    ▶ Adapted from *States and regions.* (1997). Orlando, FL: Harcourt Brace.

2. Explain that once students have decided on an organizational pattern they should write their main points on the appropriate Writing Frame. Tell students that Descriptive Frames should be used to present information that has the following relationships: compare-contrast, cause-effect, forms-functions, and advantages-disadvantages. Goal Frames should be used to display organizational structures of material such as goal-plan-action. Problem-Solution Frames should be used when problems and solutions are identified. Use your content area example or the following example to model how to list ideas in a Writing Frame.

Problems	Solutions
The states disagree on water allocation of Colorado River.	Allocate water to three states using former agreement.
Nevada anticipates growing water needs.	Create a commission to make allocation decisions.
California needs more water now.	Store less water in Lake Mead.

3. Have students use their Writing Frame as an organizational structure for their writing or presentation. Blank copies of Writing Frames follow.

Writing Frames

Cause-Effect Writing Frame

Causes	Effects	Locations

Goal-Action Writing Frame

Goals	Actions	Outcomes

Problem-Solution Writing Frame

Problems	Solutions

Based on Ryder, R.J. (1994). Using frames to promote critical writing. *Journal of Reading,* 38, 210–218.

Thinking Over-Thinking Through

When students synthesize information they have collected from their research, they need to transform it so that the ideas and words are theirs. Transforming text is the highest level of writing. When students transform text, they integrate new knowledge into their own knowledge base. Thinking Over-Thinking Through (Moffett, 1989) is a strategy that facilitates the complex cognitive act of transforming related information into a writer's own thoughts and words.

Directions and Example

1. Explain to students that, as they synthesize the information they have gathered, they will need to incorporate that information into what they already know about the topic and then transform that knowledge into new thoughts and ideas. When students restate what other authors have said, they are not making a contribution to knowledge about the research topic.

2. Tell students that they can transform texts by using the strategy Thinking Over-Thinking Through. Demonstrate the use of the strategy by employing a content area example or by using the example that follows. Begin by modeling how researchers rehearse their background knowledge and their research question. To model this, make the following comments.

    > I have been researching 20th century Chinese history. My question for this research is: How did The Long March impact the Communist China movement?

    > I know that the Communist Party of China was founded in 1921 and that it became popular early in the 1930s under the leadership of Mao Zedong (formerly Mao Tse-tung). I know that the Nationalist government attacked the Communists who escaped in a 6,000 mile journey, which is now called The Long March.

3. Explain that after they rehearse background knowledge researchers should "Think Over" what they have learned from their research. As students "Think Over" their material, they should read it, reread it, and look for answers to their research questions. Model how to use the "Think Over" strategy, as in the following example.

    > As I read about The Long March, I found that the Communists marched and fought their way from south central China to northwest China. The journey took over a year. They crossed 18 mountain ranges and 62 rivers. As they journeyed, they fought an average of one skirmish a day. As they moved through the countryside, the Communists publicized their cause in meetings and performances. They also redistributed land from the landlords to the peasants. Today The Long March is told and retold in stories and songs.

    ▶ Adapted from *Through Chinese eyes*. (1988). New York: Center for International Training and Education.

4. Tell students that after they have reread their notes they need to "Think Through" the topic by thinking about their background knowledge, remembering their research questions, and answering their research questions from the information they have learned. Tell students that in order to transform text they need

to answer their research questions, not state facts. Demonstrate how to answer a research question using information. Use an example from your content area or say the following:

> My research question is: How did The Long March impact the Communist China movement? I found out about The Long March, and now I need to answer my question. The Communist movement was being overshadowed by the Nationalist government before the journey. After the journey, several things happened. First, the high visibility of The Long March may have turned popular opinion toward Communism. Second, the March happened right before the Chinese had a long war with Japan. The war increased discontent with the Nationalist government. Therefore, the Communists looked like heroes. Finally, the March became one of the important cultural tales of China. That also indicates that it was influential in the Communist movement in China. In summary, The Long March was one of the influential factors in the Communist takeover of China. Taken with the other historical events, it may have been the impetus for the Communists' swift takeover of China.

5. Have students synthesize their information and write their reports using the Thinking Over-Thinking Through strategy. Remember that transforming text is a complex process that students learn over a long period of time and that they will need many opportunities to practice this skill before they are proficient at it.

TEACHING STRATEGY 13

I-Search

An I-Search paper is an alternative to a traditional research paper. The I-Search paper was devised by Macrorie (1984) to make writing research papers more meaningful to his students. When writing an I-Search paper, students write about their search process as they refine their research questions, locate and evaluate sources, select and organize information, and synthesize their findings. In essence, students tell the story of their research in a narrative paper. Since I-Search papers describe students' research processes as well as answers to research questions, these types of papers are useful tools when planning instruction for future research projects.

Directions and Example

1. Assign a research project that students can complete independently or in groups. (See Section 9.1 for ways to generate research questions.) As students think about their research questions, have them reflect on their process by writing in a journal or on the computer. Demonstrate how you could reflect on the process of generating a research question. Create a question that applies to your content area or use the following example.

> I have been watching the National Basketball Association (NBA) playoffs, and I decided that I could make better decisions than some of the coaches make. I have been watching basketball for my entire life, and I know most of the important statistics for players in the entire NBA. I want to use my interest and my knowledge for this research project. I know there are many directions I could take. I think what I want to do most is to create my own all-star basketball team using information I know or can find out about the players.

▶ Adapted from Roerden, L.P. (1997). *Net lessons: Web-based projects for your classroom.* Sebastopol, CA: Songline Studios.

2. Tell students that as they gather information that answers their research questions they should write both the information they located and how they found it. Model the process of narrating the search for information with an example from your content area or use the example that follows.

> To create my all-star basketball team, I accessed the NBA web site at www.nba.com. From that site, I found all sorts of statistics on the players I thought were stars. As I read that information, I decided that I would also ask others for their recommendations for my all-star team. I created a short survey with the names of 20 top players and e-mailed it to other basketball fans I know through the middle school newsgroup k12.ed.chat.junior. When my friends e-mailed me back, I added their ideas to a database that I created. Then I used the *Microsoft Explorapedia—The World of People* CD-ROM to find out additional information about my favorite players. Finally, I went to the library to find books written by and about the players on my top 20 list. I listed most of my information on I-Charts. Finally, I created my all-star team and e-mailed it to the Commissioner of the NBA for consideration. He had an assistant reply by e-mail. The assistant thanked me for my careful work.

3. Explain that, even though students are writing a narrative research paper, their work can be assessed in a manner similar to traditional research papers. Tell students that together you will be creating a rubric to assess their research papers. Divide the class into groups of three or four students. Have students generate components for assessing their research papers or use the following Research Paper Rubric Components list.

4. Use the ideas generated by the students and your own ideas to create a rubric for scoring the I-Search papers. Then use that rubric to assess the research papers. You may also want the students to assess their own papers.

Research Paper Rubric Components

	No				Yes
Topic Selection					
• Topic is compelling.	1	2	3	4	5
• Topic is realistic.	1	2	3	4	5
• Topic is important.	1	2	3	4	5
• Topic is not overly broad or too narrow.	1	2	3	4	5
Research Question					
• Question has a clear focus.	1	2	3	4	5
• Question addresses an important issue.	1	2	3	4	5
• Question is meaningful.	1	2	3	4	5
• Question is compelling.	1	2	3	4	5
Information Selection					
• Sources are appropriate.	1	2	3	4	5
• Sources are varied.	1	2	3	4	5
• Sources chosen evidence a broad search.	1	2	3	4	5
• Sources were evaluated before use.	1	2	3	4	5
Information Organization					
• Organization is apparent.	1	2	3	4	5
• Organization follows recognizable relationships.	1	2	3	4	5
• Organizational choice is appropriate.	1	2	3	4	5
Synthesizing Information					
• Information answers research question.	1	2	3	4	5
• Information is in student's own words.	1	2	3	4	5
• Information is synthesized in a compelling manner.	1	2	3	4	5

Based on Harvey, S. (1998). *Nonfiction matters: Reading, writing, and research.* York, ME: Stenhouse.

Professional Organizations

Note: The information below is subject to change, especially telephone numbers.

Art

National Art Education Association (NAEA)
1916 Association Dr.
Reston, VA 20191-1590
Phone: (703) 860-8000
FAX: (703) 860-2960
E-mail: naea@dgs.dgsys.com
Web site: http://www.naea-reston.org
Publications: *Art Education, Studies in Art Education*

Business

National Business Education Association (NBEA)
1914 Association Dr.
Reston, VA 20191-1596
Phone: (703) 860-8300
FAX: (703) 620-4483
E-mail: nbea@nbea.org
Web site: http://www.nbea.org
Publication: *Business Education Forum*

English

National Council of Teachers of English (NCTE)
1111 West Kenyon Rd.
Urbana, IL 61801-1096
Phone: (217) 328-3870
(800) 369-6283
FAX: (217) 328-0977
Web site: http://www.ncte.org
Publications: *English Leadership Quarterly, English Publication, NOTES Plus, Research in the Teaching of English, Language Arts, English Journal*

International Reading Association (IRA)
800 Barksdale Rd.
P.O. Box 8139
Newark: DE 19714-8139
Phone: (302) 731-1600
(800) 336-READ
FAX: (302) 731-1057
E-mail: 74673.3646@compuserve.com
Web site: http://www.ira.org
Publications: *Reading Research Quarterly, Reading Today, Journal of Reading, The Reading Teacher, Lectura y vida* (Spanish)

Foreign Languages

American Association of Teachers of French (AATF)
Mail Code 4510
Southern Illinois University
Carbondale, IL 62901-4510
Phone: (618) 536-5571
FAX: (618) 453-3253
E-mail: fmajatf@uiuc.edu
Publications: *AATF National Bulletin, French Review*

American Association of Teachers of German (AATG)
112 Haddontowne Ct. #104
Cherry Hill, NJ 08034
Phone: (609) 795-5553
FAX: (609) 795-9398
E-mail: AATG@compuserve.com
Web site: http://www.aatg.org
Publications: *American Association of Teachers of German Newsletter, Die Unterrichtspraxis: For the Teaching of German*

American Association for the Teachers of Spanish and Portuguese (AATSP)
c/o Dr. Lynn A. Sandstedt, Executive Director
University of Northern Colorado
210 Butler Hancock
Greeley, CO 80639
Phone: (970) 351-1090
FAX: (970) 351-1095
E-mail: lsandste@bentley.UnivNorthCo.edu
Web site: http://www.aatsp.org
Publication: *Hispania*

The American Classical League (ACL)
Miami University
Oxford, OH 45056
Phone: (513) 529-7741
FAX: (513) 529-7742
E-mail: American Classical League@muohio.edu
Web site: http://www.umich.edu/~acleague
Publication: *Classical Outlook*

American Council on the Teaching of Foreign Languages (ACTFL)
6 Executive Plaza
Yonkers, NY 10701
Phone: (914) 963-8830
FAX: (914) 963-1275
E-mail: actflhg@aol.com
Web site: http://www.actfl.org
Publications: *Foreign Language Annals, ACTFL Newsletter*

Teachers of English to Speakers of Other Languages (TESOL)
1600 Cameron St., Suite 300
Alexandria, VA 22314-2751
Phone: (703) 836-0774
FAX: (703) 836-6447 or (703) 836-7864
E-mail: tesol@tesol.edu
Web site: http://www.tesol.edu
Publications: *TESOL Journal, TESOL Quarterly*

Mathematics

National Council of Teachers of Mathematics (NCTM)
1906 Association Dr.
Reston, VA 20191-1593
Phone: (703) 620-9840
    (800) 235-7566

FAX: (703) 476-2970
Web site: http://www.nctm.org
Publications: *Mathematics Teacher, MCTN News Bulletin, Mathematics Teaching in the Middle School, Teaching Children Mathematics, Journal for Research in Mathematics*

Music

Music Educators National Conference (MENC)
1806 Robert Fulton Dr.
Reston, VA 20191
Phone: (703) 860-4000
    (800) 336-3768
FAX: (888) 275-6362
E-mail: mbmenc@aol.com
Web site: http://www.menc.org
Publications: *Music Educators' Journal, Journal of Music Teacher Education, Journal of Research in Music Education, Teaching Music, General Music Today*

Music Teachers National Association (MTNA)
441 Vine St., Suite 505
Cincinnati, OH 45202-2814
Phone: (513) 421-1420
FAX: (513) 421-2503
E-mail: MTNadmin@aol.com
Web site: http://www.mtna.org
Publication: *American Music Teacher*

Physical Education

American Alliance for Health, Physical Education, Recreation and Dance (AAHPERD)
1900 Association Dr.
Reston, VA 20191
Phone: (703) 476-3400
    (800) 213-7193
FAX: (703) 476-9527
E-mail: evp@aahperd.org
Web site: http://www.aahperd.org
Publications: *AAHPERD Update, Health Educator, Journal of Physical Education, Recreation and Dance, Journal of Health Education*

Science

National Science Teachers Association (NSTA)
1840 Wilson Blvd.
Arlington, VA 22201-3000
Phone: (703) 243-7100
FAX: (703) 243-7177
E-mail: publicinfo@NSTA.org
Web site: http://www.nsta.org
Publications: *The Science Teacher, Science and Children, Science Scope, Quantum*

National Association of Biology Teachers (NABT)
11250 Roger Bacon Dr. #19
Reston, VA 20190-5202
Phone: (703) 471-1134
      (800) 406-0775
FAX: (703) 435-5582
E-mail: NABTer@aol.com
Web site: http://www.nabt.org
Publications: *National Association of Biology Teachers—News and Views, The American Biology Teacher*

Social Studies

National Council for the Social Studies (NCSS)
3501 Newark St. N.W.
Washington, DC 20016-3167
Phone: (202) 966-7840
FAX: (202) 966-2061
E-mail: ncss@ncss.org
Web site: http://www.ncss.org
Publications: *Social Education, The Social Studies Professional, Social Studies Middle School Journal, Theory & Research in Social Education*

Technology

Association for the Advancement of Computing in Education (AACE)
P.O. Box 2966
Charlottesville, VA 22902
Phone: (804) 973-3987
FAX: (804) 978-7449
Web site: www.aace.org
Publications: *Journal of Computers in Mathematics and Science Teaching, Information Technology and Childhood Education Annual, Educational Technology*

Review, Journal of Interactive Learning Research

International Society for Technology in Education (ISTE)
1787 Agate St.
Eugene, OR 97403-1923
Web site: iste-gopher.uoregon.edu
Publications: *The Computing Teacher, Journal of Research on Computing in Education, Telecommunications in Education*

General Professional Organizations

Association for Supervision and Curriculum Development (ASCD)
1250 N. Pitt St.
Alexandria, VA 22314-1453
Phone: (703) 549-9110
      (800) 933-2723
FAX: (703) 299-8631
Web site: http://www.ascd.org
Publications: *Educational Leadership, Journal of Curriculum & Supervision*

Council for Exceptional Children (CEC)
1920 Association Dr.
Reston, VA 20191-1589
Phone: (703) 620-3660
FAX: (703) 264-9494
Web site: http://www.cec.sped.org
Publications: *Teaching Exceptional Children, Exceptional Child Education Resources, Exceptional Children*

National Association for Gifted Children (NAGC)
1707 L St. N.W., Suite 550
Washington, DC 20036
Phone: (202) 785-4268
Web site: http://www.nagc.org
Publication: *Gifted Child Quarterly*

National Middle School Association (NMSA)
2600 Corporate Exchange Dr., Suite 370
Columbus, OH 43231
Phone: (614) 895-4730
      (800) 528-6672
FAX: (614) 895-4750
Web site: http://www.nmsa.org
Publications: *Middle School Journal, High Strides, Middle Ground*

Resources for Middle and High School Content Areas

Books

Adamson, L.G. (1994). *Re-creating the past: A guide to American and world historical fiction for children and young adults.* New York: Greenwood Press.

Benedict, S. (1991). *Beyond words: Picture books for older readers and writers.* Portsmouth, NH: Heinemann.

Burroughs, L. (1988). *Introducing children to the arts: A practical guide for librarians and educators.* Boston: G.K. Hall.

Carlsen, G.R. (1980). *Books and the teenage reader: A guide for teachers, librarians, and parents.* New York: Bantam Books.

Carter, B.C., & Abrahamson, R.F. (1990). *From delight to wisdom: Nonfiction for young adults.* Phoenix: Oryx.

Carter, B.C., & Abrahamson, R.F. (1988). *Books for you: A booklist for senior high students* (5th ed.). Phoenix: Oryx Press.

Christensen, J. (Ed.). (1983). *Your reading: A booklist for junior high students.* Urbana, IL: National Council of Teachers of English.

Cline, R.K., & McBride, W.G. (1983). *A guide to literature for young adults: Background, selection, and use.* Glenview, IL: Scott Foresman.

Hartman, D.K., & Sapp, G. (1994). *Historical figures in fiction.* Phoenix: Oryx Press.

International Reading Association. (1996). *More teens' favorite books: Young adults' choices 1993–1995.* Newark, DE: International Reading Association.

International Reading Association. (1992). *Teens' favorite books: Young adults' choices 1987–1993.* Newark, DE: International Reading Association.

Kennedy, D.M., Spangler, S.S., & Vanderwerf, M. A. (1990). *Science and technology in fact and fiction: A guide to children's books.* New York: R.R. Bowker.

Kennemer, P.K. (1993). *Using literature to teach middle grades about war.* Phoenix: Oryx.

McBride, W.G. (Ed.). (1990). *High interest-easy reading: A booklist for junior and senior high school students* (6th ed.). Urbana, IL: National Council of Teachers of English.

Moss, J., & Wilson, G. (1992). *From page to screen: Children's and young adult books on film and video.* Detroit: Gale Research.

Pilla, M.L. (1990). *The best high/low books for reluctant readers.* Englewood, CO: Libraries Unlimited.

Robertson, D. (1992). *Portraying persons with disabilities: An annotated bibliography of fiction for children and teenagers.* New York: R.R. Bowker.

Rochman, H. (1993). *Against borders: Promoting books for a multicultural world.* Chicago: American Library Association.

Thiessen, D., & Matthias, M. (Eds.). (1993). *The wonderful world of mathematics: A critically annotated list of children's books in mathematics.* Reston, VA: National Council of Teachers of Mathematics.

Trelease, J. (1995). *The read aloud handbook.* New York: Penguin Books.

VanMeter, V. (1990). *American history for children and young adults: An annotated bibliographic index.* Englewood, CO: Libraries Unlimited.

Webb, C.A. (Ed.). (1993). *Your reading: A booklist for junior high and middle school students* (8th ed.). Urbana, IL: National Council of Teachers of English.

Selected Web Sites

AMAZON—a bookstore where 1.1 million titles are searchable by author.
http://www.amazon.com

Books Stacks Unlimited—a bookstore with symposiums on books.
http://www.books.com

Do You Know? Will You Remember?—books and web sites about the Holocaust.

Favorite Teenage Angst Books—lists and reviews of problem novels.
http//www.echonyc.com/~cafephrk/angstbooks.html

Internet Book Information Center—lists of books.
http://sunsite.unc.edu/ibic/IBIC-homepage.html

Internet Poetry Archive
http://dundiyr.unc.edu/dykki/poetry/

Internet School Library Media Center Historical Fiction Suggestions—lists and reviews of historical fiction.
http://falcon.jmu.edu/~ramseyil/historical.htm

Kids In Between—suggested materials and books with lower reading levels for secondary school students.
http://.kidsinbetween.com

Online Literature Library—books online.
http://www.cs.cmu.edu/Web/books.html

Recommended Young Adult Reading—book picks from a young adult librarian.
http://www.st-charles.lib.il.us/low/ygadread.htm

The Children's Literature Web Guide
http://www.ucalcary.ca/dkbrown/index.html

World Wide Web Virtual Literature Library
http://sunsite.unc.edu:bic/IBIC-homepage.html

Journals That Publish Trade Book Reviews and Lists

ALAN Review. Assembly on Literature for the Adolescent, National Council of Teachers of English. Published 3 times per year.

Appraisal: Science Books for Young People. Children's Science Book Review Committee. Published 3 times per year.

Booklist. American Library Association. Published 22 times per year.

English Journal. National Council of Teachers of English. Published 8 times per year.

Interracial Books for Children Bulletin. Council of Interracial Books for Children. Published 8 times per year.

Journal of Adolescent and Adult Literacy. International Reading Association. Published 8 times per year.

Journal of Youth Services in Libraries. Association of Literacy Service for Children and the Young Adult Services Division of the American Library Association. Published 4 times per year.

Kirkus Reviews. Kirkus Service. Published 4 times per year.

School Library Journal. R. R. Bowker Company. Published 12 times per year.

The Horn Book Magazine. Horn Book. Published 6 times per year.

Assessing Text Difficulty: Using Readability Formulas

Overview

Texts have varying degrees of difficulty. Consider the following sentence from *Chemistry* (1995, p. 87): "An electron carries exactly one unit of negative charge and its mass is 1/1840 the mass of a hydrogen atom." Note the length of the sentence, the vocabulary, and the concepts. These are some of the factors that can have an impact on the difficulty of a text. Such factors are called text variables. In addition to text variables, students vary in their reading levels, motivation, and interests. These factors, called reader variables, can also influence the difficulty of a text for a particular student. Some text and reader variables are shown below.

Text Variables	Reader Variables
• vocabulary difficulty	• reading level
• sentence complexity	• motivation
• format	• background knowledge
• typography	• interests
• content	• engagement
• literary form	• intellectual abilities
• literary style	• topic familiarity
• concept load	
• cohesiveness	

Harris and Hodges (1995, p. 203) note that "text and reader variables interact in determining the readability of any piece of reading material for any individual reader." Readability refers to estimating the difficulty of understanding a particular text by using some of the text variables listed above. One way to estimate the difficulty of a text is to use a readability formula. It can provide one answer to the question "How difficult is this text or book?"

The first true readability formula was probably published in 1923 (Klare, 1963). Since that time, over 100 readability formulas have been published. A few of the more popular formulas include the Dale-Chall, Spache, Flesch, and Fry. Below is a step-by-step procedure for using the Fry readability graph to make a readability calculation by hand.

Procedure for Using Fry Readability Formula

1. Randomly select three sample passages and count out exactly 100 words in each, starting with the beginning of a sentence. Count proper nouns, initialisms, and numerals.

2. Count the number of sentences in the 100 words, estimating the length of the fraction of the last sentence to the nearest one-tenth.

3. Count the total number of syllables in the 100-word passage. If you don't have a hand counter available, an easy way is to simply put a mark above every syllable over one in each word. When you get to the

end of the passage, count the number of marks and add 100. Small calculators can also be used as counters by pushing numeral 1 and then pushing the + sign for each word or syllable when counting.

4. Enter the graph with *average* sentence length and *average* number of syllables; then plot a dot where the two lines intersect. The area where the dot is plotted will give you the approximate grade level.

5. If a great deal of variability is found in the syllable count or sentence count, putting more samples into the average is desirable.

6. A word is defined as a group of symbols with a space on either side; thus, *Joe, IRA, 1945,* and *&* are each one word.

7. A syllable is defined as a phonetic syllable. Generally, there are as many syllables as vowel sounds. For example, *stopped* is one syllable and *wanted* is two syllables. When counting syllables for numerals and initialisms, count one syllable for each symbol. For example, *1945* is four syllables. *IRA* is three syllables, and *&* is one syllable.

Fry's Graph for Estimating Readability

Average Number of Syllables per 100 Words

Adapted from Fry, E. (1968). A readability formula that saves time. *Journal of Reading, 11,* 513–516 and Fry, E. (1977). Fry's readability graph: Clarifications, validity, and extension to level 17. *Journal of Reading, 21,* 242–252. The Fry Readability Graph is not copyrighted. Reproduction is permitted. From Susan Davis Lenski, Mary Ann Wham, and Jerry L. Johns, *Reading & Learning Strategies for Middle & High School Students.* Copyright © 1999 by Kendall Hunt Publishing Company (1-800-228-0810).

A Few Notes on the Fry Readability Technique

1. It is recommended that a *minimum* of three samples from a book be evaluated for readability. The procedure is exemplified below.

	Sentences Per 100 Words	Syllables Per 100 Words
100-word sample, page 5	4.0	148
100-word sample, page 89	3.6	152
100-word sample, page 163	5.0	144
	12.6÷3=4.2	444÷3=148

By plotting the average sentence length (4.2) and the average number of syllables (148) on the graph, the readability is tenth grade. If great variability is encountered in either sentence length or in the syllable count for the three samples, randomly select several more passages and average them before plotting the results on the graph. Be certain to note that the book has uneven readability.

2. The readability estimate is probably accurate within a grade level.

3. The readability estimate is given in terms of a grade level. There are **no** fine distinctions such as 3.1, 7.4, or 11.2. Readability is given in terms of whole grade levels.

4. The Fry formula correlated highly with the Dale-Chall (r=.94) and the Flesch (r=.96) readability formulas.

Example of Applying the Fry Readability Formula

Below is one sample from *Algebra 2* (1995, p. 122). At least two additional samples should be evaluated, but they are not included in the example.

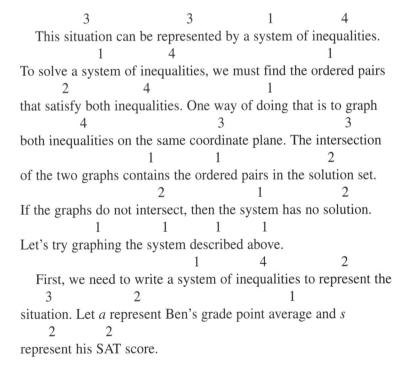

3   3   1   4
This situation can be represented by a system of inequalities.
1   4   1
To solve a system of inequalities, we must find the ordered pairs
2   4   1
that satisfy both inequalities. One way of doing that is to graph
4   3   3
both inequalities on the same coordinate plane. The intersection
1   1   2
of the two graphs contains the ordered pairs in the solution set.
2   1   2
If the graphs do not intersect, then the system has no solution.
1   1   1   1
Let's try graphing the system described above.
1   4   2
First, we need to write a system of inequalities to represent the
3   2   1
situation. Let *a* represent Ben's grade point average and *s*
2   2
represent his SAT score.

5. Count the number of sentences. The number of sentences is 8.

6. Count the number of syllables. Begin with 100 (the number of words) and then put numerals above each word for *every syllable over one.* The number of syllables is 164.

7. Enter the graph with the sentence length (8) and number of syllables (164). Place a dot where the two lines intersect. The area where the dot is plotted gives the approximate grade level. In this example, the approximate grade level is 10.

Using Personal Computers to Estimate Text Readability

With the growing use of personal computers, it is not necessary to go through the laborious process of doing the numerous calculations by hand to estimate the readability of a piece of writing. You can type in selections from the text or piece of writing, and the computer does the rest. Word-processing programs will often contain one or more readability formulas. In addition, separate readability programs can be purchased; these programs are usually available in Macintosh and Windows versions. Listed below are two readability programs that can be used with personal computers.

Readability Master 2000 (Brookline Books, P.O. Box 1047, Cambridge, MA 02238) 800-666-BOOK.

> Macintosh and Windows versions of this program give scores based on the New Dale-Chall Readability Formula, the Spache Readability Formula, and the Fry Readability Formula.

Readability Calculations (Micro Power & Light Company, 8814 Sanshire Avenue, Dallas, TX 75231) 214-553-0105.

> Macintosh and Windows versions of these programs provide scores for seven or eight readability formulas, depending on the particular program purchased. Among the readability formulas are Fry, Flesch, FOG, and Dale-Chall.

The same sample from the high school mathematics book was used with *Readability Calculations.* Below is the resulting printout (with numerals added on the left).

1. Sample Begins: This situation can be
    Sample Ends: and *s* represent his SAT score.

2. Words: 100
3. Syllables: 159
4. Syllables (Fry): 161
5. Monosyllabic Words: 75
6. Words of 3 or More Syllables: 21
7. Difficult Words (FOG): 18
8. Difficult Words (Dale-Chall): 31
9. Sentences: 8

10. Syllables / Word: 1.60
11. Syllables / 100 Words: 159.01
12. Syllables / 100 Words (Fry): 161.01
13. Monosyllabic Words / 100 Words: 75.01
14. Polysyllabic Words / 100 Words: 21.01
15. Sentences / 100 Words: 8.01
16. Words / Sentence: 12.51
17. % of Words Not on the Dale-Chall List: 31.01

18. Dale-Chall Grade Level: 9.2
19. Flesch Reading Ease: 59.64
20. Flesch Grade Level: 8.0
21. FOG Grade Level: 12.2
22. Powers* Grade Level: 6.0
23. SMOG Grade Level: 11.9
24. FORCAST Grade Level: 8.8

Item 1 refers to the first and last phrases of the sample passage selected for the readability analysis. Items 2 through 17 refer to various aspects of the sample passage. These items are used in calculating the various readability formulas. For example, items 2, 4, and 8 are used in the Fry readability formula. The computer program automatically uses this information and plots the resulting grade level on a graph that can be viewed on the computer screen. In this case, the result is grade 10—the same level we obtained by doing the formula by hand. (The difference in the syllable count is due to the abbreviation SAT. The computer program apparently considered SAT one word; however, initialisms should be counted as one syllable for each symbol. In addition, *average* can be counted as two or three syllables.)

Items 18 through 24 present the resulting readabilities for the passage when six different readability formulas were used. Note that the results range from grade 6.0 to 12.2. It is not unusual for formulas to give different results for the same passage. Because readability formulas use information in different ways, the results should be expected to vary. Making sense of the results is the challenge.

The Powers-Sumner-Kearl Formula is used most often for the primary grades, and it seldom produces scores above the seventh-grade level. The FOG and SMOG results are often higher than other formulas because they estimate the reading level necessary to understand the material completely. Based on experience, we recommend that the results from the Fry and Dale-Chall formulas be given priority in estimating text difficulty. Both formulas are widely known and used. In addition, the Dale-Chall formula has been updated recently (Chall & Dale, 1995). If the results of these formulas applied to the mathematics textbook sample are considered, the grade levels are 9.2 and 10. Such results, when based on several samples from the text, suggest that the book may be suitable for students who read at the ninth-grade and tenth-grade levels.

Some Things to Remember about Readability Formulas

When using readability formulas, there are some general cautions to keep in mind. With regard to text variables, readability formulas do not consider graphic aids (charts, diagrams, photographs, etc.) that may help make the text more readable. Instead, the formulas rely heavily on word length and sentence length, thereby assuming that shorter words and sentences are easier to understand than longer words and sentences. There are times, however, when a longer sentence that links two thoughts may actually be more comprehensible than the same information in two shorter sentences. Remember that all readability formulas are only estimates of a book's difficulty, and the resulting grade-level score is not exact. A Fry readability estimate, for example, is probably accurate within plus and minus one grade level.

Readability formulas can often be a useful beginning point for assessing text difficulty. The results of formulas should also be combined with qualitative judgments of the text's overall organization, other physical features of the text (e.g., photographs, illustrations, charts, headings, marginal notes), and your students' backgrounds.

Perhaps the most important reader variable to remember is that readability formulas do not directly consider the student who will read the book. A student's interests and motivation, for example, are generally not taken into account. All the reader variables listed above are important in determining the suitability of a book for a student or class.

Assessing Text Difficulty: Developing Cloze Tests to Determine Textbook Appropriateness

Simply stated, a cloze test is a passage from a text in which 50 words have been deleted. Here is a partial example from *Mechanical Drawing* (1990, p. 22):

Engineering has evolved into _____ specialized branches, including aerospace,

_____, architectural, chemical, civil, electrical, _____, mechanical,

mining and metallurgical, _____, petroleum, plastics, and safety. _____

branch uses specialized drafting _____.   The science and mathematics

_____ to each branch help _____ natural resources into processes

_____ provide useful new material _____ products and machines.

Answers: 1. many 2. agricultural 3. industrial 4. nuclear 5. Each 6. skills 7. common 8. convert 9. that 10. for.

You can use cloze tests to help determine the suitability of a text for your classes. If a particular text is judged to be difficult for most students in the class, preparation and guidance before, during, and after reading may help reduce the difficulty of the material. Cloze tests are "a better way to test the difficulty of instructional materials and evaluate their suitability for students" (Bormuth, 1975, p. 65).

It is important to match students with books of appropriate difficulty. Content area books are frequently written above the average student's reading ability, thereby making the book difficult to understand. The situation that occurs because of a mismatch between a student and a book is even more serious when the range of reading ability within the classroom is considered. Students will experience frustration if they are asked to glean information from books that are too difficult for them to read. The cloze procedure helps you determine whether a book is at the student's independent, instructional, or frustration level.

The independent level is that level at which the student demonstrates excellent comprehension and can pronounce practically all of the words. The student would generally not make more than one significant error in each 100 words. With respect to comprehension, the student's score should be no lower than 90% when various types of comprehension questions are asked (Johns, 1997).

The instructional level is that level at which the student is challenged but not frustrated. To be considered at the student's instructional level, materials should be read with not more than five significant errors in each 100 words. In terms of comprehension, the student should be able to achieve a score of 75% (Johns, 1997).

The frustration level is that level at which the student should not be asked to read. Students at their frustration levels mispronounce many words and are unable to understand the reading material. Generally, students make 10 or more errors in every 100 words (90% or less) and achieve comprehension scores of 50% or less (Johns, 1997).

Developing and Administering Teacher-Made Cloze Tests

The first step in developing a cloze test is to select a number of passages from the book being evaluated. Bormuth (1975) suggests that as few as one to three passages can be adequate for evaluating a text for class use. Additional samples (up to 12) may provide further information. We recommend that five samples, randomly selected from the book, be used. After the five samples have been selected, each one should be inspected to determine whether comprehension of the passage depends heavily on preceding text material. If it does, another passage should be selected. Also, the passage should be unified and should not contain many mathematical symbols or numerals.

The second step is to count approximately 250 words in each passage and then randomly choose any word at the beginning of the passage. Delete this word and every fifth word until 50 words have been deleted. A number such as 1492 is counted as one word and hyphenated words that can stand alone as separate words may be counted as separate words (e.g., empty-handed). After the words have been deleted, type the passage. In place of every fifth word that has been deleted, type a 15-space underline. Do *not* deviate from the standard underlined blank. Any deviation from this procedure invalidates the test for evaluating textbook appropriateness. Butler (1990) discusses how a computer program can be used to construct cloze tests.

The third step is to run off copies of the cloze passages and administer them to students in your class. The sample test should orient the students to the testing procedure. Students should also be told that the cloze tests may be harder than most tests they have taken previously.

Each of the five cloze tests should be given to approximately 25 students. If five classes of 25 students each are using the text to be evaluated, each of the five passages could be randomly assigned within each class. Teachers have found that cooperation with colleagues makes it quite easy to secure the necessary classes to evaluate a particular book.

Scoring and Interpreting Teacher-Made Cloze Tests

After the tests have been given, they are scored by accepting only exact words as correct (disregarding misspellings). The omission of plural or tense endings (e.g., "neutron" for "neutrons" or "translate" for "translated") is scored as incorrect. Bormuth (1975, p. 72) answers a question that many teachers raise when scoring tests:

> Some argue that when a student writes in a synonym for the deleted word this shows that he or she understood the passage and therefore synonyms should be scored as correct. Their speculations are correct in asserting that a synonym reflects comprehension. Scores based on synonyms show a fairly high correlation with other measures of comprehension, such as scores on standardized tests of comprehension achievement and cloze test scores based on exactly matching responses. The chief problem is that scorers disagree on what is an acceptable synonym and, so far, it has been impossible to devise a set of rules for settling these disputes. Consequently, scoring synonyms correct detracts from the reliability of the scores.

Since cloze tests contain 50 items, the number of correct items can be doubled to determine the percentage of items answered correctly by each student. Scoring may be facilitated by using a window key with holes cut in a sheet of paper so that only the students' responses are visible. The correct response can be written near each window for ease in scoring.

After each of the five passages has been scored, the arithmetic average (mean) for each passage is determined. To compute the average, the teacher should add all of the percentage scores for that particular passage and divide by the number of students who completed it. Below are some sample resulting percentages.

Cloze Passage	Mean Percentage
1	52
2	44
3	36
4	54
5	40

Next, the mean percentages for the five passages are averaged by adding the five percentages and dividing by five. In the example above, the resulting percentage is approximately 45. Then, the passage whose mean is closest to the mean of 45 is selected as being representative of the book. In the example above, the representative passage is number 2, whose mean is 44. This passage would then be used in future classes for determining the suitability of the text. It would no longer be necessary to administer all five passages.

Finally, passage 2 is administered to all students who have not yet read that passage. The percentage for each student is then determined and compared to the appropriate criterion scores developed by Bormuth (1975, p. 80) and contained in the following table. A ninth-grade student, for example, would need a cloze score of approximately 52% if the book is to be used as a textbook in the classroom. If the book is to be used for reference, the cloze score should be 47%. The criterion scores should serve as guidelines, not rigid cut-off points. Bormuth found that students who made cloze scores below 35% gleaned little or no information from the selections. It would be appropriate for teachers to use 35% as the lowest acceptable cloze score. Bormuth (1975, p. 81) states the case more strongly: "materials falling below that level [35%] are essentially worthless for teaching that student." When materials are selected for instructional purposes, teachers should try to choose a text where the mean cloze score is slightly above the textbook criterion score for a particular grade level. This practice will help ensure that the text is partially comprehensible to nearly every student.

Criterion Percentage Scores for Cloze Readability Tests								
Use to be Made of the Materials	Grade Level of Student							
	4	5	6	7	8	9	10	11	12
Textbook	58	57	56	55	53	52	50	50	49
Reference	53	52	51	49	48	47	45	45	44
Voluntary	62	54	50	49	46	44	40	34	34

Directions for Taking Cloze Tests

Following these directions is a sample cloze test. This test was made by copying a few paragraphs from a book. Every fifth word was left out of the paragraphs and replaced by a blank space.

Your job will be to guess what word was left out of each space and to write that word in the blank space. It will help you in taking the test if you remember these things.

1.   Write only one word in each blank.

2.   Try to fill every blank. Don't be afraid to guess.

3.   You may skip difficult blanks and come back to them when you have finished.

4.   Incorrect spelling will not count against you if we can figure out what word you mean.

5.   Most of the blanks can be answered with ordinary words but a few will be words like the following ones.

numbers like . . . . 3,427 or $12 or 1954
contractions like . . . . can't or weren't
abbreviations like . . . . Mrs. or U.S.A.
parts of hyphenated words like . . . . self- in the word self-made
entire hyphenated words like . . . . surface-point

Sample Test

Below is a sample cloze test from *Biological Sciences: An Ecological Approach* (1995, p. 348). Fill each blank with the word you think is missing. You may check your paper when you finish by looking at the answers, which are written upside down at the bottom of the page. Write neatly.

Many common conifers are _____ adapted to life in _____ habitats.

For example, although _____ trees may grow where _____ is much

snow, the _____ is really frozen water _____ is not available for

_____. In the spring, much _____ the snow evaporates, and

_____ melted snow may run _____ into streams before it

_____ into the soil. The _____ of pines are well _____

for growth in dry _____. The long, narrow needles _____ the

amount of water _____ by evaporation. In addition, _____ pine

needle often is _____ by a thick, waxy _____ that further reduces

water _____.

Answers: 1. well 2. dry 3. pine 4. there 5. snow 6. and 7. growth 8. of 9. the 10. off 11. soaks 12. leaves 13. adapted 14. places 15. reduce 16. lost 17. a 18. covered 19. cuticle 20. loss

Adapted from Bormuth, J.R. (1975). Literacy in the classroom. In W.D. Page (Ed.), *Help for the reading teacher: New directions in research* (pp. 60–90). Urbana: ERIC Clearinghouse on Reading and Communication Skills. From Susan Davis Lenski, Mary Ann Wham, and Jerry L. Johns, *Reading & Learning Strategies for Middle & High School Students.* Copyright © 1999, Kendall Hunt Publishing Company (1-800-228-0810). May be reproduced for noncommercial educational purposes.

Appendix E

Professional Material Cited in this Book

Afflerbach, P. (1996). Engaged assessment of engaged readers. In L. Baker, P. Afflerbach, & D. Reinking (Eds.), *Developing engaged readers in school and home communities* (pp. 191–214). Mahwah, NJ: Erlbaum.

Alexander, J., & Tate, M. (1998, April 8). *The web as a research tool: Evaluation techniques* [On-line]. Available: http://www.science.widener.edu/~withers/advoc.htm

Alvermann, D.E. (1992). The discussion web: A graphic aid for learning across the curriculum. *The Reading Teacher, 45*, 92–99.

Alvermann, D.E., & Moore, D.W. (1991). Secondary school reading. In R. Barr, M.L. Kamil, P. Mosenthal, & P.D. Pearson (Eds.), *Handbook of reading research* (Vol. II) (pp. 951–983). White Plains, NY: Longman.

Alvermann, D.E., & Phelps, S.F. (1998). *Content reading and literacy* (2nd ed.). Boston: Allyn and Bacon.

Alvermann, D.E., & Qian, G.G. (1994). Perspectives on secondary school reading: Implications for instruction. *Reading & Writing Quarterly: Overcoming Learning Difficulties, 10*, 21–38.

Amendment deprives faithful of protections. (1998, June 1). *USA Today*, p. A10.

Anderson, R.C., & Pearson, P.D. (1984). A schema-theoretic view of basic processes in reading comprehension. In P.D. Pearson (Ed.), *Handbook of reading research* (pp. 255–291). New York: Longman.

Anderson, T.H., & Armbruster, B.B. (1991). The value of taking notes during lectures. In R.F. Flippo & D.C. Caverly (Eds.), *Teaching reading & study strategies at the college level* (pp. 166–194). Newark, DE: International Reading Association.

Anderson, T.H., & Armbruster, B.B. (1984). Studying. In P.D. Pearson (Ed.), *Handbook of reading research* (pp. 657–679). New York: Longman.

Antes, R.L. (1989). *Preparing students for taking tests* (Fastback 291). Bloomington, IN: Phi Delta Kappa Educational Foundation.

Armbruster, B.B. (1986, December). *Using frames to organize expository text*. Paper presented at the annual meeting of the National Reading Conference, Austin, TX.

Armbruster, B.B., Anderson, T.H., & Ostertag, J. (1989). Teaching text structure to improve reading and writing. *The Reading Teacher, 43*, 130–137.

Armbruster, B.B., Anderson, T.H., & Ostertag, J. (1987). Does text structure/summarization instruction facilitate learning from expository text? *Reading Research Quarterly, 22*, 331–346.

Artley, A.S. (1943). Teaching word meaning through context. *Elementary English Review, 20*, 68–74.

Au, K.H. (1993). *Literacy instruction in multicultural settings*. New York: Harcourt Brace Jovanovich.

Baker, L. (1991). Metacognition, reading, and science education. In C.M. Santa & D.E. Alvermann (Eds.), *Science learning: Processes and applications* (pp. 3–13). Newark, DE: International Reading Association.

Baker, L., & Brown, A.L. (1984). Metacognitive skills and reading. In P.D. Pearson (Ed.), *Handbook of reading research* (pp. 353–394). White Plains, NY: Longman.

Baskin, B.H., & Harris, K. (1995). Heard any good books lately? The case for audiobooks in the secondary classroom. *Journal of Reading, 38,* 372–376.

Baumann, J.F., & Kameenui, E.J. (1991). Research on vocabulary instruction: Ode to Voltaire. In J. Flood, J. Jensen, D. Lapp, & J. Squire (Eds.), *Handbook of research on teaching the English language arts* (pp. 604–632). New York: Macmillan.

Bean, T.W., Sorter, J., Singer, H., & Frazee, C. (1986). Teaching students how to make predictions about events in history with a graphic organizer plus options guide. *Journal of Reading, 29,* 739–745.

Beck, I.L., & McKeown, M.G. (1991). Social studies texts are hard to understand: Mediating some of the difficulties. *Language Arts, 68,* 482–490.

Beck, I.L., McKeown, M.G., Hamilton, R.L., & Kucan, L. (1997). *Questioning the author: An approach for enhancing student engagement with text.* Newark, DE: International Reading Association.

Blachowicz, C.L.Z. (1986). Making connections: Alternatives to the vocabulary notebook. *Journal of Reading, 29,* 543–549.

Bormuth, J.R. (1975). Literacy in the classroom. In W.D. Page (Ed.), *Help for the reading teacher: New directions in research* (pp. 60–90). Urbana, IL: ERIC Clearinghouse on Reading and Communication Skills.

Bransford, J.D., & McCarrell, N.S. (1974). A sketch of a cognitive approach to comprehension. In W.B. Weimer & D.S. Palermo (Eds.), *Cognition and the symbolic processes* (pp. 52–74). Hillsdale, NJ: Erlbaum.

Braun, J.A., Fernlund, P., & White, C.S. (1998). *Technology tools in the social studies curriculum.* Wilsonville, OR: Franklin, Beedle.

Brechtel, T. (1992). *Bringing the whole together: An integrated whole-language approach for the multilingual classroom.* San Diego: Dominic Press.

Brophy, J. (1986). Teacher influences on student achievement. *American Psychologist, 41,* 1069–1077.

Brozo, W.G., & Simpson, M.L. (1995). *Readers, teachers, learners: Expanding literacy in secondary schools* (2nd ed.). Columbus, OH: Merrill.

Buehl, D. (1995). *Classroom strategies for interactive learning.* Schofield, WI: Wisconsin State Reading Association.

Bulgren, J., & Scanlon, D. (1997/1998). Instructional routines and learning strategies that promote understanding of content area concepts. *Journal of Adolescent & Adult Literacy, 41,* 292–302.

Butler, G. (1990). Using FrEd writer to create "cloze" reading lessons. *The Writing Handbook, 7,* 39.

Carr, E., & Wixson, K. (1986). Guidelines for evaluating vocabulary instruction. *Journal of Reading, 50,* 588–595.

Cassady, J.K. (1998). Wordless books: No-risk tools for inclusive middle-grade classrooms. *Journal of Adolescent & Adult Literacy, 41,* 428–432.

Caverly, D.C., Mandeville, T.F., & Nicholson, S.A. (1995). PLAN: A study-reading strategy for informational text. *Journal of Adolescent & Adult Literacy, 39,* 190–199.

Chall, J.S., & Dale, E. (1995). *Readability revisited.* Cambridge, MA: Brookline Books.

Chapman, A. (1993). *Making sense: Teaching critical reading across the curriculum.* New York: College Board.

Childress, H. (1998). Seventeen reasons why football is better than high school. *Phi Delta Kappan, 78,* 616–619.

Clewell, S., & Haidemenous, J. (1982, April). *Organizational strategies to increase content area learning: Webbing, pyramiding, and think sheets.* Paper presented at the annual meeting of the International Reading Association, Chicago, IL.

Cline, Z. (1998). *Buscando su voz en dos culturas*—Finding your voice in two cultures. *Phi Delta Kappan, 79,* 699–702.

Countryman, J. (1992). *Writing to learn mathematics.* Portsmouth, NH: Heinemann.

Crawley, S.J., & Mountain, L. (1995). *Strategies for guiding content reading* (2nd ed.). Boston: Allyn and Bacon.

Crowder, R.G. (1976). *Principles of learning and memory.* Hillsdale, NJ: Erlbaum.

Cummins, J. (1994). The acquisition of English as a second language. In K. Spangenberg-Urbschat & R. Pritchard (Eds.), *Kids come in all languages: Reading instruction for ESL students* (pp. 36–54). Newark, DE: International Reading Association.

Cunningham, R., & Shabloak, S. (1975). Selective reading guide-o-rama: The content teacher's best friend. *Journal of Reading, 18,* 380–382.

Daniels, H. (1994). *Literature circles: Voice and choice in the student-centered classroom.* York, ME: Stenhouse.

Davis, S.J. (1990). Applying content study skills in co-listed reading classrooms. *Journal of Reading, 33,* 277–281.

Delpit, L.D. (1988). The silenced dialogue: Power and pedagogy in educating other people's children. *Harvard Educational Review, 58,* 280–298.

Denner, P.R., & McGinley, W.J. (1986). The effects of story-impressions as a prereading/writing activity on story comprehension. *Journal of Educational Research, 82,* 320–326.

Dillner, M. (1993/1994). Using hypermedia to enhance content area instruction. *Journal of Reading, 37,* 260–270.

Doctrow, M., Whittrock, M.C., & Marks, C. (1978). Generative processes in reading comprehension. *Journal of Educational Psychology, 70,* 109–118.

Dole, J.A., Duffy, G.G., Roehler, L.R., & Pearson, P.D. (1991). Moving from the old to the new: Research on reading comprehension instruction. *Review of Educational Research, 61,* 239–264.

Eanet, M., & Manzo, A.V. (1976). REAP—A strategy for improving reading/writing/study skills. *Journal of Reading, 19,* 647–652.

Feathers, K.M. (1993). *Infotext: Reading and learning.* Scarborough, Ontario: Pippin.

Flavell, J.H. (1981). Cognitive monitoring. In W.P. Dickson (Ed.), *Children's oral communication skills* (pp. 35–60). New York: Academic.

Flippo, R.F., & Caverly, D.C. (Eds.). (1991). *Teaching reading & study strategies at the college level.* Newark, DE: International Reading Association.

Flood, J., & Lapp, D. (1995). Broadening the lens: Toward an expanded conceptualization of literacy. In K.A. Hinchman, D.J. Leu, & C.K. Kinzer (Eds.), *Perspectives on literacy research and practice* (pp. 1–16). Chicago: National Reading Conference.

Fry, E. (1978). *Skimming and scanning.* Providence: Jamestown.

Fry, E. (1977). Fry's readability graph: Clarifications, validity, and extensions to level 17. *Journal of Reading, 21,* 242–252.

Fry, E. (1968). A readability formula that saves time. *Journal of Reading, 11,* 513–516.

Galica, G.S. (1991). *The blue book: A student's guide to essay examinations.* New York: Harcourt Brace Jovanovich.

Gambrell, L.B., & Morrow, L.M. (1996). Creating motivating texts for literacy learning. In L. Baker, P. Afflerbach, & D. Reinking (Eds.), *Developing engaged readers in school and home communities* (pp. 115–137). Mahwah, NJ: Erlbaum.

Garner, R., Gillingham, M.G., & White, C.S. (1989). Effects of "seductive details" on macroprocessing and microprocessing in adults and children. *Cognition and Instruction, 6,* 41–58.

Gauthier, L.R. (1996). Using guided conversation to increase students' content area comprehension. *Journal of Adolescent and Adult Literacy, 39,* 310–312.

Gillet, J., & Kita, M.J. (1979). Words, kids and categories. *The Reading Teacher, 32,* 538–542.

Gipe, J.P. (1979). Investigating techniques for teaching word meaning. *Reading Research Quarterly, 14,* 624–644.

Goodman, K.S. (1986). *What's whole in whole language?* Portsmouth, NH: Heinemann.

Grant, R. (1993). Strategic training for using text headings to improve students' processing of content. *Journal of Reading, 36,* 482–487.

Graves, M.F., Juel, C., & Graves, B. (1998). *Teaching reading in the 21st century.* Boston: Allyn and Bacon.

Graves, M.F., & Prenn, M.C. (1986). Costs and benefits of various methods of teaching vocabulary. *Journal of Reading, 50,* 596–602.

Gunning, T.G. (1998). *Assessing and correcting reading and writing difficulties.* Needham Heights, MA: Allyn and Bacon.

Guthrie, J.T., McGough, K., Bennett, L., & Rice, M.E. (1996). Concept-oriented reading instruction: An integrated curriculum to develop motivations and strategies for reading. In L. Baker, P. Afflerbach, & D. Reinking (Eds.), *Developing engaged readers in school and home communities* (pp. 165–190). Mahwah, NJ: Erlbaum.

Haggard, M.R. (1986). The vocabulary self-collection strategy: Using student interest and world knowledge to enhance vocabulary growth. *Journal of Reading, 29,* 634–642.

Harris, T.L., & Hodges, R.E. (1995). *The literacy dictionary: The vocabulary of reading and writing.* Newark, DE: International Reading Association.

Hartman, D.K. (1995). Eight readers reading: The intertextual links of proficient readers reading multiple passages. *Reading Research Quarterly, 30,* 520–561.

Harvey, S. (1998). *Nonfiction matters: Reading, writing, and research.* York, ME: Stenhouse.

Hayes, D.A. (1989). Helping students GRASP the knack of writing summaries. *Journal of Reading, 33,* 96–101.

Hemmrich, H., Lim W., & Neel, K. (1994). *Primetime!* Portsmouth, NH: Heinemann.

Herber, H.L. (1978). *Teaching reading in content areas* (2nd ed.). Englewood Cliffs, NJ: Prentice-Hall.

Hidi, S., & Baird, W. (1988). Strategies for increasing text-based interest and students' recall of expository text. *Reading Research Quarterly, 23,* 465–483.

Hoffman, J.V. (1992). Critical reading/thinking across the curriculum: Using I-Charts to support learning. *Language Arts, 69,* 121–127.

Hoffman, J.V. (1979). The intra-act procedure for critical reading. *Journal of Reading, 22,* 605–608.

Igoa, C. (1995). *The inner world of the immigrant child.* New York: St. Martin's Press.

International Reading Association & National Council of Teachers of English. (1996). *Standards for the English language arts.* Newark, DE and Urbana, IL: Author.

Irwin, J., & Baker, I. (1989). *Promoting active reading comprehension strategies.* Englewood Cliffs, NJ: Prentice-Hall.

Jacobson, J. M. (1998). *Content area reading: Integration with the language arts.* New York: Delmar Publishers.

Johns, J.L. (1997). *Basic reading inventory* (7th ed.). Dubuque, IA: Kendall/Hunt.

Johns, J.L., & Lenski, S.D. (1997). *Improving reading: A handbook of strategies* (2nd ed.). Dubuque, IA: Kendall/Hunt.

Johnson, D.D., & Pearson, P.D. (1984). *Teaching reading vocabulary* (2nd ed.). New York: Holt, Rinehart and Winston.

Kameenui, E.J., Dixon, S.W., & Carnine, R.C. (1987). Issues in the design of vocabulary instruction. In M.G. McKeown & M.C. Curtis (Eds.), *The nature of vocabulary acquisition* (pp. 129–145). Hillsdale, NJ: Erlbaum.

Klare, G.R. (1963). *The measurement of readability.* Ames, IA: Iowa State University Press.

Klemp, R.M., Hon, J.E., & Short, A.A. (1993). Cooperative literacy in the middle school: An example of a learning-strategy based approach. *Middle School Journal, 24,* 19–27.

Laffey, D.G., & Laffey, J.L. (l986). Vocabulary teaching: An investment in literacy. *Journal of Reading, 50,* 651–657.

Langer, J.A. (1981). From theory to practice: A prereading plan. *Journal of Reading, 25,* 152–156.

Lara, J. (1994). Demographic overview: Changes in student enrollment in American schools. In K. Spangenberg-Urbschat & R. Pritchard (Eds.), *Kids come in all languages: Reading instruction for ESL students* (pp. 9–21). Newark, DE: International Reading Association.

Lazarus, B.D. (1988). Using guided notes to aid learning disabled students in secondary mainstream settings. *The Pointer, 33,* 32–36.

Lenski, S.D., & Johns, J.L. (1997). Patterns of reading-to-write. *Reading Research & Instruction, 37,* 15–38.

Lenski, S.D., Marciniec, P.V., & Johns, J.L. (1998). *Study smart and test terrific.* Normal, IL: Illinois Reading Council.

Lester, J.H., & Cheek, E.H. (1997/1998). The "real" experts address textbook issues. *Journal of Adult & Adolescent Literacy, 41,* 282–291.

Lowry, L. (1993). *The giver.* New York: Bantam Doubleday Dell.

Lyman, H.B. (1986). *Test scores and what they mean* (4th ed.). Englewood Cliffs, NJ: Prentice-Hall.

Macrorie, K. (1984). *Searching writing.* Upper Montclair, NJ: Boynton/Cook.

Manzo, A.V. (1969). The ReQuest procedure. *Journal of Reading, 13,* 123–126.

Manzo, A.V., & Casale, U.P. (1985). Listen-read-discuss: A content reading heuristic. *Journal of Reading, 28,* 732–734.

Manzo, A.V., & Manzo, U.C. (1990a). *Content area reading.* New York: Macmillan.

Manzo, A.V., & Manzo, U.C. (1990b). Note cue cards: A comprehension and participation training strategy. *Journal of Reading, 33,* 608–611.

Marzano, R.J. (1992). *A different kind of classroom: Teaching with dimensions of learning.* Washington, DC: Association for Supervision and Curriculum Development.

Mathison, C. (1989). Activating student interest in content area reading. *Journal of Reading, 33,* 170–176.

McKenna, M.C., & Robinson, R.D. (1997). *Teaching through text: A content literacy approach to content area reading* (2nd ed.). New York: Longman.

McKenna, M.C., & Robinson, R.D. (1990). Content literacy: A definition and implications. *Journal of Reading, 34,* 184–186.

McNamara, T., Miller, D., & Bransford, J. (1991). Mental models and reading comprehension. In R. Barr, M.L. Kamil, P. Mosenthal, & P.D. Pearson (Eds.). *Handbook of reading research* (Vol. II) (pp. 490–511). White Plains, NY: Longman.

Mendels, P. (April 28, 1998). Study shows students use internet primarily for research. *New York Times,* p. 4.

Mendrinos, R.B. (1997). *Using educational technology with at-risk students.* Westport, CT: Greenwood.

Mikulecky, L., & Drew, R. (1991). Basic literacy skills in the workplace. In R. Barr, M.L. Kamil, P. Mosenthal, & P.D. Pearson (Eds.), *Handbook of reading research* (Vol. II) (pp. 669–689). White Plains, NY: Longman.

Miller, E.F. (1994). Book dialogues. *Journal of Reading, 37,* 415–416.

Miller, T. (1998). The place of picture books in middle-level classrooms. *Journal of Adolescent & Adult Literacy, 41,* 376–381.

Moffett, J. (1989). *Bridges: From personal writing to the formal essay.* Berkeley, CA: Center for the Study of Writing.

Moore, D.W., & Moore, S.A. (1986). Possible sentences. In E.K. Dishner, T.W. Bean, J.E. Readence, & D.W. Moore (Eds.), *Reading in the content areas: Improving classroom instruction* (2nd ed.) (pp. 174–179). Dubuque, IA: Kendall/Hunt.

Moore, D.W., Moore, S.A., Cunningham, P.M., & Cunningham, J.W. (1998). *Developing readers & writers in the content areas K–12.* New York: Longman.

Morgan, R.F., Meeks, J.W., Schollaert, A., & Paul, J. (1986). *Critical reading/thinking skills for the college student.* Dubuque, IA: Kendall/Hunt.

Mullis, I.V.S., Campbell, J.R., & Farstrup, A.E. (1993). *NAEP 1992 reading report card for the nation and the states* (Report No. 23-ST06). Washington, DC: National Center for Education Statistics, U.S. Department of Education.

Nagy, W.E., & Anderson, R.C. (1984). How many words are there in printed school English? *Reading Research Quarterly, 19,* 304–330.

Nagy, W.E., & Herman, P.A. (1987). Breadth and depth of vocabulary knowledge: Implications for acquisition and instruction. In M.G. McKeown & M.E. Curtis (Eds.), *The nature of vocabulary acquisition* (pp. 19–35). Hillsdale, NJ: Erlbaum.

Nist, S.L., & Simpson, M.L. (1989). PLAE, a validated study strategy. *Journal of Reading, 33,* 182–186.

Ogle, D.M. (1986). K-W-L: A teaching model that develops active reading of expository text. *The Reading Teacher, 39,* 564–570.

Oldfather, P. (1992, December). *Sharing the ownership of knowing: A constructivist concept of motivation for literacy learning.* Paper presented at the annual meeting of the National Reading Conference, San Antonio, TX.

Oldfather, P., & Wigfield, A. (1996). Children's motivations for learning. In L. Baker, P. Afflerbach, & D. Reinking (Eds.), *Developing engaged readers in school and home communities* (pp. 89–113). Mahwah, NJ: Erlbaum.

Paris, S., Wasik, B., & Turner, J. (1991). The development of strategic readers. In R. Barr, M.L. Kamil, P. Mosenthal, & P.D. Pearson (Eds.), *Handbook of reading research* (Vol. II) (pp. 609–640). White Plains, NY: Longman.

Pauk, W. (1974). *How to study in college.* Boston: Houghton Mifflin.

Paul, R.W. (1993). *Critical thinking: How to prepare students for a rapidly changing world.* Santa Rosa, CA: Foundation for Critical Thinking.

Paul, R.W. (1991). Dialogical and dialectical thinking. In A.L. Costa (Ed.), *Developing minds: A resource book for teaching thinking* (pp. 42–54). Alexandria, VA: Association for Supervision and Curriculum Development.

Pearson, P.D., & Camperell, K. (1994). Comprehension of text structures. In R.B. Ruddell, M.R. Ruddell, & H. Singer (Eds.), *Theoretical models and processes of reading* (4th ed.) (pp. 448–468). Newark, DE: International Reading Association.

Pearson, P.D., & Fielding, L. (1991). Comprehension instruction. In R. Barr, M.L. Kamil, P. Mosenthal, & P.D. Pearson (Eds.), *Handbook of reading research* (Vol. II) (pp. 815–860). White Plains, NY: Longman.

Perkins, D.N. (1994). *Knowledge as design: A handbook for critical and creative discussion across the curriculum.* Pacific Grove, CA: Critical Thinking Press and Software.

Perkins, D.N. (1986). *Knowledge as design.* Hillsdale, NJ: Erlbaum.

Peters, J. (1991). *The elements of critical reading.* NY: Macmillan.

Randall, S.N. (1996). Information charts: A strategy for organizing student research. *Journal of Adolescent & Adult Literacy, 39,* 536–542.

Readence, J.E., Bean, T.W., & Baldwin, R.S. (1992). *Content area reading: An integrated approach* (4th ed.). Dubuque, IA: Kendall/Hunt.

Reasoner, C. (1976). *Releasing children to literature* (Rev. ed.). New York: Dell.

Risko, V.J., Fairbanks, M.M., & Alvarez, M.C. (1991). Internal factors that influence study. In R.F. Flippo & D.C. Caverly (Eds.), *Teaching reading & study strategies at the college level* (pp. 237–293). Newark, DE: International Reading Association.

Ritter, S., & Idol-Maestas, L. (1986). Teaching middle school students to use a test-taking strategy. *Journal of Educational Research Quarterly, 79,* 350–357.

Robinson, H.A. (1975). *Teaching reading and study strategies: The content areas.* Boston: Allyn and Bacon.

Roerden, L.P. (1997). *Net lessons: Web-based projects for your classroom.* Sebastopol, CA: Songline Studios.

Rothstein, R. (1998). Bilingual education: The controversy. *Phi Delta Kappan, 79,* 672–684.

Routman, R. (1994). *Invitations.* Portsmouth, NH: Heinemann.

Ryder, R.J. (1994). Using frames to promote critical writing. *Journal of Reading, 38,* 210–218.

Ryder, R.J., & Graves, M.F. (1998). *Reading and learning in content areas* (2nd ed.). Saddle River, NJ: Merrill.

Ryder, R.J., & Graves, M.F. (1996/1997). Using the internet to enhance students' reading, writing, and information-gathering skills. *Journal of Adolescent & Adult Literacy, 40,* 244–254.

Santa, C.M., Dailey, S.C., & Nelson, M. (1985). Free-response and opinion proof: A reading and writing strategy for middle grade and secondary teachers. *Journal of Reading, 28,* 346–352.

Scanlon, D., Schumaker, J.B., & Deshler, D.D. (1994). Collaborative dialogue between teachers and researchers to create education interventions: A case study. *Journal of Educational and Psychological Consultation, 5,* 69–76.

Schmidt, B., & Buckley, M. (1991). Plot relationships chart. In J.M. Macon, D. Bewell, & M. Vogt (Eds.), *Responses to literature: Grades K–8* (pp. 7–8). Newark, DE: International Reading Association.

Schwartz, R. (1988). Learning to learn vocabulary in content area textbooks. *Journal of Reading, 32,* 108–117.

Schwartz, R., & Raphael, T. (1985). Concept of definition: A key to improving students' vocabulary. *The Reading Teacher, 39,* 198–205.

Simpson, M.L. (1994). Talk throughs: A strategy for encouraging active learning across the content areas. *Journal of Reading, 38,* 296–304.

Simpson, M.L. (1993, December). *An examination of elaborative verbal rehearsals and their impact on college freshmen's cognitive and metacognitive performance.* Paper presented at the annual meeting of the National Reading Conference, Charleston, SC.

Simpson, M.L. (1986). PORPE: A writing strategy for studying and learning in the content areas. *Journal of Reading, 29,* 407–414.

Smith, C.C., & Bean, T.W. (1980). The guided writing procedure: Integrating content reading and writing improvement. *Reading World, 19,* 290–302.

Speigel, D.L. (1981). Six alternatives to the directed reading activity. *The Reading Teacher, 34,* 914–922.

Spivey, N.N. (1997). *The constructivist metaphor.* San Diego: Academic Press.

Stahl, N.A., King, J.R., & Henk, W.A. (1991). Enhancing students' notetaking through training and evaluation. *Journal of Reading, 34,* 614–622.

Stahl, S. (1986). Three principles of effective vocabulary instruction. *Journal of Reading, 50,* 662–668.

Stahl, S.A., Hynd, C.R., Glynn, S.M., & Carr, M. (1996). Beyond reading to learn: Developing content and disciplinary knowledge through texts. In L. Baker, P. Afflerbach, & D. Reinking (Eds.), *Developing engaged readers in school and home communities* (pp. 139–163). Mahwah, NJ: Erlbaum.

Stauffer, R.G. (1969). *Directing reading maturity as a cognitive process.* New York: Harper and Row.

Stotsky, S. (1991). *Connecting civic education and language education: The contemporary challenge.* New York: Teachers College Press.

Sturk, A. (1992). Developing a community of learners inside and outside the classroom. In P. Shannon (Ed.), *Becoming political* (pp. 263–273). Portsmouth NH: Heinemann.

Taba, H. (1967). *Teacher's handbook for elementary social studies.* Reading, MS: Addison Wesley.

Tanner, M.L., & Casados, L. (1998). Promoting and studying discussions in math classes. *Journal of Adolescent & Adult Literacy, 41,* 342–351.

Taylor, B.M., & Beach, R.W. (1984). The effects of text structure instruction on middle-grade students' comprehension and production of expository text. *Reading Research Quarterly, 19,* 134–146.

Tierney, R.J., & Pearson, P.D. (1994). Learning to learn from text: A framework for improving classroom practice. In R.B. Ruddell, M.R. Ruddell, & H. Singer (Eds.), *Theoretical models and processes of reading* (4th ed.) (pp. 496–513). Newark, DE: International Reading Association.

Thompson, R., Mixon, G., & Serpell, R. (1996). Engaging minority students in reading: Focus on the urban learner. In L. Baker, P. Afflerbach, & D. Reinking (Eds.), *Developing engaged readers in school and home communities* (pp. 43–63). Mahwah, NJ: Erlbaum.

Thornburg, D. (1997, June 27). *2020 visions for the future of education* [On-line]. Available: http://www.tepd.org/handouts/thornburg/2020.html

Tomlinson, L.M. (1995). Flag words for efficient thinking, active reading, comprehension, and test taking. *Journal of Reading, 38,* 387–388.

Unrau, N.J. (1997). *Thoughtful teachers, thoughtful learners: A guide to helping adolescents think critically.* Scarborough, Ontario: Pippin.

Vacca, R.T., & Vacca, J.L. (1996). *Content area reading* (5th ed.). New York: HarperCollins.

Vytgotsky, L.S. (1978). *Mind in society.* Cambridge, MA: MIT Press.

Wade, S.E., & Reynolds, R.E. (1989). Developing metacognitive awareness. *Journal of Reading, 33,* 6–14.

Weaver, C.A., & Kintsch, W. (1991). Expository text. In R. Barr, M.L. Kamil, P. Mosenthal, & P.D. Pearson (Eds.), *Handbook of reading research* (Vol. II) (pp. 230–245). White Plains, NY: Longman.

Weir, C. (1998). Using embedded questions to jump-start metacognition in middle school readers. *Journal of Adolescent & Adult Literacy, 41,* 458–467.

Wilson, E.A. (1996). *The internet roadmap for educators.* Arlington, VA: Educational Research Service.

Wong-Kam, J., & Au, K.H. (1988). Improving a fourth grader's reading and writing: Three principles. *The Reading Teacher, 41,* 768–772.

Wood, K.D. (1984). Probable passages: A writing strategy. *The Reading Teacher, 37,* 496–499.

Wray, D., & Lewis, M. (1997). *Extending literacy.* New York: Routledge.

Content Area Texts Used as Examples in this Book

A history of multicultural America: The new freedom to the new deal. (1993). Austin, TX: Raintree Steck-Vaughn.

A more perfect union. (1991). Boston: Houghton Mifflin.

Accounting. (1992). Lake Forest, IL: Macmillan/McGraw-Hill.

Africa. (1998). Needham, MA: Prentice-Hall.

Algebra 2. (1995). New York: Glencoe/McGraw-Hill.

America: Pathways to the present. (1998). Needham, MA: Prentice-Hall.

American government. (1999). Westerville, OH: Macmillan/McGraw-Hill.

An Edgar Allan Poe reader: Adapted classic tales. (1979). New York: Globe.

Anne Frank: Diary of a young girl. (1995). New York: Doubleday.

Art: Images and ideas. (1992). Worcester, MA: Davis Publications.

Art scholastic. (1993). Jefferson City, MO: Scholastic.

Beginning & intermediate algebra: An integrated approach. (1996). New York: Brooks/Cole.

Bienvenue. (1994). New York: Glencoe/McGraw-Hill.

Biodiversity: Understanding the variety of life. (1995). New York: Scholastic.

Biological science: An ecological approach. (1992). Dubuque, IA: Kendall/Hunt.

Biology. (1994). Menlo Park, CA: Addison-Wesley.

Biology. (1981). New York: Macmillan.

Biology: A human approach. (1997). Dubuque, IA: Kendall/Hunt.

Biology: The study of life. (1993). Englewood Cliffs, NJ: Prentice-Hall.

BSCS biology: An ecological approach. (1998). Dubuque, IA: Kendall/Hunt.

Business: Stock market and investment practice set. (1993). Englewood Cliffs, NJ: Prentice-Hall.

Career directions. (1991). St. Paul, MN: EMC Publishing.

Celtic myths. (1995). London: British Museum Press.

ChemCom: Chemistry in the community (3rd ed.). (1998). Dubuque, IA: Kendall/Hunt.

Chemistry. (1995). Menlo Park, CA: Addison-Wesley.

Civics: Responsibilities and citizenship. (1992). New York: Glencoe/McGraw-Hill.

Consumer math. (1983). Cincinnati, OH: South-Western.

Discovering geometry: An inductive approach (2nd ed.). (1997). Berkeley, CA: Key Curriculum Press.

Drive right (9th ed.). (1993). Glenview, IL: Scott Foresman.

Earth science. (1997). New York: Glencoe/McGraw-Hill.

Earth science. (1993). Westerville, OH: Macmillan/McGraw-Hill.

Ecology: A systems approach—water. (1998). Dubuque, IA: Kendall/Hunt.

Economics today & tomorrow. (1995). Westerville, OH: Macmillan/McGraw-Hill.

English: Composition and grammar. (1988). Orlando, FL: Harcourt Brace Jovanovich.

Enjoying literature. (1985). New York: Macmillan.

Explore: A course in literature. (1991). Circle Pines, MN: AGS.

Exploring art. (1992). Mission Hills, CA: Macmillan/McGraw-Hill.

Exploring careers. (1990). Indianapolis, IN: JIST Works.

Exploring our world: Eastern hemisphere. (1980). Chicago: Follett.

Exploring our world: Latin America and Canada. (1980). Chicago: Follett.

Fitness for life. (1993). Glenview, IL: Scott Foresman.

From gutterballs to strikes. (1998). Chicago: Contemporary Books.

Government in the United States. (1990). New York: Glencoe/McGraw-Hill.

Health for life. (1992). Glenview, IL: Scott Foresman.

History of England. (1974). London: Collins.

How matter changes: Exploring the structure of matter. (1995). New York: Scholastic.

Human development: How human beings grow and change. (1995). New York: Scholastic.

Human heritage: A world history. (1989). Columbus, OH: Merrill.

Latin America. (1998). Needham, MA: Prentice-Hall.

Latin for Americans. (1997). New York: Glencoe/McGraw-Hill.

Life science. (1993). Englewood Cliffs, NJ: Prentice-Hall.

Literature. (1984). Evanston, IL: McDougal, Littell.

Literature & language. (1994). Evanston, IL: McDougal, Littell.

Literature & language. (1992). Evanston, IL: McDougal, Littell.

Literature and the language arts: The British tradition. (1996). St. Paul, MN: EMC/Paradigm.

Married and single life (6th ed.). (1997). New York: Glencoe/McGraw-Hill.

Math curse. (1995). New York: Viking.

Math trailblazers: A mathematical journey using science and language arts. (1998). Dubuque, IA: Kendall/Hunt.

Mathematics in action. (1994). New York: Macmillan/McGraw-Hill.

Mechanical drawing (11th ed.). (1990). Lake Forest, IL: Glencoe/McGraw-Hill.

Moving on: The American people since 1945. (1994). Englewood Cliffs, NJ: Prentice-Hall.

Our country. (1991). Morristown, NJ: Silver Burdett & Ginn.

Perception. (1985). New York: McGraw-Hill.

Pride and prejudice. (1998). St. Paul, MN: EMC.

Prentice-Hall literature: Bronze. (1991). Englewood Cliffs, NJ: Prentice-Hall.

Science and technology: Changes we make. (1985). San Diego, CA: Coronado.

Science anytime. (1995). Orlando, FL: Harcourt Brace.

Science for life and living: Balance and decisions. (1992). Dubuque, IA: Kendall/Hunt.

Science interactions. (1995). New York: McGraw-Hill.

Self-Discovery: Alcohol and other drugs. (1984). Boston: Management Sciences for Health.

Share the music. (1995). New York: Macmillan/McGraw-Hill.

Southeast Asia. (1978). Evanston, IL: McDougal, Littell.

States and regions. (1997). Orlando, FL: Harcourt Brace.

Succeeding in the world of work (5th ed.). (1992). New York: Glencoe/McGraw-Hill.

Technology: Science and math in action. (1995). New York: Glencoe/McGraw-Hill.

Technology today & tomorrow. (1993). New York: Glencoe/McGraw-Hill.

The African American experience: A history. (1992). Englewood Cliffs, NJ: Globe.

The American nation. (1998). New York: Longman.

The American nation (3rd ed.). (1991). Englewood Cliffs, NJ: Prentice-Hall.

The American tradition in literature. (1974). New York: Grosset & Dunlap.

The Americans. (1999). Evanston, IL: McDougal, Littell.

The developing child: Understanding children and parenting. (1994). New York: Glencoe/McGraw-Hill.

The pit and the pendulum: Interactive mathematics program. (1997). Berkeley, CA: Key Curriculum Press.

Through Chinese eyes. (1988). New York: Center for International Training and Education.

Today's teens. (1994). New York: Glencoe/McGraw-Hill.

Transition mathematics. (1995). Glenview, IL: Scott Foresman.

Treasury of literature: Voices and reflections. (1995). Orlando, FL: Harcourt Brace.

Understanding business and personal law (9th ed.). (1993). New York: Glencoe/McGraw-Hill.

Voices in African American history: The colonies. (1994). Cleveland, OH: Modern Curriculum Press.

What on earth?: Insights in biology. (1998). Dubuque, IA: Kendall/Hunt.

World geography. (1992). New York: Glencoe/McGraw-Hill.

World geography: People and places. (1989). Columbus, OH: Merrill.

World geography today. (1995). Austin, TX: Holt, Rinehart and Winston.

World history. (1994). Lexington, MA: D.C. Heath.

World history: People and nations. (1990). Orlando, FL: Harcourt Brace Jovanovich.

World regions. (1998). Chicago: Macmillan/McGraw-Hill.

World regions. (1991). Chicago: Macmillan/McGraw-Hill.

Index

D

Database organization, 284–285
Decision making, 29–31
Definitions, 42–48
Concept of Definition Map, 45–47
Four Square, 48
magic squares, 43–45
Definitions, vocabulary, 42–48
Developing Child, The, 175
Discovering Geometry, 120
Discussion groups, 164–167
Discussion web, 170–173
Drive Right, 145, 147

E

Earth Science, 11, 41
Easy-to-read texts, 115–117
Ecology: A Systems Approach, 71
Economics Today & Tomorrow, 45
Edgar Allan Poe Reader, 116
Editorial perspectives, 180–182
Embedded questions, 122–123
English: Composition and Grammar, 212
Enjoying Literature, 171
Essay evaluation rubric, 188
Essay tests, 239–249
PORPE strategy, 242–246
strategy for, 239–242
three parts of, 246–249
Exclusion brainstorming, 39–40
Expectation outline, 94–95
Experience/text linking, 124–129
Concept Rating Guide, 124–126
concept-text-application, 126–127
guided writing procedure, 127–129
Explore: A Course in Literature, 213–214
Exploring Art, 50
Exploring Careers, 284
Exploring Our World, 154, 162

F

Factstorming, 258
Fill-in-the-blank test, 237–238
Fitness for Life, 258

Flag words, 88–89
Four Square, 48
From Gutterballs to Strikes, 134
Fry Readability Formula, 305–308

G

General reading ability, 2–4
Generative writing, 190–191
Giver, The, 61
Government in the United States, 155
Graduate Record Examination (GRE), 223
Graphic organizers, 75–79
GRASP strategy, 221–222
Grolier's Encyclopedia, 269
Group frame, 120–121
Guided conversation, and argument, 184–185
Guided notes, 131–132
Guided Reading And Summarizing Procedure (GRASP), 221–222
Guided writing procedure, 127–129

H

Health for Life, 190
History of England, 155
History of Multicultural America, A, 141
How Matter Changes, 215
Human Development, 136
Human Heritage, 105

I

Idea-Map, 80–84
Improving Reading, 96, 232
Information, about testing, 225–226
Information, identifying, 130–133
guided notes, 131–132
note cue cards, 132–133
selective reading guide, 130–131
Information charts, 285–288
Information organization, of research, 280–288
database organization, 284–285

information charts, 285–288
questioning the author, 281–283
Information synthesis, 289–296
I-Search strategy, 294–296
Thinking Over-Thinking Through strategy, 293–294
writing frames, 290–292
Interest, creating, 11–17
anticipation guide, 11–12
people search, 13–14
problematic situation, 14–16
story impressions, 16–17
Internet, reading flexibility and, 204–205
Intertextual links, 159–167
discussion groups, 164–167
Intra-Act, 162–164
Text Connect strategy, 159–161
Intra-Act, 162–164
I-Search strategy, 294–296

J

Journal, response, 103–104

K

Know-Want-Learn (K-W-L), 28–29
Knowledge as Design, 178–179
Knowledge as design strategy, 176–179
Knowledge rating scale, 37–38
K-W-L strategy, 28–29

L

Latin for Americans, 158
Learning environment, creation of, 6–7
Learning to study, 195–199
collaborative, 195
monitoring study habits, 199
preplan-List-Activate-Evaluate strategy, 196–197
study management, 197–198
Lifelong learning, encouragement of, 7
Limited English Proficiency (LEP), 113
Listen-read-discuss strategy, 121–122